Workplace Basics Training Manual

Anthony P. Carnevale
Leila J. Gainer
Ann S. Meltzer

WORKPLACE BASICS TRAINING MANUAL

A Publication of the
American Society for Training and Development

Jossey-Bass Publishers
San Francisco • Oxford • 1990

WORKPLACE BASICS TRAINING MANUAL
by Anthony P. Carnevale, Leila J. Gainer, and Ann S. Meltzer

Copyright © 1990 by: Jossey-Bass Inc., Publishers
350 Sansome Street
San Francisco, California 94104

Jossey-Bass Limited
Headington Hill Hall
Oxford OX3 0BW

American Society for Training and Development
1630 Duke Street, Box 1443
Alexandria, Virginia 22313

Library of Congress Cataloging-in-Publication Data

Carnevale, Anthony Patrick.
  Workplace basics training manual / Anthony P. Carnevale, Leila J. Gainer,
Ann S. Meltzer. — 1st ed.
    p.   cm. — (The Jossey-Bass management series)
  Includes bibliographical references.
  ISBN 1-55542-204-7
    1. Employees—Training of—United States—Handbooks, manuals, etc.
2. Employer supported education—United States.   I. Gainer, Leila J.
II. Meltzer, Ann S.   III. Title.   IV. Series.
HF5549.5.T7C2985 1990 suppl.
658.3′124—dc20
                                                            89-48805
                                                                 CIP

Manufactured in the United States of America

The paper in this book meets the guidelines for
permanence and durability of the Committee on
Production Guidelines for Book Longevity of the
Council on Library Resources.

The case study from Mazda presented in Resource A is included herein
with permission of the Mazda Motor Manufacturing (USA) Corporation.

The case study from Harrison Radiator presented in Resource B
is included herein with permission of Harrison Radiator Division,
General Motors Corporation.

JACKET DESIGN BY WILLI BAUM
FIRST EDITION

Code 9012

The Jossey-Bass Management Series

ASTD Best Practices Series:
Training for a Changing Work Force

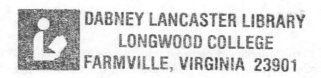

The material in this project was prepared under Grant No. 99-6-0705-75-079-02 from the Employment and Training Administration, U.S. Department of Labor, under the authority of Title IV, part D, of the Job Training Partnership Act of 1982. Grantees undertaking such projects under government sponsorship are encouraged to express freely their professional judgment. Therefore, points of view or opinions stated in this document do not necessarily represent the official position or policy of the Department of Labor.

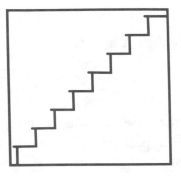

Contents

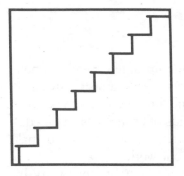

Preface

As more and more employers are discovering basic skills deficiencies in their workers, they are beginning to seek assistance in how to establish training programs to meet their needs. However, little practical information has been available on the actual how-to part of setting up workplace basics programs. Our research has revealed that employers and other private and public training providers could benefit from a manual that would provide step-by-step guidance on establishing basic skills training programs.

The *Workplace Basics Training Manual* lays out a blueprint for the successful establishment and implementation of a workplace basics program. The blueprint is based on an innovative concept called the applied approach. This model was selected because it motivates learners by linking learning to improved job performance. In turn, applied training may lead to improvement in learners' careers and earnings, encourage learner retention by requiring immediate and repeated use of newly gained knowledge, and improve job performance by creating learning experiences based on actual job needs. The model includes everything from advice on how to win internal political support to the latest information on modifying an instructional systems design concept to fit the individual needs of a company.

The information in this manual represents only some of the findings gathered during a thirty-month research effort that explored training practices among America's corporate employers. Other findings are detailed in three companion books published by Jossey-Bass: *Workplace Basics: The Essential Skills Employers Want,* which explores both the theoretical and practical aspects of the sixteen basic skills that employers say are essential to success in the workplace, *Training the Technical Work Force,* and *Training in America: The Organization and Strategic Role of Training.* In addition, the project produced several booklets: *Workplace Basics: The Skills Employers Want, The Learning Enterprise, Train America, Training Partnerships: Linking Employers and Providers,* and *The Next Economy* (available from the American Society for Training and Development, 1630 Duke Street, Box 1443, Alexandria, Va. 22313).

The American Society for Training and Development (ASTD), which undertook this project in conjunction with the U.S. Department of Labor (DOL), is a nonprofit professional association representing approximately 50,000 practitioners, managers, administrators, educators, and researchers in the field of human resource development.

How the Research Was Conducted

The ASTD-DOL research project team was made up of ten members: both professionals and support staff. This team was greatly assisted by ASTD members who volunteered their expertise and provided access to their corporations. In addition, experts from the fields of economics, adult education, training, public policy, and strategic management contributed analyses that provided a contextual backdrop for our work.

In all study areas, including basic skills, we launched our work by surveying the current literature, looking for trends and patterns; this effort helped us to identify the leaders in various disciplines and to draw some preliminary conclusions. We tested our preliminary findings on a cadre of individual experts drawn from ASTD's membership and asked those members to identify other experts and practitioners who might provide feedback and insights. We continued along this path, and our list of contacts grew. From them we formed advisory panels that met during 1987 to advise us on our direction and findings. We also built networks of more than 400 experts and practitioners (the basic skills network alone had 175 members) who received periodic updates of findings and were asked for feedback.

Corporations and other private and public employer institutions were tapped extensively to provide actual examples of successful training systems and practices. We conducted some on-site studies and much telephone interviewing, using specially constructed interview instruments that ensured we would gather uniform information. The resulting employer snapshots are used throughout this manual to complement and illustrate the step-by-step instructions.

After developing our first-draft reports, we enlisted more than thirty experts and practitioners to review them and give their comments. Their insights are reflected in this final version.

Who Should Read This Manual

This manual is designed to provide readers with an understanding of how to establish a workplace basics program. It contains political insights and suggestions, as well as basic training methodology. We believe that it can serve as a useful reference book, but it is primarily designed to be a tool. When used in concert with our book *Workplace Basics*, it provides a complete picture of the who, what, where, when, and how of basic workplace skills training. Its intended audience includes practitioners and managers responsible for providing private or public training programs; administrators and instructors involved in the various basic skills (including literacy) programs across the nation; business and management consultants; secondary, postsecondary, and adult educators (including vocational educators).

Organization and Content

Readers should view this manual as an instructional aid. It is organized to emphasize the step-by-step instructions it contains.

The Introduction explains what skills employers want and why, as well as how to create a blueprint for success in basic skills instruction.

How to Use the Manual explains the format of this manual and what various symbols mean throughout.

Step One explores how to identify job changes or problems related to basic workplace skills.

Step Two charts a course for building management and union support for workplace basics training programs.

Step Three illustrates how to develop and present an action plan to management and the unions, as well as giving guidelines for selecting outside training providers.

Step Four outlines how to perform a task analysis.

Step Five explains how to design a curriculum.

Step Six examines how to develop a curriculum.

Step Seven looks at implementation of the program.

Step Eight explores how to evaluate and monitor the program.

Each step also includes references and additional suggested readings.

The Glossary contains definitions of the key concepts used in the manual.

Resources A and B profile two actual workplace basics training program experiences, at Mazda Motor Manufacturing (USA) Corporation and at the Harrison Radiator Division of General Motors.

Resource C gives information on locating providers of basic skills training programs and getting help in setting up a workplace basics program.

Resource D provides a sample form that can be used to request proposals from potential providers.

Resource E provides generic curriculum guidelines.

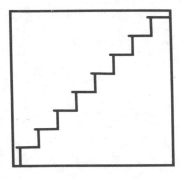

Acknowledgments

Special thanks to Shari L. Holland, who served as research assistant on the project; Dawn Temple, Kim Genevro, and Stacey Wagner, who provided administrative assistance; Diane L. Charles, who managed our research symposium, as well as the production aspects of report preparation; Diane Kirrane, who provided editorial assistance; Gerald Gundersen and Ray Uhalde of DOL who provided insights and guidance along the way; and J. R. Reingold and Associates, for their help in producing this manual.

The project team also wishes to acknowledge the contributions of the following people who worked closely with us on the four workplace basics publications: Elaine M. Brady, Janet G. Elsea, Greta Kotler, Stephen K. Merman, Jorie W. Phillippi, Virginia Polytechnic Institute (Libby Hall, Charles W. Humes, Linda Kunder, Martha Livingston, Ronald L. McKeen, Harold W. Stubblefield, and Albert K. Wiswell), and Dale Yeatts.

We also wish to thank our advisory panel and network participants, who contributed their advice and counsel.

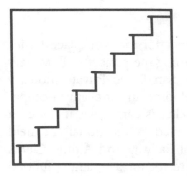

The Authors

Anthony P. Carnevale was principal investigator for this ASTD-DOL project. Carnevale is chief economist and vice president of national affairs for ASTD. His education, experience, and numerous published works on employment and training illustrate both practical and theoretical involvement with human resource aspects of the nation's economic performance. Some of his publications include *Human Capital: A High Yield Corporate Investment* (1983), *Jobs for the Nation: Challenges for a Society Based on Work* (1985), and *Skill Change in Financial Services* (1987). Prior to joining ASTD, Carnevale was a consulting economist to Congress, business and international associations, and labor unions, as well as a research associate at both Harvard and Ohio State universities. He has served as a fiscal analyst with the U.S. Senate Committee on the Budget and as a senior policy analyst with the Department of Health, Education and Welfare. Carnevale has a Ph.D. degree with a concentration in public finance economics from the Maxwell School of Public Affairs, Syracuse University.

Leila J. Gainer directed the daily operations of the ASTD-DOL project, coauthored the four resulting volumes, and served as the principal researcher and writer for strategic management issues. Gainer is ASTD's director of national affairs and, as such, manages the society's external relations and national affairs programs, which include research, congressional relations, and building partnerships with the business and educational communities. Before joining ASTD, Gainer was director of federal liaison for the National Association of Regional Councils (NARC), working with elected officials at the state and local levels around the nation. As head of NARC's Center for Regional Action, she directed the association's research, policy development, communications, and government relations efforts. During her tenure, research projects focused on public-private partnerships and on linking economic development and job training. Prior to joining NARC, Gainer was a Washington, D.C.–based reporter and editor for Commerce Clearing House, covering urban affairs, education, and commodity futures. In the early 1970s, she was an editor on the staff of *Labor Law Report* and managing editor of *Labor Law Guide*. Gainer has a B.A. degree from Frostburg State College in Maryland.

Ann S. Meltzer was the writer and researcher for the workplace basics portion of the ASTD-DOL project. Prior to joining the project staff, Meltzer was a member of the planning staff of the San Diego Private Industry Council, where she was responsible for developing an innovative occupation-specific training program for adults. Meltzer's career has included a number of training assignments; she has served as vocational and field training coordinator for the Brotherhood of Railway and Airline Clerks Manpower Training Department, project director for a federally funded program to train Job Corps members, and labor liaison for the Interstate Commerce Commission's reorganization of the northeast and midwest railroads. As president of ASM Associates, a Washington, D.C., consulting firm, Meltzer managed a variety of domestic and international projects, including the development of federal Job Corps program training materials, an assessment of the training needs of the Malayan Railway, and a survey on the federal Job Training Partnership Act. Her clients included the American Vocational Association, the Agency for International Development, the National Alliance of Business, and the Solar Energy Industries Association. She has an M.A. degree in international relations from Johns Hopkins School of Advanced International Studies and an M.B.A. degree with a concentration in organizational development from National University, San Diego.

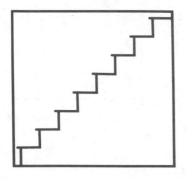

Workplace Basics Advisory Panel

Joseph Cooney
Regional Representative
The National Alliance
of Business

Brian Elrod
Skills Enhancement
Program Associate
UAW-Ford National Education
Development Center

Mike Fox
Executive Director
Push Literacy Action Now

Karl O. Haigler
Director
Adult Literacy Initiative
U.S. Department of Education

Renee Lerche
Education Consultant
Ford Motor Company
(formerly with
General Motors)

Larry Mikulecky
Director
Learning Skills Center
Indiana University, Bloomington

Robert E. Norton
Senior Research Development
Specialist
National Center for Research
in Vocational Education

Phillip M. Plott
Manager
Professional Development
Duke Power Company

Thomas G. Sticht
President
Applied Behavioral and
Cognitive Sciences, Inc.

Linda E. Stoker
Vice President
Cox Educational Services, Inc.
(formerly with
Polaroid Corporation)

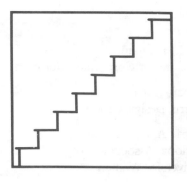

Workplace Basics Skills Network

Mike Allen
Dana Corporation

Ray Balcer
Datapoint Corporation

Renate Banks
Xerox Corporation

Mary Jo Beans
Center for Applied Linguistics

Sue Berryman
Columbia University

Kathy Blair
AT&T Communications

Richard Blue
Dayton Progress Corporation

Francine Boren
Consortium for Worker
Literacy Program

Susan Bourgeois
Penn Valley Community College

Ron Bradley
Blue Cross/Blue Shield
of Massachusetts

Franklin Brown
Horizon's Technology, Inc.

Christina Caron
British Embassy

Ivan Charner
National Institute for Work
and Learning

Mat Chavez
Rockwell International

Susan Chipman
Office of Naval Research

Andrea Couture
United Negro College Fund

Doug Crawford
Athabasca University

Kerry Crist
70001 Training and
Employment Institute

Susan P. Cuman
Brandeis University

Judy B. Dailey
Ashland Oil Foundation, Inc.

Richard Danakowski
Ford Motor Company

Louis D. Dantiago
Amalgamated Clothing &
Textile Workers

E. Jewell Dassance
U.S. Basics

Dr. Leland Davies
Victoria Hospital Corporation

Libert V. P. Diaforli
McGraw-Hill, Inc.

Ralph Dosher
Texas Instruments

John Dresher
Merck, Sharp and Dohme

Paula Duggan
Northeast-Midwest Institute

Amy Dyar
Northern Telecom

Michael Emmott
Manpower Services Commission

Michael Erickson
National Job Training Partnership

Carol Ewart
Rhode Island Hospital

Cheryl Feldman
Philadelphia Hospital &
Health Care

Robert Fenn
The Travelers

Joseph Fernandez
City Bank

Ernest Fields
National Center for Research
in Vocational Education

Arlene Fingeret
NCSU Governor's Commission
on Literacy

David M. Finley
Southland Corporation

Badi G. Foster
Aetna Institute

Charlotte Frank
Twin County Credit Union

Dewey L. Gilbertson-Winbume
Creative Rapid Learning Center

Irvin Gordon
Independence Bancorp

Bill Grace
Central Kansas Cooperative
Education

Susan Greenblatt
D.C. Office of
Family Assistance

Norman T. Halls
Massachusetts Career
Development Institute

Al Halseth
Upjohn Corporation

Mary Ann Haney
Michigan Consolidated
Gas Company

William L. Hardy
Florida Department
of Transportation

David Harman
Institute for Corporate Education

Robert Harris
Harris Design Group

Carrie A. Haynes
National Association of
University Women

Sara Hayward
3M Corporation

Curtis Heath
Brown & Williamson Tobacco
Corporation

Roberta Henrichs
Michigan Consolidated
Gas Company

Larry Hirschhorn
Wharton Center for
Applied Research

Ross L. Hodgkinson
TACK

Jo Hogin
IBM/Rolm Systems

C. E. Jannetti, Director
Kepner-Tregoe, Inc.

Norfleet Jones
Aqualon Company

Sue Jones
Planters Peanuts

Pauline R. Jordan
General Electric Company

Paul Jurmo
Business Council on
Effective Literacy

Barbara Kairson
District Council 37, AFSCME

Jan Kakela
Capital Area Career Center

Dianne Kangisser
Robert Bowne Founation

Gary M. Kaplan
Jobs for Youth–Boston, Inc.

Rita Kaplan
Honeywell

George R. G. Karlsson
Growth Communications, Inc.

Leslie Kelly
Kelly and Associates

George R. Kent
Milwaukee Electric Tool
Corporation

Daryl Kinney
Arizona State University

Paula Kirby
UniSys Corporation

Robert Knight
National Association of
Private Industry Councils

Susan L. Koen
MATRICES Consultants, Inc.

Judith Ann Koloski
American Association for Adult
and Continuing Education

Robert Koppes
Gillette Company

Linda Lampkin
AFSCME

Wendy Lawson
Washington Gas and
Light Company

Luba B. Lewytzkyj
Control Data Corporation

Harvey S. Long
IBM

Jerry Lord
Higher Education &
Adult Learning

Leonard Lund
Conference Board

Robert McCarthy
70001 Training and
Employment Institute

Sherman McCoy
D.C. General Director

Maggy McFerron
Center for Applied Linguistics

E. H. McGrath, S.J.
Xavier Labour Relations Institute

P. Alistair MacKinnon
New York State
Education Department

Susan McLean
DelCo Products

Donald C. Mann
Prudential Insurance Company

John Marciari
Long Island Railroad

Jorie Lester Mark
Pennsylvania State University

Rupert H. Marsh
William Carter Company

Kimbol Martin
Easco Handtools

Jack Mastrianni
North Carolina National Issues
Chair

Christine Mattern
R. J. Reynolds Tobacco Company

David J. Matuszak
Planters/Lifesavers Company

David Meier
Center for Accelerated Learning

Jerry Meyer
ONAN Corporation

Michael D. Mierau
Emerald Corporation

Susan Miller
Continental Illinois Bank and Trust

T. R. Mizzies
Kelly-Springfield Tire Company

Tim Moore
Polaroid/Inner City, Inc.

Richard Moreno
Tucson Fire Department

Sandra Mosso
Institute for Scientific Information

Dorothy R. Murphree
Poynor Adult Center

John L. Murphy
American Institute of Banking

Charlotte Nesbitt
American Correctional Association

Marcia R. Newman
Phoenix Special Programs

Tom Newport
Allied Fibers

Thierry Noyelle
Conservation of Human Resources

James O'Connell
Control Data Corporation

Barbara Oliva
Pratt & Whitney Aircraft

Jack O'Toole
Saturn Corporation

Cindy Owen
Duke Power Company

Arnie Packer
Hudson Institute

Philip J. Papola
Consolidated Edison

Jeanne Perovich
ONAN Corporation

Susan A. Peterson
ONAN Corporation

Ron Pugsley
U.S. Department of Education

John Purnell
Digital Equipment Corporation

Don Robbins
Florida Steel Corporation

Ned Roberts
Citicorp

Bernard Robinson
Washington Hospital Center

Raymond Romero
SER-Jobs for Progress

Veda Ross
St. Vincent Hospital

Trenda Rusher
EAST-WALTEC

Carol Russo
UpState Federal
Credit Union

James T. Ryan
District 1199C

Thomas C. Saba
Plymouth (Minnesota)
Police Department

Mike Sack
Public/Private Ventures

Debra Savage
Honeywell

Robert E. Scarborough
Greater Cincinnati Industrial
Training Corporation

Betty Scharfman
Valley National Bank

Katherine Schrier
District Council 37, AFSCME

Ruth Ann Sieber
Ohio Department of Human
Services

Jane Baldus Smith
Manpower, Inc.

Ron Smith
Ford Motor Company

William F. Smith
General Motors

Rena Soifer
Ford Motor Company

Sheryl Soifer
Walgreen Company

Benita Somerfield
U.S. Department of Education

Sister Madellene Sophie, C.S.C.
St. Joseph's Medical Center

Donna Sosnowski
The Provident

Gail Spangenberg
Business Council for
Effective Literacy

Sondra Stein
Commonwealth Literacy
Campaign

Mary Louise Strom
Northeast Iowa Technical
Institute

Lori Strumpf
Center for Remediation Design

Fred A. Swan
University of Massachusetts,
Amherst

Bob Taggart
Remediation Training Institute

James O. Tatro
Aetna Institute

Jackie Taylor
Kelly Springfield Tire Company

Mary L. Tenopyr
AT&T Communications

Sara B. Toye
National SER Policy and
Research Institute

Sarah Turner
Xerox Corporation

L. L. Vickery
Buick-Oldsmobile-Cadillac
Headquarters

Dale Wade
Fisher Controls

Bill Waite
Cigna Corporation

James E. Wall, Jr.
Pratt & Whitney

Jim Walace
Newport News Shipbuilding

Thomas J. West
Michelin Tire Corporation

Philip K. Williams
Celina Insurance Group

Lois S. Wilson
Ford Aerospace Corporation

Dewey Winburne
American Institute for Learning

Robert A. Wisher
Army Research Institute

Peggy Zapple
WQED-Pittsburgh

William Zeigler, Jr.
Aetna Institute

Bob Zelnick
Jobs for Youth–Boston, Inc.

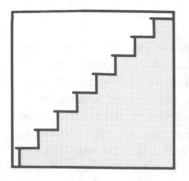

INTRODUCTION
Building a Training Program Around Essential Skills

New technology. Participative management. Sophisticated, statistical quality controls. Customer service. Just-in-time production. The workplace is changing, and so are the skills that employees must have to be able to change with it.

But many workers do not have the workplace basics essential for acquiring more sophisticated job-related skills.

While not a new problem, deficiency in basic workplace skills is a growing one. It is a challenge arising from a volatile mix of demographic, economic, and technical forces. These combined forces are propelling the nation toward a human capital deficit among both new and experienced workers, threatening the competitiveness of economic institutions, and acting as a barrier to the individual opportunity of all Americans.

Our nation is facing a startling demographic reality that will be with us for a long time. The sixteen-to-twenty-four-year-old age group that is the traditional source of new workers is shrinking; consequently, employers will be forced to reach into the ranks of the less qualified to find their entry-level work force. This means that an increasing number of entry-level workers will come from groups where, historically, human resource investments will have been deficient.

If that's news to you, don't feel bad; it's news to most. Americans are predisposed to the view that there are too many qualified people and not enough good jobs to go around. Our recent history encourages us to believe that people are superfluous while machinery, financial capital, and natural resources are hard to come by. But things are rarely as they first appear: Closely examined, the apparent excess of American workers proves illusory. In the future, there will likely be too few well-educated and trained American workers looking for their first jobs.

Ironically, this demographic reality is on a collision course with the idea that today's employees must be able to understand and acquire new and different skills quickly. As technology becomes more abundant and instantaneously available worldwide, employees' skills become an employer's competitive edge. The workplace now demands that workers have more than just a good command of the three R's. Employers want and need workers with a broad set of workplace skills—or at least with a strong foundation of basics that facilitates learning on the job.

For employers, the basic workplace skills challenge has been slowly coming into focus for some time. Inadequate reading, writing, and computation skills have been the first deficiencies to be clearly seen in the workplace. Increasingly, skills such as problem solving, listening, negotiating, and knowing how to learn also are being viewed as essentials in short sup-ply. Lack of competence in these basic workplace skills is a barrier to entry-level employees, experienced employees, and dislocated workers trying to adapt to economic and technological change within their companies.

Employer interest in improving basic workplace skills derives from economic concern. When workers' skills deficiencies affect the bottom line, employers respond with training or replacement. But the time-honored choice, replacement, is becoming less practical because the supply of work-ers is shrinking. As more and more employers are compelled to "make" rather than "buy" productive employees, employer interest in providing training in basic workplace skills is growing.

Employee interest in skills development is growing too, because work-ers are being challenged as never before. For those already employed, defi-ciencies in basic workplace skills threaten adaptation, short-circuiting successful job transitions and career growth. Employees find themselves less supervised but more frequently called upon to identify problems and make crucial decisions. The ground under them is shifting as the range of skills needed for successful participation in this economy expands.

Perhaps the most devastating impact of basic workplace deficiencies falls on the disadvantaged who are outside the economic mainstream, struggling to get in. For those attempting to enter the work force and those who have been displaced from their jobs, such deficiencies inhibit entry into productive and well-paying work, further ensuring that those already at a disadvantage will remain at the bottom of the economic ladder.

The "upskilling" of work in America is necessitated by technical changes, the need for innovation, and a sense of heightened competition. The picture is further complicated by the competitive challenges driving companies to pursue an array of strategies that require adaptive and inno-vative workers with strong interpersonal skills. Current business strate-gies—such as collaboration through work teams, exemplary customer service, and emphasis on quality—demand skills related to teamwork, lis-tening, goal setting, creativity, and problem solving.

Simultaneously, there is movement toward more participative manage-ment as employers aggressively involve workers in decision making at the point of production, service, or sale. In light of these trends, it is easy to see that new skills must be applied if employees—and their employers—are to succeed in the marketplace.

In fact, one might even say that a new kind of American worker is being ordered up. This new worker will be expected to have a broad set of skills that previously were required only of supervisors and managers.

For example, one industry in which jobs are in transition is banking. Competitive shifts and new technologies have had a profound effect on the structure, organization, and management of banks. A new customer-service philosophy demands that traditional institutional and professional special-ties give way to a one-stop-shopping approach for financial services.

Traditionally, a bank teller's primary role was to perform a series of repetitive tasks (checks and money in, money out, tally reconciliation) very well. Competitive pressures to satisfy the customer's wish for one-stop ser-vices have expanded the role of jobs at the bank teller level to include advising customers on a wide range of customized financial services. Employees in this new role are privy to diverse information previously in the domain of midlevel managers, are empowered to advise customers, and are charged with making judgment calls on the line—that is, at the point of customer contact. Moreover, these employees are linked with data via computer terminals and must have or learn a new range of skills for operating the equipment to access relevant data quickly.

In short, to be effective in the workplace, this new bank employee may not need the same degree of skills in a narrow area of expertise but instead must have good knowledge of a wide range of skills.

The Skills Employers Want

So what are the skills—the basic workplace skills—that employers want? They certainly still include the basic skills associated with formal schooling, such as reading, writing, and computation. But these are simply the tip of the iceberg.

Learning how to learn is the most basic of all skills because it is the key to lifelong learning. Equipped with this skill, a person can achieve competence in all other basic workplace skills, from reading through leadership. Without this skill, the learning process is difficult and frequently inefficient, frustrating would-be learners and leading them to give up on learning tasks.

From an employer's perspective, an employee who knows how to learn—who knows how to approach and master any new situation—is more cost effective because time and other resources spent on training can be reduced. More importantly, however, by applying new knowledge efficiently to job duties, employees who have learned how to learn can greatly assist an employer in meeting strategic goals and competitive challenges.

Reading, writing, and computation are, as has been noted, fundamental to achieving success in the workplace. The workplace of the past was one where those with limited academic skills could still succeed because many jobs required only the ability to learn a regularized or repetitive task with little or no machine interaction. In that fast-disappearing workplace, illiteracy and innumeracy could be hidden or ignored.

In contrast, today's workers often interface with sophisticated, computerized machinery. Operating that machinery safely and efficiently requires good reading skills. And the introduction of measures such as statistical process control (SPC) demands better employee mastery of high-level computation skills. Meanwhile, writing often is the first line of contact for interacting with customers, communicating with machines, documenting competitive transactions, and successfully moving new ideas from the drawing board to the workplace.

America is fortunate in that the majority of her workers are literate and numerate. But frequently employees cannot transfer these skills to the workplace. Sometimes this is because workers are suddenly called on to use mathematical principles they have not practiced for twenty years or more. Sometimes it is because skills must be used in a different context from that in which they were originally learned. So even when the base knowledge is there, workers may lack understanding of how to expand and apply it.

Reading and writing are not the only essential communication tools; it is through **listening** and **oral communication** that we most frequently interact with others. Most workers spend much of their day in some form of direct communication. In person and by phone, they communicate with each other about procedures and problems and they relay information to and receive it from customers and suppliers. Job success is strongly linked to good communication skills. In fact, recent studies indicate that only job knowledge ranks above communication skills as a factor in workplace success.

Employees who lack proficiency in oral communication and listening skills are handicapped in both learning and communication, which in turn hampers their personal and professional development. Business leaders estimate that deficiencies in these skills annually cost employers millions of dollars because of errors and lost productivity.

An organization's achievement of its strategic objectives often depends on how quickly and effectively it can transcend barriers to improved productivity and competitiveness. These pressures put **creative thinking** and **problem solving** at a premium on all organizational levels.

Problem-solving skills include the ability to recognize and define problems, to invent and implement solutions, and to track and evaluate results. Cognitive skills, group interaction skills, and information-processing skills are all crucial to successful problem solving. Creative thinking in the workplace generally relates to creative problem solving or innovative processing.

Unresolved problems create dysfunctional workplace relationships. Ultimately, these become impediments to an organization's flexibility and its ability to deal with strategic change in open-ended and creative ways. Conversely, an ability to come up with creative solutions helps an organization move toward its strategic goals.

Organizations traditionally have viewed **self-esteem, motivation, goal setting,** and **employability/career development** as skills an individual should acquire outside the workplace. But the demands of today's evolving workplace are influencing employers to recognize that when workers do not have these skills, organizations must provide training opportunities to build them.

Individual effectiveness in the workplace can be linked directly to positive self-esteem and motivation. A good self-image helps employees take pride in their work. Workers' abilities to set goals and meet them are demonstrated when production quotas are met or exceeded and when deadlines are met. Solid career development skills are evidenced by efficient integration of new technology or processes, creative thinking, high productivity, and a pursuit of skills enhancement through training or education.

Significantly, employees who exhibit these skills increase their value in the workplace and the marketplace. Employers value these skills because their presence usually leads employees to successful job transitions and effective training experiences.

Whenever people work together, successful interaction depends on effective **interpersonal** skills, focused **negotiation,** and purposeful **teamwork.** The quality of these three factors defines and controls working relationships. In the past two decades, the use of teams in the workplace has increased markedly because the team approach has been linked conclusively to higher productivity and product quality, as well as to improved quality of work life. And change strategies usually depend on the ability of employees to pull together and refocus on a new common goal.

Finally, employers want employees to have a basic level of skill in *organizational effectiveness* and *leadership.* To be effective in an organization, employees need a sense of its workings and of how their actions affect organizational and strategic objectives. A worker skilled in discerning the forces and factors that may interfere with the organization's ability to carry out its tasks can become an accomplished problem solver, innovator, and team builder.

Organizations are a tapestry of explicit and implicit power structures. In the explicit structure, leadership is conferred and represented by title and authority. In the implicit structure, leadership is a delicately sculpted image, crafted by cultivating the respect of peers and projecting a sense of reliability, goal orientation, and vision.

At all levels, employers require employees who can operate effectively within organizational parameters, assume responsibility willingly, and motivate co-workers toward exemplary performance. Organizational effectiveness and leadership skill, once identified with employees on the fast track, are now basic ingredients for all workers up and down the organizational hierarchy.

Taking the First Step

The nation is already taking the first step toward addressing basic workplace skills deficiencies. The voices of business and government leaders are joined in a dialogue aimed at effecting damage control—at meeting the challenge of basic skills deficiencies before the problem grows larger. This challenge will be difficult to surmount unless policy makers and training providers are equipped with the proper tools.

This manual and its companion book *Workplace Basics: The Essential Skills Employers Want* are both intended to provide public- and private-sector trainers and all human resource professionals with some of the tools they need for meeting this serious challenge.

Public-sector providers of training who work to enhance the skills of economically and educationally disadvantaged clients can use this manual to format their course work in a systematic fashion to meet the needs of local employers. These providers should find steps One to Three particularly useful in gaining an understanding of what kind of preparation and skills it takes to sell a program to management. Steps Four to Eight provide a clear example of how to go about establishing instructional course work to meet the rigorous standards of those who will eventually employ program completers.

Blueprint for Success: How to Create a Workplace Basics Training Program

The model discussed in this manual is a framework for using tried-and-true elements of training practice in an innovative fashion that better reflects the needs of today's workplace. This approach links three operational components to create a new training model in which the whole performs more efficiently and effectively than its parts. These components are:

- *A plan:* an in-house marketing plan to convince management and union leadership of the need to be active in linking workplace basics training programs to strategic planning and organizational goals;

- *A design:* a modified instructional system design for developing and implementing training programs; and

- *A learning method:* a job-specific, performance-oriented learning methodology for training delivery.

Combining these three components results in an applied approach to training in business organizations. This approach takes into account the constraint of scarce dollars and the rapid pace of technological change and marries them to state-of-the-art thinking about how to ensure that training is appropriate and relevant, providing the best return on investment.

Throughout the post–World War II period, American military and civilian employers have been experimenting with training practices that might enable them to link training needs directly with job requirements. This experimentation in the practical art of workplace training has evolved into an applied approach. The strength of the applied approach is that it strays as little as possible from the reality of the job and the employee. It begins and ends with the individual on the job.

Research and experience in adult training tell us that an applied approach works best because it:

- Motivates learners by linking learning to improved job performance, which in turn may lead to improvement in learners' careers and earnings;

- Encourages learner retention by requiring immediate and repeated use of newly gained knowledge; and

- Improves job performance by creating learning experiences based on actual job needs.

Embedded in the applied approach is a pragmatic, work-based program development and implementation system that can effect positive changes in employee behavior. This practical and systematic training methodology is a result of the coming together of two factors: employers' needs for training programs that will consistently improve employee job performance, and emergence of a systematic method for the design, development, and delivery of training.

The applied approach methodology first proceeds in a step-by-step fashion to measure the gap between job requirements and employee skills.

Then human resource professionals create training programs that, when fully operational, are able to translate each job's separate duties and tasks into practical learning experiences that successfully reduce or eliminate employee skill deficiencies.

The following are brief descriptions of the applied approach activities:

- *Investigate* in broad, comprehensive terms which jobs and workers need training because of changes in the nature of the work or as a result of emerging workplace problems.

- *Advocate* (a two-step process) support of a training program to management and senior union officials as an integral part of the strategic planning and goal-setting process.

- *Analyze* jobs and tasks to determine where the need is and thereby determine what training should focus on.

- *Design* the program's instructional content, related performance objectives, and criterion-referenced tests. Determine the content's structure and sequence, decide on documentation, and plan for program evaluation.

- *Develop* objectives that represent the actual learning activities workers need to master and develop documentation and evaluation instruments that measure training's impact on improving an employee's job effectiveness.

- *Implement* the program while trying out and revising materials, expanding program publicity, and putting support systems in place.

- *Evaluate* the program: first, through program monitoring that provides continuous feedback on how well learners are meeting training objectives on a day-to-day basis; and about three months later, through a program evaluation procedure activated after learners are back on their jobs and have had opportunities to put their newly gained skills into operation.

At first glance, these stages may appear to be separate and distinct, but in practice they are only roughly sequential. At a given stage of training program development, a particular activity will dominate, but all the activities exert significant and continuous influence throughout. The stages, therefore, should not be viewed as totally independent from one another. Rather, they are dynamic and interactive like the changing patterns of a kaleidoscope.

For example, the interpretation of a needs assessment will inevitably have to be rethought as new knowledge is acquired during design and implementation. Evaluation of training's effects on actual job performance will invariably test not only training program design and implementation but also the interpretation of the original needs assessment.

As an applied training program moves from inception through to completion, emphasis will rest on different roles played by personnel charged with program responsibilities. Although different roles dominate at different stages of the process, the talents and perspectives implicit in each role thread their way in and out as needed.

Initially, the talents of an investigator are needed for front-end analysis of the need for, and appropriate size of, a training program initiative. If initial investigation indicates that a significant training effort is required, then the organizational skills of an advocate are used to secure management and union approval, acceptance, and action. Next employee support must be won. Once the support of employees, management, and the unions has been secured, training experts will need to conduct a task analysis and to design, develop, implement, and evaluate the training program. These activities require training specialists with skills and experience in the areas of design, development, implementation, and evaluation.

The chart on page nine graphically displays the applied approach to creating a basic workplace skills training program. In the following chapters is an in-depth, step-by-step discussion of what is involved in preparing, promoting, and operating such a program.

Case Studies, at the conclusion of the manual, provides a description of how two companies, Mazda Motor Manufacturing (USA) Corporation and Harrison Radiator Division of General Motors, used the applied approach as a proactive strategy for ensuring quality production.

The steps discussed in the manual need not be carried out in the exact format presented. But progressing through all the steps in some logical order will significantly increase the likelihood of establishing and implementing a successful workplace basics program. As in baseball, to score a home run, you must touch all the bases!

Resource C provides separate generic training outlines for each of the sixteen skills discussed in the introduction.

Blueprint for Success

Step 1: Identify Job Changes or Problems Related to Basic Workplace Skills

- Assess the extent of the need for training because of job changes or problems
- Form a company-wide representative advisory committee
- Perform a job analysis for selected jobs
- Document employee performance deficiencies on the selected jobs
- Identify population to be targeted for training
- Build cooperation with unions

Step 2: Build Support for Training Through Alliances with Management and Unions

- Make the case for skills training in workplace basics
- Build support for skills training in workplace basics

Step 3: Present the Strategy and Action Plan for Approval

- Present the strategy and action plan for training
- Select a training program architect: in-house staff versus external providers

Step 4: Perform a Task Analysis

- Perform a task analysis
- Determine whether to select a quick route through task analysis and determine which process is most appropriate
- Review the generic elements of the task analysis process

Step 5: Design the Curriculum

- Design performance-based, functional context instructional program
- Design evaluation system
- Design documentation and record-keeping system
- Obtain final budget approval to implement

Step 6: Develop the Program

- Prepare the instructional format
- Select instructional techniques
- Select facilities site and designate equipment requirements
- Develop evaluation and monitoring instruments

Step 7: Implement the Program

- Select and train the instructional staff
- Develop a learning contract: yes or no?
- Run pilot test (optional)

Step 8: Evaluate and Monitor the Program

- Carry out initial evaluation
- Begin on-going program monitoring
- Advise and consult with management on program status

How to Use the Manual

The different elements in this manual are designed to make it easy to use, both as a reference on specific topics and as an instructional text on how to design a workplace basics skills training program from beginning to end. The symbols and conventions used to indicate the different elements in the manual are listed below.

Major headings are printed in blue boldface type.

Secondary headings are in black boldface type.

Chapters/Steps: Each step in Designing a Workplace Basics Skills Training Program is discussed in a separate chapter. The page numbering tells the reader the step and page number.

Learning Objectives: Each chapter begins with a set of learning objectives that describes what the learner should know or be able to do as a result of reading and using the materials in that particular step.

Case Study: Case studies are provided to give the manual user some real-life examples of experiences of other organizations or corporations.

Examples: Examples are provided to illustrate a particular point or to provide several alternative approaches to a similar task.

Checklists: Checklists are provided to help the manual user review material just covered or to ensure that the user has considered every step in a multistep process.

Tables: Tables are provided to supplement the text with an experiential exercise so that the user can work through a particular process firsthand and better understand how a particular task or activity is accomplished.

The *Remember Box* reiterates an important point made in the text so that the user's memory will be refreshed before moving on.

Definitions: A definition is pulled out of the text where the word is first used and is italicized for easy reference.

Glossary: Terms are defined in the glossary at the end of the manual.

Resources: Resources are located at the end of the manual and provide relevant supplemental material.

References and Suggested Readings: References and Suggested Readings are located at the end of each step to provide the manual user with additional resources on the topics covered.

A *Notes* section is provided at the end of each step so that the manual user can have a place to jot notes for further reference.

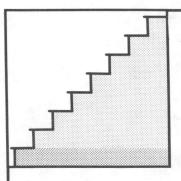

STEP ONE

Identify Job Changes or Problems Related to Basic Workplace Skills

Learning Objectives

The reader will be able to:

1. List the circumstances under which basic workplace skills problems are likely to become apparent.

2. Determine the composition of a representative advisory committee for the basic workplace skills training program.

3. Establish a process for selecting members of the advisory committee.

4. Develop and implement a plan for winning employee acceptance and support in both union and nonunion situations.

5. Develop a job description.

6. Select jobs for an in-depth analysis.

7. Document employee performance problems.

8. Identify populations to be targeted for required or voluntary basic workplace skills training.

9. Develop a plan for building support and cooperation with the union.

Introduction

To win management support for training in basic workplace skills, there needs to be a front-end job review to identify job problems and job changes that may require new or up-graded training. This is a preliminary **needs analysis.**

Needs analysis is a systematic process for determining and ordering goals, measuring needs, and deciding on priorities for action.

A job review is the process of gathering, recording, and analyzing job descriptions and job performance information necessary to make good training decisions. The results of a good job review can be critical to the proper allocation of an institution's limited training resources in a manner that will contribute to the achievement of its strategic goals. Useful research data are relevant, accurate, current, and sufficient (Silver, 1985, p. 17).

The job preliminary review is the equivalent of an in-house marketing research effort. It is generally initiated as a response to two basic circumstances:

- Uncertainties about performance that may be the result of basic workplace skills problems reported on a case-by-case basis, or

- Broader institutional performance needs.

Often managers, supervisors, or employees observe and report problems or employee behavior patterns that indicate the presence of one or more basic workplace skills problems. Problems may become more apparent when employees try to:

- Meet new regulatory requirements,

- Adapt to technological or procedural changes, or

- Comply with policies designed to advance new corporate strategies.

Where organizations have institutionalized basic workplace skills training as an employee benefit, individual employees will be less fearful of losing their jobs and often will report their own problems and seek assistance.

Case Study

General Motors: Employee-Reported Skills Problems

Ten thousand employees at a General Motors plant in Ypsilanti, Mich., were polled to determine what kind of basic skills training they thought would be helpful. The pollsters helped workers who had trouble completing the questionnaire. Of the 5,700 who responded, 22 percent said they needed training in "understanding simple words, signs, and labels," and 31 percent asked for help in understanding "basic written directions, charts, and procedures." The plant management and local union leadership both thought the assessment to be accurate (Ross, 1986, p. 49).

The four examples given here show the kind of new regulatory requirements, changes in job requirements, and institutional and strategic goals that a company might have to respond to by training employees.

Examples

Safety and Health Regulations

Regulations of the Occupational Safety and Health Administration require that workers using particular kinds of hazardous substances be trained in safety procedures for both the use and disposal of the materials. There are also monetary considerations. Chrysler Corporation estimated that it saves $1.3 million by training workers about the dangers of hazardous substances in the workplace (U.S. Congress, Office of Technology Assessment, 1988).

Fair Hiring Practices

If the regulations concerning discrimination in hiring on the basis of sex or race were altered, employers would have to ensure, probably by training affected personnel, that the regulations were understood and followed.

New Technology

When a company changes from manually operated to computerized tools, machine operators must acquire a whole new set of abilities that may require training in basic workplace skills like reading, problem solving, and computation.

Quality Circles or Work Teams

A decision by management to move toward more employee participation in decision making through quality circles or self-directed work teams will change workers' jobs in a way that may require training in communication and interpersonal skills.

The Investigator: Assess the Extent of the Problem

*The **investigator** explores the nature and scope of all reported problems in order to determine an appropriate response.*

After the initial report of a basic workplace skills problem, the basic workplace skills **investigator**'s role takes center stage. The investigator assesses the extent of the basic skills problem and may ascertain that a training remedy is necessary and cost effective.

First, however, the investigator must discover whether the reported problem requires a comprehensive training effort or whether an alternative, and perhaps less expensive, remedy will be just as effective.

Self-reporting and special case reporting of basic workplace skills problems are often the most obvious clues in a basic workplace skills investigation. But there are other, more subtle clues.

Case Study

Preventing Accidents at a Public Utility

In one public utility, employee accidents occurred regularly despite extensive posting of warnings in dangerous areas. Management first assumed a basic literacy problem. But a thorough investigation revealed that the employees had grown so accustomed to the sight of the warning signs that they no longer paid them any attention. When new, eye-catching color signs were substituted for old black and white signs, the incidence of accidents declined markedly. Changing the signs was apparently effective and certainly less expensive than providing a basic workplace reading program for employees who did not really need it.

Reports of quality problems or safety and regulatory violations should be examined with an eye toward uncovering basic workplace skills problems. Any substantial change in work requirements that might increase job skill requirements is equally deserving of an investigator's attention.

It is critical that the investigator explore the nature and scope of all reported problems in order to determine an appropriate response. When examining a self-reported case of basic workplace skills problems, the investigator must determine if the individual report should be regarded as an indication of more pervasive problems.

Case Study

Duke Power Company: Reactive Response

When Duke Power Company was ending its construction phase, it wanted to retain some of the construction workers for maintenance jobs inside the plant. The prospective employees, however, could not pass a written test mandated by the Nuclear Regulatory Commission and the company, even after it was extensively rewritten. Duke Power set up a task force to look into the literacy problem and is developing a job-specific program aimed at employees who do not have the skills they need, as well as at other employees whose jobs have rising skill requirements (Lee, 1988, p. 32).

Allowing these problems to go undetected and uncorrected could threaten other crucial areas of an organization such as safety and regulatory compliance, the ability to adapt successfully to institutional changes, achievement of institutional strategies and goals, or the career development of broad classes of employees.

This means that an investigator will always need to move from a reactive to a proactive role in order to ascertain the true magnitude of the problem.

Case Study

General Motors: Proactive Response

In 1984, General Motors (GM) underwent a massive reorganization that included its automotive assembly division. The divisional reorganization and introduction of robotics systems required extensive training to prepare plant personnel to operate, maintain, and repair the new equipment. After trying a combination of resources to provide the training, GM developed an in-house instructor team that over a two-and-a-half-year period trained 200 production-oriented personnel and over 200 skilled tradespeople in operating and troubleshooting. One of the most important lessons learned was the value of providing basic training to employees prior to equipment-specific vendor training (Casner-Lotto and Associates, 1988, pp. 188–199).

Formalize the Representative Advisory Committee

When an investigation is initiated that could affect employee job status, an investigator must be sensitive to the possibility of an adverse reaction to the process. Any action taken in conjunction with work in progress, such as observing employees on the job or going through their work records, could be misconstrued as having a possible negative impact on job security.

As a protection against such misunderstanding, a formal representative task force or advisory committee should be formed to oversee the analysis, design, development, implementation, and evaluation process. This should help to build acceptance company-wide for the training program.

The composition of such a committee will vary from company to company. Typically these committees include representatives from training and human resources, department heads and supervisors directly affected by the program, plant managers, union or other employee representatives, and employees themselves.

A balanced committee will ensure the input of all points of view, from top management who are familiar with the company goals and policies to the relatively inexperienced worker who knows firsthand the specific learning needed to successfully perform on the job. Checklist 1 gives the range of personnel you should consider including on such a committee.

Checklist

Checklist 1. Members to Include on a Workplace Basics Advisory Committee.

☐ Training department representative

☐ Human resources department representative

☐ Manager or assistant from affected department

☐ Front-line supervisor(s)

☐ Union steward or representative

☐ One or two respected, experienced workers

☐ One or two skilled, exemplary workers

☐ One or two enthusiastic, newer workers

The announcement that the company is exploring the development of a basic workplace skills training program should highlight the establishment of the formal advisory committee to oversee the project.

The announcement should include the items listed in Checklist 2.

Checklist

Checklist 2. Information to Include in the Announcement.

☐ The general make-up of the committee

☐ The size of the committee

☐ The committee's assignment

☐ The approximate work schedule to projected date of completion

☐ The selection process

The process must not appear to be prejudiced or closed, giving the whole project the appearance of preselection and manipulation. One should not be able to say, "They have already made up their minds. Why should I get involved?"

It may even be desirable to invite a skeptical person from any level of the organization to serve on the committee. Involvement is the surest way to convert negative, destructive energy into positive, constructive action and support.

This is, of course, a judgment call that should be made only with great caution. The project leader should consider in making this decision that such people are likely to serve only if they have some real interest in the project that can be channeled in a positive direction.

Keep the committee relatively small at first so that you can show flexibility by adding interested and qualified personnel who might later express a desire to participate.

Remember, it is better to have to expand the group because of growing interest in the project than to be forced to proceed with a smaller-than-announced group because of apathy toward basic workplace skills training.

Demonstrating flexibility at this point can establish a spirit of openness for the entire project that encourages involvement and support.

When the committee has been formed, make a positive announcement with a restatement of its goals and anticipated schedule of work. Checklist 3 lists the questions that need to be answered when selecting an advisory committee.

 Checklist

Checklist 3. Advisory Committee Selection Process and Considerations.

☐ Has administrative clearance been given for people to work on the project?

☐ Has the approximate number of personnel on the committee been determined?

☐ What mechanism(s) can be used to ensure that the announcement is circulated to all affected personnel at about the same time?

☐ Is it clear to whom and by when interested people should respond? Keep in mind that it may be necessary to ask certain key people to participate. It is often not enough just to offer the opportunity.

☐ Is the selection process clear?

☐ Does the committee composition have the balance suggested in the previous list of committee members?

☐ Does the committee include more than just experienced workers?

☐ Are the individuals under consideration relatively confident, open, and communicative?

☐ Can they relate well both up and down the organizational hierarchy?

☐ Are any of them threatened by authority?

☐ Do any of them have a history of personal animosity toward one another?

☐ In a union situation, has the union been sufficiently involved in the selection of employee representatives so as not to endanger its support of the project?

☐ Are different work sites adequately represented?

Once the advisory committee is formalized, a core group from the committee should be designated the *task analysis subcommittee.*

People with expert knowledge of the job to be analyzed should be designated as members of the *job-specific review committee.* This second committee will review the work of the task analysis subcommittee to ensure that it is correct. These committees will validate the final task listing for each job or job family in their own areas of expertise.

Win Employee Acceptance and Support

Besides including employee representatives on the committee, it is essential to begin and follow through on a strategy for gaining employee acceptance. It is politically and strategically essential to gain the support of all employees.

Some ideas for approaching this task might include:

- Make the program highly visible. Use internal newsletters, union and employee representatives, and other communications sources to let employees know that a new training program will be developed for implementation at a given start-up date.

- Include an address and telephone number where employees can obtain more detailed information.

- Brief union and employee representatives. Use union or other employee representatives who are knowledgeable about the program to allay any fears that this and related activities will have a negative impact on employment status.

- Emphasize positive aspects of the program:
  a. Characterize the program as an effort to improve company-wide technical readiness,
  b. Characterize the program as an effort to offer employees a chance for improving their promotion possibilities, and
  c. Characterize the program as an effort to maximize limited training dollars to improve both company and individual performance.

People are motivated most strongly by self-interest, either for defense (keeping what they have and value) or for gain (achieving something they want).

The most successful strategy will, therefore, address the employees' needs for job security, personal growth, career advancement, recognition, and so on, as well as addressing the company's future well-being.

The future of the company should also be important to the employees, but it should be explained from their point of view.

Employee Support in a Union Situation

To gain employee acceptance and support in a union situation:

- Contact the union through the appropriate official. An understanding of the union's structure will be necessary to determine whether this should be a steward or a higher official in the union.

- Approach the initial meeting with the union with an open mind. Announce in general terms what is contemplated in basic workplace skills training and also indicate that both the union's acceptance of the program and its participation and support are sought.

    You might ask whether the local's national affiliate headquarters has a training or education department that could assist with the project.

- A subsequent meeting with the union would be useful to broaden its involvement in the project. Include shop stewards and rank-and-file members who might contribute to the project.

Although the company may indicate its intention to involve the most productive, or most successful workers, it would be unwise to attempt to dictate to the union specifically whom it should bring to such a meeting.

- Work with the union in announcing the program to the workers. Joint communications would, of course, indicate clearly that the union and employer are collaborating on the project.

See Table 1 later in this chapter (p. 1.20) for further details.

Employee Support in a Nonunion Situation

The chain of command in the company must, of course, be respected when seeking to win the acceptance and support of workers for the basic workplace skills training program.

When there is no formal union structure, it will require some sensitivity on the part of the trainer to avoid the appearance of management co-optation. The enthusiastic involvement of the workforce requires that there be not even the suggestion of worker manipulation.

Attempt to identify the natural work leaders, those who have won the respect of their co-workers and whose support will draw a positive response to the project from their peers. The emphasis should be on the opportunity to participate in a new and exciting program.

The process might go as follows:

1. Speak with supervisors to:
    a. Identify exemplary workers and
    b. Suggest possible work leaders.

2. Announce purpose of basic workplace skills program:
    a. Voluntary or required,
    b. Nonevaluative,
    c. Designed to improve worker satisfaction and productivity.

3. Outline employee participation and involvement:
    a. Advisory committee,
    b. Program design,
    c. Instruction,
    d. Program review and revision, and
    e. Program evaluation.

4. Participation in project activities is:
    a. Desirable and
    b. Voluntary.

5. Method of contact:
    a. Meeting and/or
    b. Questionnaire or survey.

Perform a Job Analysis

*A **job analysis** is a process designed to determine whether a basic workplace skills problem exists that warrants a special training effort for a substantial number of employees.*

Once the preliminary needs analysis has verified that a particular job situation needs attention, the next step is to analyze a current or future discrepancy between what is and what ought to be. This process, the **job analysis,** is phase two of the needs analysis.

Job description research and analysis does not require a heavy upfront commitment of staff or dollars. The activity can be carried out by inhouse personnel with some experience in job analysis.

If no experienced in-house person is available, a specialized provider can be hired to perform this limited task at relatively little cost.

In larger companies job descriptions are normally found on file in company personnel offices. Companies that do not maintain job description files can find adequate substitutes in the *Dictionary of Occupational Titles,* published by the U.S. Department of Labor, or through a literature search on job descriptions developed by other companies in their industry or related industries.

It may turn out that existing job descriptions no longer fit the work being done. In that case a new analysis may need to be undertaken (see Step Four).

The difference between the job analysis at this point and the task analysis described in Step Four is mainly one of detail. The objective of the job analysis is to determine in broad terms whether a basic workplace skills problem exists of a magnitude large enough to consider mounting a specialized training effort for a substantial number of employees.

The purpose of gathering this preliminary information is to have a strong case to present to management. If management approves the development of a new training effort, then a more detailed task analysis will need to be undertaken. The focus of the subsequent task analysis is to determine precisely the behavior necessary to perform appropriate learning objectives.

Job Description

*A **job description** is a tool for describing general information about what a person does on a job and the conditions under which she or he works. It is composed of a number of duty statements, that is, statements that describe a worker's major job duties and responsibilities.*

A **job description** is a tool for describing general information about:

- What a person does on a job, and
- The conditions under which she or he works.

It is composed of a number of duty statements, that is, statements that describe a worker's major job duties and responsibilities.

The example given here is a generic description of the duties and responsibilities for the position of machinist.

Case Study

Machinist 600-280.022

Sets up and operates machine tools and fits and assembles parts to make or repair metal parts, mechanisms, tools, or machines, applying knowledge of mechanics, shop mathematics, metal properties, and layout and machining procedures. Studies specifications such as blueprint, sketch, damaged parts, or description of parts to be replaced to determine dimensions and tolerance of piece to be machined, sequence of operations and tools, and materials and machines required. Measures, marks, and scribes dimensions and reference points to lay out stock for machining. Sets up and operates metal-removing machines, such as lathe, milling machine, shaper, or grinder, to machine parts specifications using measuring instruments, and so on (adapted from U.S. Department of Labor, 1977, p. 488).

Obviously, a job description is only the outline of a job. It does, however, provide enough information for determining what is essential to perform competently in a particular job.

The next step is to match the duties that make up a job or family of jobs with the basic workplace skills required to perform these duties. A preliminary analysis of the machinist's job description would indicate that certain basic workplace skills are required for competent performance including:

- Problem solving—the worker must be able to select the proper tools and the appropriate machines;

- Reading for technology—the worker must be able to interpret blueprints and read precision instruments; and

- Computation—the worker must be able to apply principles to shop mathematics.

A job description provides only a guideline for determining whether there is a discrepancy between the written statements that describe what a worker ought to be doing on a job and what an employee actually does on a job.

Job Identification Phase

During this preliminary job identification phase, it is particularly important how jobs are selected for analysis. When employees or managers report basic workplace skills problems, jobs targeted for further analysis are at first limited to those of the self-reported or manager-reported employees. If an investigator is satisfied that a basic workplace skills problem is restricted to those identified jobs, the selection process ends and a limited training opportunity may be implemented.

If an investigator suspects that the reported problems are indicative of a larger problem, it is appropriate to select further jobs in order to verify the information.

When certain jobs are flagged from outside a department because they affect organizational performance, selection of these jobs for further analysis depends on how important they are to meeting institutional goals. If basic workplace skills problems can be isolated and identified as having a significant negative impact on company performance, then the selected jobs should be those that demonstrate a strong likelihood for improving that performance. For example, if there is a concern that basic workplace skills problems are resulting in production of defective products, then jobs most critical to correcting those defects should be analyzed.

Document Employee Performance Problems

Once relevant job descriptions are compiled, the basic workplace skills investigator gathers information about the performance levels of individual employees or groups of employees who work at the selected jobs. The investigator then compares the written job skill requirements against each employee's performance on the selected job in order to make a preliminary determination as to whether worker performance, in the aggregate, matches the requirements listed in the job description.

The investigator must take into account the skill levels required for each pay step within the job family. Using the machinist as an example, pay step three may require only skill at hand lathe operation, while pay step nine may involve mastery of a numeric control machine.

Information about an employee's basic workplace skills and educational background can be obtained in various ways depending upon the original purpose of the basic workplace skills investigation and the reactive or proactive approach of the investigator. All current employees in jobs critical to the performance problem are candidates for review. If the performance problems of prior job holders are consistent with those of current job holders, both will be useful in providing clues. At a minimum, the skill profiles of prior job holders provide a useful and nonthreatening starting point for an analysis of the basic workplace skill requirements for a particular job family. Depending on available financial resources and time constraints, an investigator may review employee performance using one or more of the following tools:

- Anecdotal information obtained through informal conversation with workers, union representatives, and supervisors discussing their perceptions of skills and proficiencies needed to perform a job competently;
- Selected observation of behavior by training department members who are skilled in observational analysis;
- Oral or written questionnaires developed and administered by the training department;
- Union grievance records or other legal records accessed through requests for information from the union or legal department;
- Performance appraisal records accessed through the personnel department; and
- Compensation records accessed through the personnel department. These provide accurate tallies of how many people do what and what they are paid.

At all times it is of utmost importance to provide and maintain confidentiality and to publicize this fact.

Basic workplace skills problems may become particularly obvious when the job responsibilities of workers are changing. The investigator should look for situations where new responsibilities may require additional skills on the part of employees like those in the examples given here.

Examples

Government Regulations

New government regulations require emission control tests on automobiles. The employees of a chain of auto repair facilities need to learn how to operate new specialized equipment, how to carry out proper procedures for determining whether a given vehicle passes the test, how to complete the required forms correctly, and how to advise customers of necessary corrective action.

Auto Repair

The responsibilities of repairing automobiles have changed so dramatically with the introduction of computerized devices to replace mechanical ones that the job title has been changed from auto mechanic to automobile service technician. Rather than searching for the broken part, the technician uses computerized analysis to determine what repairs are necessary.

Health Care

The increased use of outpatient procedures in the health care industry requires employees to be able to read and explain complicated follow-up directions to patients before they go home.

Automated Tools

A small manufacturing company is changing over from hand-operated to automated machine tools. The new job description reveals that employees must be able to read and apply directions from the operator's manuals for the machines and perform conversion to metric values.

Banking Deregulation

Banking deregulation leads a savings and loan to offer new services to its customers. Job descriptions reveal that new terminology, procedures, and decisions must be learned by employees so they can deal with the changes.

The beginning of job description development and preliminary determination of employee problems should be carried out with care; good documentation must be maintained. These records may later be useful to:

- Help target the jobs and populations for which a new training program will be developed, if a training program is recommended;

- Support a request for allocating funds for a new training program; or

- Satisfy a union or employee representative's request for back-up information verifying that employee skills problems are significant enough to warrant establishing a new training program.

If the evidence demonstrates that individual job performance is related to problems in basic workplace skills, a training plan should be presented to management that details the corrective action necessary to rectify the problems.

Identify Populations to Be Targeted for Training

Although curriculum design will be strongly influenced by a careful analysis of the jobs and the targeting of performance problems, it will also be heavily influenced by the population identified to receive the training.

There are circumstances in which a company will need to train all employees in a given job classification, such as the introduction of a new technology, a new service, or a new operating procedure (required training).

In other situations, when management, supervisory personnel, or the workers themselves have identified a problem, training may be offered to a group of employees (voluntary training). In either case, certain fundamental principles of adult learning need to be applied if the training is to be effective:

- Adults resist learning anything because someone says they should. They need to have an inner motivation to develop a new skill or acquire new knowledge.

- If employees themselves are satisfied with the status quo, they will feel little need to change.

- Adult learners need to see how the situation concerns them, how the training will be directly helpful to them, and how it will pay off for the company.

So, whether the training is to be required or voluntary, sell it to the employees. The best-conceived and best-delivered program will fail if the trainees do not buy it.

Populations for Required Training

A major issue for any company providing training is whether it ought to be required. Required training often raises fears among employees that the training is a management scheme for weeding out the less effective members of the work force. Unless required training has employee support, cooperation is likely to be nonexistent, especially in a unionized institution.

A training plan must be carefully introduced to demonstrate relevance to the jobs in question and to head off any legal issues that might be raised. It is likely that employees will participate enthusiastically if the training is consistent with the goals of the work teams as well as with individual career development goals.

The way in which required training is presented is very important. The word *required* can have several different meanings. For example:

- New technology is changing the nature of the jobs, and training is required to maintain employee skills;

- Possibilities for employee promotion will require additional training; or

- A new approach to production is being implemented, and employees will be subject to job reclassification that requires additional skills.

There are many ways in which required training can be introduced. One example is currently popular among high-tech companies. It is referred to as learning by objectives (LBO). A manager and an employee sit down together and negotiate in advance a written agreement on the training the employee will undertake in the coming year. At the end of that year, they review the outcomes and decide if any further training is necessary. Both parties understand that the employee's career will be shaped and furthered by these decisions.

In addition to LBO, some other ways to provide positive reinforcement for required training are to:

- Assure employees that the company values them and that is why the program is being offered;

- Ensure confidentiality of all records;

- Avoid any public characterizations that expose personal problems;

- Appeal to the employees' pride in working for an innovative, up-to-date organization; and

- Point out choices the training will open for employees.

Positive and Negative Motivating Tools

There are a number of reasons workers might become motivated, some of which are positive and some negative. Here are some examples:

- *Job security and other factors.* Job security is an especially critical issue for workers today. It is fine to talk of opportunities for promotion and advancement, but almost everyone knows that there is currently a steady upward shift in the basic skill requirements for well-paying jobs. Keeping something they value (a well-paying job) offers workers strong motivation for training.

Other negative-sounding but very real motivators are: fear of loss of self-esteem, guilt at not performing as well as one's peers, failure to achieve accepted standards, and being unsuccessful at reaching career and personal goals.

These factors should not be underestimated. Some individuals are not moved to action by anything other than fear of failure. Management and supervisory personnel should be very forthright about the possible consequences for workers who do not take advantage of training opportunities to upgrade their skills. Do not allow them to complain later that "no one ever explained it to me that way."

- *Employee-identified need.* Required training is particularly effective if the need for it is identified by the employees themselves. When a study team at Onan Corporation in Minneapolis, Minn., asked the workers to assess their own readiness for dealing with new technology being introduced, 60 percent indicated they needed help in reading blueprints and specifications. And when the firm offered technical courses to prepare them for the automation, many individuals could not complete the preliminary survey instrument (Lee, 1988, pp. 30–31).

- *Supervisory support.* Supervisors should be informed about the purpose and content of the program. Their support can be invaluable in convincing workers that the training will be useful. Similarly, their interest after the training is completed will encourage workers to apply their new skills and knowledge to the job.

On the other hand, supervisors' lack of knowledge and support will send a strong message to workers that they view the training as an intrusion and really do not expect much change or improvement to result.

Populations for Voluntary Training

Voluntary training falls into two categories:

- Training for professional growth and development, which is related to the individual's career or job; for example, upgrade training in computation to handle a move to statistical process control.

- Training for personal growth, which is strictly related to an individual's desire to improve her or himself; for example, a course in Spanish.

To ensure participation in job-related voluntary training, costs should be picked up by the company, and training should be offered either in-house or through outside providers working on-site.

But if an employee wants non-job-related education or training to improve her or his general quality of life rather than to affect job performance directly and the employer wishes to pay for it, it is probably more cost effective for an employer to contract with an external provider or use tuition reimbursement than to try to develop an in-house program to meet multiple goals and objectives.

From a management perspective, employee training not directly tied to job improvement is not a good business investment because it does not directly relate to the bottom line.

When providing job-related voluntary training opportunities, remember that on-site instruction and full or partial time off from work will attract more of an audience because it will not inconvenience participants and will be perceived as an employee benefit.

If instruction is given off-site, the company might also consider picking up fees and transportation costs to encourage participation.

Small, discrete work groups might be especially receptive audiences for voluntary training. People who work closely together are usually aware of their needs, and, in situations where they identify a particular problem, the basic workplace skills trainer can help by designing a program for them or finding them an appropriate course of instruction offered by an outside provider.

Build Cooperation with the Unions

The establishment of a consensus position between labor and management on common training needs, both required and voluntary, will reap big benefits later, when more difficult decisions are made, because the precedent for agreement will already have been set.

Some successful programs are jointly funded, designed, administered, and operated by union and management. Jointly funded programs can create a sense of shared responsibility for management of the training and for its results.

Union involvement in training can be limited or extensive. Involvement can be limited to funding, setting goals or selecting courses, and contracting with outside providers to conduct training. On the other hand, it may include participating in course development, content development, and delivery, as well as selecting trainers from the union ranks.

Experience at the Ford Motor Company and elsewhere demonstrates that the more inclusive the union involvement is, the more cooperation there will be, and the more durable the learning will be (Rosow and Zager, 1988).

Union representation on the company's planning team can be immensely valuable. Historically, unions have a commitment to education. Many already are heavily involved in providing basic skills services, sometimes as a partner with management, sometimes by directly initiating and running programs themselves.

Case Study

United Auto Workers, General Motors, and Ford

In 1984 the United Auto Workers union (UAW) negotiated agreements with both General Motors and Ford to establish basic skills programs. More than $200 million a year was made available at General Motors and some $120 million over three years at Ford. The programs cover all forms of adult education, including language training and remedial reading. Chrysler began to consider basic skills programming in 1985–1986 and has since allocated substantial funds to its effort.

At the local level, each company's program is governed by a joint body consisting of two or three UAW officials and three company representatives. This group has overall responsibility for deciding how and what basic skills instruction should be given and how it should fit into the overall education and health program.

At Ford, it was agreed that the program would be built from the elicited interests of the workers themselves. Of six areas of training requested, one was a basic skills enhancement program. Since 1983, 45,000 UAW members have participated in the various programs, 8,300 in basic skills.

The skills enhancement program is jointly administered from the companies and from UAW national headquarters in Dearborn, Mich. The union also provides guidance and support for the projects at the plant level, where they are jointly governed by union and management representatives.

Along with standard materials, teachers are expected to develop customized curricula related to each individual's work and personal life (Business Council for Effective Literacy, 1987).

In very large industries, such as auto making, unions often provide major financial backing for educational activities. Most see the provision of educational benefits for their members as a key area for contract negotiation.

Unions can play a key role in efforts to recruit employees. Because they are trusted by their members, their endorsement of the program will help convince potential trainees that it is a good thing. And union publications are an excellent vehicle for promoting programs and giving employees information about program activities, goals, and procedures.

Many unions also are experienced in developing job-specific basic skills curricula. This could be an important resource in efforts to analyze the basic skills requirements of jobs and later in designing an effective program (Business Council for Effective Literacy, 1987).

Case Study

International Ladies Garment Workers Union and T.J. Maxx

The International Ladies Garment Workers Union operates a training program with the management of T.J. Maxx, a subsidiary of Newton Buying Corporation located in Worcester, Mass. This project started as a collaboration between labor, management, and a local community college.

Management and labor both sit on the project advisory committee, which established the program philosophy and hired the program coordinator, and both sides are accountable for making the program work.

The union provides material for curriculum development and assists in student recruitment and support. Management has given teachers access to the shop floor so that they are exposed to authentic work site language needs and can directly encourage line supervisors to support the program.

The program coordinator regularly attends the weekly meetings of supervisors. And department production quotas have been adjusted to permit personnel to attend classes on released time (Business Council for Effective Literacy, 1987).

It will obviously be difficult to work with the union if past relationships have not been harmonious. The present climate, however, generally favors joint efforts between labor and management to maintain the competitive position of American industry. Thoughtful preparation before the initial meeting will maximize the chances for a positive response from the union.

In Table 1 are suggestions for preparing to meet with the union.

Table

Table 1. How to Prepare to Meet with the Union.

1. Meet with staff from the labor relations department. Ask them to:

   - Review the company's general relationship with the union.

   - Identify the key union leaders to be contacted.

   - Review any contractual provisions that might affect the proposed basic workplace skills training.

   - Anticipate any particular union concerns for which you should be prepared.

   - Introduce yourself to the key leaders of the local union.

2. Review records of:

   - Any joint union-management projects.

   - Union participation in or reactions to past training programs.

   - Grievance or regulatory complaints that might be related to basic workplace skills problems.

3. Research the local and international union's involvement in basic skills training.

4. Follow protocol. Hold an initial meeting with the local union president or other appropriate official. She or he will determine who else should be included in subsequent meetings.

5. Anticipate the union's questions. Be ready to:

   - Discuss the reasons for the proposed training program.

   - Present any documentation you have of basic workplace skills problems.

   - Outline the plan of action.

   - Clarify the program's relationship to job security.

   - Specifically request that the union be involved in the project.

   - Commit the company to release time for union-named employees who might be involved in the project.

Explore Possible Training Options

The questions in Table 2 illustrate the possible options in the applied approach that could be modified and accomplished through off-the-shelf purchase or a nontraining solution. They demonstrate that flexible response and an awareness of the multiple training opportunities available are the best way to ensure that the most cost-effective, least intrusive solution is promoted.

Table

Table 2. Questions to Ask to Identify Possible Training Options.

1. What is the performance discrepancy?

   - What is the difference between what workers are doing and what they should be doing?
   - What is not being accomplished that causes dissatisfaction?

2. Is the discrepancy important?

   - What does it cost the company?
   - What happens if nothing is done?

3. Is the performance discrepancy caused by a basic workplace skills problem?

   - Could the workers perform if required to do so?
   - Are the workers' skills deficient?
   - If so, in what way?

4. If the performance discrepancy is not caused by a problem in basic workplace skills, why are skilled workers not performing up to standards?

- Is it caused by some obstacle to performance, such as faulty tools, equipment, or materials? Are superior workers punished by being given more and harder work than their less productive peers?
- Are nonperformers rewarded in some way?
- Are performance expectations unclear?

5. If the performance discrepancy is caused by a basic workplace skills problem, how can that problem be resolved?
   - Can the job be changed so that the workers can produce the desired output with their present level of skills?
   - Can some job aids be provided to compensate for the skills problems and enable the workers to perform satisfactorily?
   - Do the workers have the potential to learn the skills required for satisfactory performance?

6. If skills must be improved, can the problem be resolved by on-the-job training or is a more formal training program required?

7. If an extensive, formal training program is required, what is the most cost-effective way it can be provided?
   - Are programs available at a local community college or some other institution?
   - Can suitable programs be purchased and adapted to meet the need?

8. If the program must be developed in-house, to what extent is in-house expertise sufficient and available to do the job?

9. What outside providers are available to contribute to development and implementation of the training program?

10. Of all the possible courses of action available to correct the performance discrepancy, which is the most cost effective in terms of meeting the company's goals and objectives?
    - Have all possible courses of action been considered?
    - For which course of action are the company's capabilities best suited?
    - Which course of action will best suit the long-term interests of the company?
    - Which course of action is most favored by management?

REMEMBER

A note of caution: Before moving ahead with plans for development of a basic workplace skills program, pause to examine and separate out those caused by difficulties not resolvable through training.

The problem of deficiency in job performance can be evaluated in terms of doing something about the operator or about the job (or both, if the situation requires). Figure 1 shows some solutions for both situations.

It is important to avoid the solution of overtraining, which can have negative results such as:

- More and longer courses than are necessary;

- Money unnecessarily spent on training-related personnel and equipment;

- Overtraining of personnel, thus raising expectations for jobs that workers will not be able to fill; and

- Training as an end in itself.

Figure 1. Options for Tackling the Problem of Job Deficiencies.

FITTING THE PERSON TO THE JOB

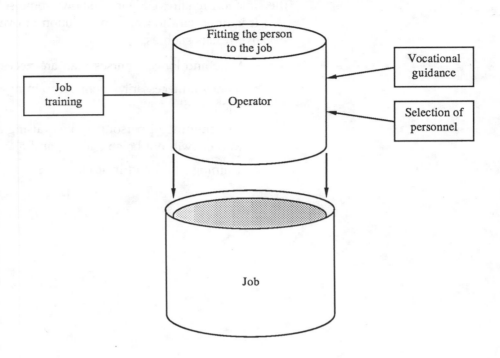

FITTING THE JOB TO THE PERSON

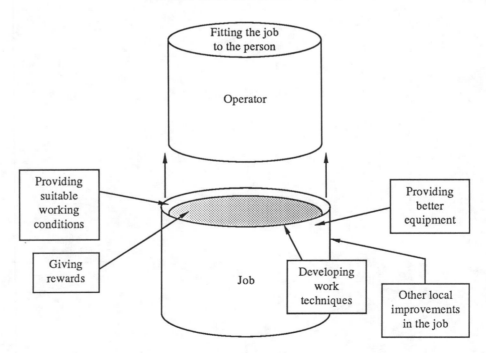

Source: Adapted from Wilson, 1987, p. 16. Used by permission of The Parthenon Publishing Group, Inc.

References and Suggested Readings

Abella, K. T. *Building Successful Training Programs: A Step-by-Step Guide.* Reading, Mass.: Addison-Wesley, 1986.

American Society for Training and Development. "Basics of Instructional Systems Development." *INFO-LINE,* Mar. 1988.

Bishop, H. "Accurate Job Descriptions: First Things First." *Performance and Instruction,* Feb. 1988, pp. 15–18.

Business Council for Effective Literacy. *Job-Related Basic Skills: A Guide for Planners of Employee Programs.* New York: Business Council for Effective Literacy, 1987.

Campbell-Thrane, L., Manning, K., Okeafor, K., and Williams, E. J. *Building Basic Skills: Models for Implementation.* Columbus, Ohio: The National Center for Research in Vocational Education, 1983.

Carkhuff,, R. R., and Fisher, S. G. *Instructional Systems Design I: Designing the Instructional System.* Amherst, Mass.: Human Resources Development Press, 1984.

Carlisle, K. E., and Arwady, J. P. *Analyzing Jobs and Tasks.* Englewood Cliffs, N.J.: Educational Technology Publications, 1986.

Casner-Lotto, J., and Associates. *Successful Training Strategies: Twenty-Six Innovative Corporate Models.* San Francisco: Jossey-Bass, 1988.

Charner, I., and Rolzinski, C. A. *Responding to the Educational Needs of Today's Workplace.* San Francisco: Jossey-Bass, 1987.

Davies, I. K. *Competency Based Learning: Technology, Management and Design.* New York: McGraw-Hill, 1973.

Gooch, B., and McDowell, B. "Using Anxiety to Motivate." *Personnel Journal,* 1988, *67* (4), 51–54.

Gossman, J. R., and Martinetz, C. "The Missing Link—A Bridge Between Task Analysis and Training Strategy." *Performance and Instruction,* Feb. 1988, 26–28.

Grant, P. "What Job Descriptions Don't Work." *Personnel Journal,* 1988, *67* (2), 52–59.

Henry, J. F., and Raymond, S. U. *Basic Skills in the U.S. Work Force.* New York: Center for Public Resources, 1982.

Knox, A. B. *Helping Adults Learn.* San Francisco: Jossey-Bass, 1986.

Lee, C. "Basic Training in the Corporate Schoolhouse." *Training,* 1988, *25* (4), 27–36.

Lillard, L. A., and Tan, H. W. *Private Sector Training: Who Gets It and What Are Its Effects?* Santa Monica, Calif.: Rand Corporation, 1986.

Mager, R. F., and Beach, K. M., Jr. *Developing Vocational Instruction.* Belmont, Calif.: David S. Lake Publishers, 1967.

Mager, R. F., and Pipe, P. *Analyzing Performance Problems: Or You Really Oughta Wanna.* (2nd ed.) Belmont, Calif.: Pitman Learning, 1984.

Markowitz, J. "Managing the Job Analysis Process." *Training and Development Journal,* 1987, *41* (8), 64–66.

National Academy of Sciences. *High Schools and the Changing Workplace: The Employers View.* Washington, D.C.: National Academy Press, 1984.

O'Neil, F., Jr. *Procedures for Instructional Systems Development.* New York: Academic Press, 1979.

Rosow, J. M., and Zager, R. *Training—The Competitive Edge.* San Francisco: Jossey-Bass, 1988.

Ross, I. "Corporations Take Aim at Illiteracy." *Fortune,* Sept. 29, 1986, pp. 48–54.

Silver, M. *Marketing First Handbook.* Washington, D.C.: National Alliance of Business, 1985.

U.S. Congress, Office of Technology Assessment. *Technology and the American Economic Transition: Choices for the Future.* Washington, D.C.: U.S. Government Printing Office, 1988.

U.S. Department of Labor. *Dictionary of Occupational Titles.* (4th ed.) Washington, D.C.: U.S. Government Printing Office, 1977.

Venezky, R. L., Kaestle, C. F., and Sum, M. *The Subtle Danger: Reflections on the Literacy Abilities of America's Young Adults.* Princeton, N.J.: Educational Testing Service, 1987.

Notes

_____

_____

_____

_____

_____

_____

_____

_____

_____

_____

_____

_____

_____

_____

_____

_____

_____

_____

_____

_____

_____

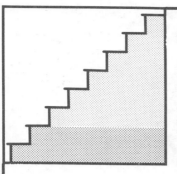

STEP TWO

Build Support for Training Through Alliances with Management and Unions

Learning Objectives

The reader will be able to:

1. Discuss the different types of organizational problems or needs that might make basic workplace skills training necessary.

2. List people in strategic leadership positions in both the organization and the union who might support, or should be convinced to support, a basic workplace skills training program.

3. Discuss how to approach those in strategic leadership positions to relate the training program to their role in achieving organizational goals.

4. List people at all levels of the organization whose support is necessary for the success of the basic workplace skills training program.

5. Discuss how one might approach organization members to relate their training needs to organizational goals in order to build coalitions.

6. Discuss how a basic workplace skills training program can become an institutionalized part of the organization.

Introduction

If the preliminary job analysis and market research effort conclude that basic workplace skills training is necessary to counteract either current or anticipated job problems, then a recommendation to develop a basic workplace skills program should be presented to management and senior union officials.

If the need for a basic workplace skills effort has been clearly established, the program advocate takes center stage.

The Program Advocate: Making the Case for Skills Training

Making the case for basic workplace skills training begins by linking the need for competency in basic workplace skills to work force problems, quality problems, regulatory or safety problems, and changes in work requirements such as technical changes, product changes, organizational changes, and strategic changes.

Work-Force Problems

Work-force problems that are frequently hidden in the form of high absenteeism, excessive tardiness, or low productivity may, in reality, be an effort to hide insufficient skills in literacy, computation, or other more nontraditional workplace skills such as problem solving, teamwork, and so on.

 Case Study

Aetna Life and Casualty Company

In many areas of the United States companies are experiencing a shortage of qualified applicants for entry-level positions. Aetna Life and Casualty Company in Hartford, Conn., found that on a given day it had between 50 and 100 such vacant positions, mostly clerical. Many of the available applicants for these jobs lacked a high school education or had done very poorly in school, and the skill requirements for even these entry-level positions were continually being upgraded.

Aetna, in cooperation with an outside community agency, developed a curriculum for unemployed people in basic business skills: reading, math, writing, oral communications, and computer skills. Those who satisfactorily complete the program are not guaranteed a job, but the backlog of openings practically assures them of one. It also offers opportunities for current employees to strengthen their basic skills in order to qualify for promotional opportunities or to cope with retraining requirements of their present jobs (Lee, 1988, pp. 29–30).

Quality Problems

Quality problems can be the result of an employee's lack of competence in basic cognitive skills (such as reading and arithmetic), which can reduce ability to follow directions or implement quantitative quality controls.

Quality can also be influenced by basic workplace skills problems in such areas as interpersonal skills, teamwork skills, leadership skills, negotiation skills, and so on.

Case Study

Metal Fab Corporation

The Metal Fab Corporation, a manufacturer of bellows based in Ormond Beach, Fla., estimates that it could save up to $1.2 million a year if its employees had stronger mathematical and reading skills. Because some employees have trouble measuring, the company's level of wasted material is higher than it should be.

In addition, workers too often have trouble reading blueprints, forcing the plant to redo orders and pay overtime ("Business Teaching Three R's . . ." 1988, pp. 1, 29).

Xerox Corporation

In 1983 Xerox chief executive David Kearns initiated an employee involvement program called Leadership Through Quality intended to keep the company's products competitive with similar machines from Japan. Today, virtually all of the company's 110,000 employees have gone through at least twenty-one hours of training in problem solving, quality improvement, and communications skills to help the employee involvement program work (Jacobson, 1988, pp. 23–27).

Regulatory or Safety Problems

Regulatory or safety problems can be caused by an employee's inadequacy in reading, inability to follow directions, or inability to adapt work requirements to new regulatory standards.

Case Study

Industrial Commission of Ohio

The Safety and Hygiene Division of the Industrial Commission of Ohio provides accident and illness prevention to employers within Ohio. In a single year roughly 5,000 employers will receive some type of training-related service from the division. There are nineteen generic programs plus 300 hours of training that the division customizes for employers with special needs. The training is conducted on company sites, and the division staff works as a team with the employer (John Paulson, telephone interview, Sept. 1988).

Changes in Work Requirements

Changes in work requirements may suggest a reexamination of the inventory of basic workplace skills needed to perform the job. Changes can come from a number of different sources.

Technical changes increase the range or depth of skills required to do a job.

Case Study

A Wastewater Treatment Plant

A number of wastewater treatment workers were transferred to a new plant. The workers had to be trained to learn new equipment, new safety measures, and new processes that were imposed by the new technology being implemented at the plant. The municipality initially contracted with an engineering firm to provide technical retraining for workers.

Relatively early in the training, it became apparent that the technical training procedures would not be sufficient for a large percentage of the wastewater treatment workers. Many workers read below an eighth-grade level, while training materials ranged in difficulty from eleventh-grade to college level. A reading specialist was hired to counsel workers, redesign the course for lower-level readers, and teach other trainers how to work with lower-level readers.

Nearly half of the trainees who worked with the reading specialist passed the technical skills test, although only 5 percent were expected to before the special basic skills course was added. The retention rate for these employees was also higher than for those who did not take the special instruction (Business Council for Effective Literacy, 1987a; Sticht and Mikulecky, 1984).

Product changes often increase the need for learning new skills to develop, produce, sell, or customize product offerings.

Case Study

Ford Motor Company

In 1986 Ford Motor Company was awarded a contract for the production of a new product—a four-speed, electronically controlled automatic truck transmission—at its Sharonville transmission plant outside Cincinnati, Ohio. The retooling of the plant included the introduction of 119 new machines from forty different providers. Among the new work-force skills required were a knowledge of metrics and blueprint reading, computer awareness and keyboard skills, new forms of gauging, the fundamentals of computerized numerical control, statistical process control, geometric dimensioning, and tolerancing.

To provide training required for the new technology, it was decided to create a joint launch training team because of the success of previous joint training efforts with the union. The launch training organization consisted of a staff of five hourly and seven salaried workers, including the plant training coordinator. In addition to technical training, it was clear the new technology required upgraded basic skills. The team designed its own two-week, eighty-hour curriculum based on stand-up teaching, hands-on training, and interactive videodisc programs, with a strong preference for the hands-on experiential approach. It also relied heavily on peer teachers drawn from the work force to help remove emotional barriers to learning (Rosow and Zager, 1988).

Organizational changes may increase skill requirements by expanding the autonomy and responsibility of employees or working teams in the development, production, or delivery of products to customers.

Case Study

Tektronix

Tektronix, an Oregon-based manufacturer of electronic equipment, tried to shift its traditional assembly line work force to a flexible manufacturing system four years ago.

The company discovered that 20 percent of its production workers lacked rudimentary skills needed for the transition. Tektronix is solving its problem by contracting with nearby Portland Community College to run a remedial on-site program in basic math and English for its many non-English-speaking assemblers.

Along the way Tektronix has added courses to enhance such skills as team building, negotiating, and effective time management to create a more well-rounded workplace skills training program (Richman, 1988, pp. 42–56).

Strategic changes may require employees to deliver a new strategic emphasis when they develop, make, or deliver products to customers.

Case Study

Primerica Corporation

An example of a company that had to undergo strategic changes in order to survive is the Primerica Corporation, formerly the American Can Company.

Within an extremely short time period, the company went from being a manufacturing company to being a company primarily involved in financial services and specialty retailing.

William Woodside, chairman of the executive committee of the Primerica Corporation and former chairman of the board of the American Can Company, moved to reorganize or diversify the company in order to keep pace with economic and technological changes.

Checklist 4 can be used to track the investigation of possible basic workplace skills problems.

Checklist

Checklist 4. The Advocate: Making the Case.

1. What triggered the investigation into possible basic workplace skills problems?
   - ☐ Work-force problems
   - ☐ Quality problems
   - ☐ Regulatory or safety problems
   - ☐ Changes in work requirements (technical changes, product changes, organizational changes, and strategic changes)

2. Who triggered the investigation into possible basic workplace skills problems?
   - ☐ Request from top management
   - ☐ Report from supervisors
   - ☐ Self-reporting of employees
   - ☐ General observation by human resources or personnel department

3. What is the specific dissatisfaction with employee performance? What are employees doing that they should not be doing? Or what are they not doing that they should be?
   - ☐ Quantity or quality of output
   - ☐ Frequency of errors
   - ☐ Waste of materials
   - ☐ Disruptive behavior

4. Who should be interviewed about this problem?
   - ☐ Management
   - ☐ Front-line supervisors
   - ☐ Employees
   - ☐ Union representatives or stewards
   - ☐ Customers

5. What evidence exists to document the performance discrepancy?
   - ☐ Production reports
   - ☐ Customer complaints
   - ☐ Failed inspection or rejected products
   - ☐ Injuries or health and safety problems
   - ☐ Employee grievances

6. What does the problem cost the company?
   - ☐ Customer dissatisfaction
   - ☐ Rejected products or errors or lost production
   - ☐ Fines or penalties
   - ☐ Overtime or remediation costs
   - ☐ Loss of competitive market position

7. What basic workplace skills problems might be causing the performance discrepancy?
   - ☐ Reading and comprehension
   - ☐ Computation
   - ☐ Problem solving

8. What is the employee profile?
   - ☐ Job experience
   - ☐ Training received
   - ☐ Performance ratings

9. What other factors might adversely affect worker performance?
   - ☐ Improper procedures, instructions, or supervision
   - ☐ Systems failure
   - ☐ Negative leadership climate
   - ☐ Faulty equipment or materials
   - ☐ Compensation

10. How might the problem be solved?
    - ☐ Formal training program
    - ☐ On-the-job training or mentoring
    - ☐ Job aids, such as procedural checklists, manuals, or job simplification
    - ☐ Clarified expectations or performance standards

11. What solution is most appropriate given organizational resources, priorities, and other factors?
    - ☐ Solves problems best
    - ☐ Suitable to employees
    - ☐ Management preference
    - ☐ Cost
    - ☐ Short-term, long-term benefit

The Program Advocate: Building Support for Skills Training

Once training is selected as the appropriate solution and the training population has been identified, the advocacy process expands. To be successful, a workplace basics advocate must skillfully use two tools—logic and politics.

The logic for establishing a workplace basics program rests on a foundation of data collected throughout Step One. The case to be made must be proactive in that it must illustrate how basic workplace skills problems can affect the employer's ability to operate effectively.

More importantly, taking a proactive stance means anticipating how problems in workplace basics will affect the employer's future plans.

The argument for establishing a workplace basics program can be persuasive. But success in making and sustaining an organizational commitment to a training program often rests upon other, sometimes less tangible, factors.

A solid foundation for launching a workplace basics program must be built—this is where politics comes into play in winning broad-based support.

Leadership

Leaders who might support a workplace basics training program need to be courted. Support from influential managers, union officials, employee representatives, and the informal leadership structure is critical to the successful launching of a basic workplace skills program.

Ideally, leadership on this issue from the chief executive officer (CEO) provides tremendous leverage in getting support from other levels of the institutional hierarchy, as well as from the top union officials or the board of directors.

 Case Study

Trucking Management Inc. and the Teamsters

Increased competition from independent haulers following deregulation of the trucking industry in 1980 has led to the failure of more than seventy major trucking companies and put over 92,000 members of the International Brotherhood of Teamsters out of work. In the fall of 1986, Arthur Bunte, president of Trucking Management Inc., and Jackie Presser, president of the Freight Industry Negotiating Committee, met to develop a joint plan to deal with this threat to the future of organized trucking. They established the Committee on Industry Development, which was charged with identifying problems in implementing the plan.

At a national conference in Washington, D.C., the participants concluded that if significant change were going to happen, it had to go all the way down to the terminal level of managers, supervisors, business agents, and workers.

However, polarized relationships between labor and management made it difficult for them to work cooperatively. A joint training program was initiated to break down the barriers and help representatives from both sides develop better communication, problem-solving, and teamwork skills.

To build support for the program, they began at the top with leaders of Teamsters locals and top management personnel from the corresponding companies. As the training program was presented at each organizational level, representatives from labor and management who had been through the program were present to introduce the program, explain its purpose, and provide evidence of joint leadership support.

The program has not always proceeded smoothly, but Art Kane, director of the Teamsters education department, and Sally Payne, project director, are convinced the joint training would not work at all without strong and visible support from the leaders of both labor and management (Art Kane and Sally Payne, personal interview, Sept. 1988).

Coalition Building

Coalition building is essential. The process of coalition building should begin by securing commitment from a respected leadership figure in the formal or informal authority structure of the institution. Here again, the CEO is ideal for this role, but coalition leadership may also come from farther down the management ladder, from members of the governing board or employee representatives.

Effective coalition leaders are those who can communicate both horizontally and vertically throughout the organization and who can forge networks of allies.

To be most effective, coalitions must include representatives from both the institution's formal and informal authority structures. Mistrust or resistance to the program can be short-circuited by involving nonsupervisory employees. Union or employee representatives can play an important role in efforts to reduce employee anxieties about the program.

One effective method of building coalitions is to carefully craft some formal and/or informal committees or advisory groups that facilitate expanded support throughout the organization in all directions.

To maximize the impact of this political effort, all commitments for support should be leveraged to build additional support and gather additional allies.

 Table

Table 3. How to Approach Key People When Coalition Building

1. Upper Management
   a. Display an interest in and an understanding of the corporation's strategic goals.
   b. Show an appreciation for the bottom line.
   c. Demonstrate the connection between corporate goals and the proposed training program.

2. Middle Management
   a. Be a proactive problem solver.
   b. Demonstrate an interest in learning about management problems.
   c. Suggest solutions other than training when appropriate.

3. Front-Line Supervisors
   a. Tell front-line supervisors that the program will not succeed without their support.
   b. Explain how the program will address performance problems.
   c. Demonstrate an understanding of their concern over lost production if training is to be conducted during work time.

4. The Employees
   a. Approach them as valued resources to be conserved and developed.
   b. Demonstrate sensitivity to employee needs and concerns such as:

- Job security,
- Anxiety about returning to school, and
- Confidentiality of evaluation.

c. Explain how the training experience will be immediately useful on the job.

d. Explain the company's willingness to invest in employees:
- Training as investment.
- Training on work time.

5. The Union

a. Assume the union's interest in the future well-being of both the employer and its own members.

b. Explain the program in terms that will appeal to the union, such as job security.

Case Study

United Auto Workers and Ford Motor Company

The United Auto Workers–Ford Motor Company Employee Development and Training Program (EDTP) was created at the bargaining table in 1982. The agreement established an organizational framework supported by the Nickel Fund: 5 cents an hour to be paid by the company for each hour worked by hourly employees, an amount that was doubled in 1984 to generate $120 million over three years.

The program, developed from the elicited interests of workers, provides six different avenues for training, including a basic skills enhancement program that is conducted at forty-two work sites around the country.

The skills enhancement program is jointly administered from a national headquarters in Dearborn, Mich., by both union and management representatives. The national center staff provides guidance and support for the local project at the plants, each of which is locally governed by union and management representatives.

That national staff provides a structure for identifying the interests of the workers and helps locate local providers who can best serve those interests. It also helps identify federal or state support for the program where available (Business Council for Effective Literacy, 1987b, p. 4).

Institution Building

This is also the time to begin laying the groundwork for a sustained institutional commitment to the training program. Leadership is a powerful and necessary ingredient for launching any program, but it is fragile and often temporary.

Programs that flourish under one leader often wither when that leader's tenure ends—unless the leader's vision is institutionalized through administrative processes and structures.

Budget and staffing commitments are key here, but they too will be seen as temporary solutions unless basic workplace skills training is linked to the strategic decision-making structure of the employer.

Efforts to build an institutional commitment must focus on destigmatizing basic workplace skills training by making it an accepted and integral part of the employer's overall training agenda rather than a remedial add-on.

Whenever training needs are being examined, questions about basic workplace skills problems should be a subset of that discussion. With training (including basic workplace skills) linked to the strategic management process, inventorying of employee skills (including the basics) will become somewhat routine. It will be triggered in anticipation of events like shifts in institutional strategies, creation of new jobs, or adoption of new safety regulations.

REMEMBER
Build interest and support through involvement.

References and Suggested Readings

Business Council for Effective Literacy. *Job-Related Basic Skills: A Guide for Planners of Employee Programs.* New York: Business Council for Effective Literacy, 1987a.

Business Council for Effective Literacy. *Unions: Bread, Butter, and Basic Skills.* New York: Business Council for Effective Literacy, 1987b.

"Business Teaching Three R's to Employees in Effort to Compete." *New York Times,* May 1, 1988, pp. 1, 29.

Jacobson, B. "Employee Relations at Xerox: A Model Worth Copying." *AMA Management Review,* Feb. 1988, pp. 22–27.

Lee, C. "Basic Training in the Corporate Schoolhouse." *Training,* 1988, 25 (4), 27–36.

Lusterman, S. *Trends in Corporate Education and Training.* New York: The Conference Board, 1985.

Richman, L. S. "Tomorrow's Jobs: Plentiful, but. . . ." *Fortune,* Apr. 11, 1988, pp. 42–56.

Rosow, J. M., and Zager, R. *Training—The Competitive Edge.* San Francisco: Jossey-Bass, 1988.

Sticht, T. G., and Mikulecky, L. *Job-Related Basic Skills: Cases and Conclusions.* Columbus: National Center for Research in Vocational Education, Ohio State University, 1984.

Woodside, W. *A Message on Managing Change.* Arlington, Va.: American Association of School Administrators. (Reprint of speech.)

Notes

_____

_____

_____

_____

_____

_____

_____

_____

_____

_____

_____

_____

_____

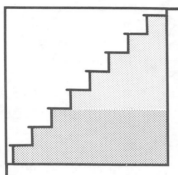

STEP THREE

Present the Strategy and Action Plan for Approval

Learning Objectives

The reader will be able to:

1. Develop a written plan to present to management and unions.

2. Prepare a training budget for the basic workplace skills programs.

3. Develop a cost/benefit analysis and list the elements that might be considered under each category.

4. Conduct a cost/benefit analysis using these three different methods: training benefit subtraction, return on investment, proportional model of responsibility.

5. Weigh the advantages of using an outside provider in different circumstances.

6. Focus on provider institutions that can best serve the particular needs of individual employer institutions.

7. Solicit and review providers' proposals against sound selection criteria.

Introduction

As part of building support, the advocate must develop and present a strategy and action plan for training.

This constitutes the final phase of the in-house marketing effort to sell the basic workplace skills training plan to internal decision makers, just as a marketing department would sell a company product to an outside client.

Any proposed plan must also take into account the need to obtain concurrence of the union or employee representatives.

Therefore, the plan should be careful to anticipate and address employee concerns that might arise.

If it is determined that the union is to be a training program co-funder and operator, the union will need to have an equal vote with management in order for the program to advance toward its goals.

Present the Strategy and Action Plan for Training

The presentation should be well thought out, comprehensive, and concise. It should be supported by a written plan. Copies of the plan should be provided to each person who must approve it.

The plan should include the following information:

- Conclusions of the preliminary research. One- or two-page summary of the most compelling data resulting from the analysis of job descriptions.

- Strategic implications. Risks versus positive impacts.

- Options for implementation. Three budget scenarios, each including a description of:
  a. Cost,
  b. Time frame,
  c. Program content,
  d. Program development responsibilities,
  e. Program design, and
  f. Resource constraints.

- Recommendations for program development.

Elements of the Plan

The proposal should not be too long, but should contain sufficient detail to be credible. Checklist 5 contains a suggested outline.

Checklist

Checklist 5. How to Prepare and Present a Plan.

1. Introduction
   - ☐ Get right to the point.
   - ☐ Summarize the plan in a clear, succinct paragraph.
   - ☐ Include what action you want management to take.

2. Problem
   - ☐ Describe the problem addressed by the program.
   - ☐ How did it come to your attention?
   - ☐ What is its significance with regard to the company's present and future well-being?

3. Solution (Program Design)
   - ☐ Describe the characteristics of the program.
   - ☐ Give management a general picture of what will happen.
   - ☐ Emphasize the practical, job-related approach to be used.

4. Target Population
   - ☐ Who is to be trained?
   - ☐ How will they be selected?
   - ☐ How many?
   - ☐ Are there any priorities?

5. Personnel
   - ☐ Explain who has contributed and who will contribute to the project.
   - ☐ Include members of the advisory committee, supervisors, management staff, consultants, key workers, and so on.

6. Schedule
   - ☐ Lay out the projected time line for program development, implementation, hiring of key workers, and so on.

7. Evaluation
   - ☐ Explain how the success of the program will be measured, especially with regard to the bottom line. (This is extremely important for credibility.)

8. Budget
   - ☐ Costs should be projected for every type of expenditure (in-house personnel, consultants, expenses, administration, outside ser vices, facilities, equipment, and so on) for each of the major steps of the project.

9. Cost/Benefit Analysis
   - ☐ Compare the budget costs of the program to the probable financial benefits to the company.
   - ☐ Assure management you understand that the decision whether to proceed must be a businesslike one and confirm that your projections of return on investment are reliable.

10. Summary
    - ☐ Make a clear restatement of the training proposal, its benefits to the company, and the action you want management to take.

> **REMEMBER**
>
> In writing the plan, try to anticipate and answer the questions management might ask. Attach appendixes as necessary to provide detailed information. The form of the presentation is important. Make it as professional and readable as possible, using graphs and charts wherever appropriate to illustrate important points.

There is a rule of thumb for determining which training option to recommend; it is based on a company's available resources and willingness to commit them to training. This is frequently identified as the "shoulda, oughta, wanna" principle.

- "Shoulda" refers to a basic training plan that will cover essential needs;
- "Oughta" is the type of training program that would be nice to have if money and other resources could be freed up; and
- "Wanna" is the comprehensive, sophisticated training program every organization would love to have in the best of all possible worlds.

In a few organizations management might be able to afford the last option, and might even see it as "shoulda" training. In many organizations, recommending the second option ("oughta") may also necessitate a hard sell to unsympathetic management.

Yet, while recommending only the "shoulda" option may look good in short-term costs and may be easier to achieve, it could, in fact, prove more costly in long-term dollars if additional funds for catch-up training are required later on.

Developing a Training Program Budget

If a project budget has not been developed before, the first one may be a bit difficult. Once a system for costing out training projects has been developed, however, subsequent budgets are much easier to handle. It is well worth the effort, because with a realistic projection of program costs in hand, the trainer can present a cost/benefit proposal to management.

Appropriate records should, of course, have been kept of the costs associated with the job review. To the extent possible, the regular financial records and reporting procedures of the organization should be used.

Financial personnel can also help by providing daily or hourly cost figures for in-house personnel and services. If that information is available, it is necessary only to project the time required to perform the various parts of the project and multiply by the appropriate figures for the various personnel involved in the project.

It is important for the training plan presentation to contain cost estimates for implementing the program once it is ready. During an initial presentation there is probably not enough information available for a full-blown operational budget, but an estimated figure should be possible. (See Step 5 for a discussion of the operating budget.)

When implementation becomes a near-term reality, decision makers need to have firm cost figures before approving the final operational budget and time frame.

Table

Table 4. Sample Training Budget Work Sheet.

Analysis

Personnel		$ _____
Human resource development staff	_____	
Support personnel	_____	
Other in-house	_____	
Expenses (meals, travel)	_____	
Office supplies	_____	
Printing and reproduction	_____	
Equipment	_____	
Outside services (consultants)	_____	
Administration and overhead	_____	
Miscellaneous	_____	
Total cost of analysis		$ _____

Design

Personnel		$ _____
Human resource development staff	_____	
Support personnel	_____	
Other in-house	_____	
Expenses (meals, travel)	_____	
Office supplies	_____	
Printing and reproduction	_____	
Equipment	_____	
Outside services (consultants)	_____	
Administration and overhead	_____	
Miscellaneous	_____	
Total cost of design		$ _____

Development

Personnel		$ _____
Human resource development staff	_____	
Support personnel	_____	
Other in-house	_____	
Expenses (meals, travel)	_____	
Office supplies	_____	
Program materials and supplies	_____	
Films and videotapes	_____	
Slides and transparencies	_____	

Other _____

Printing and reproduction _____

Equipment _____

Outside services (consultants) _____

Administration and overhead _____

Miscellaneous _____

Total cost of development $ _____

Delivery

Personnel $ _____

    Instructors _____

    Support _____

    Other in-house _____

    Expenses (meals, travel) _____

Participants _____

    Salaries _____

    Expenses _____

    Replacements _____

Program materials and supplies _____

Facilities _____

Equipment _____

Outside services (consultants) _____

Administration and overhead _____

Miscellaneous _____

Total cost of delivery $ _____

Evaluation

Personnel $ _____

    Human resource development staff _____

    Support personnel _____

    Other in-house _____

    Expenses (meals, travel) _____

Participants _____

Office supplies _____

Printing and reproduction _____

Equipment _____

Outside services (consultants) _____

Administration and overhead _____

Miscellaneous _____

Total cost of evaluation $ _____

      Total cost of program $ _____

Cost/Benefit Analysis

Management must consider possible alternatives and select the most cost-effective strategy for solving performance problems caused by basic workplace skills deficiencies.

Cost/benefit analysis (contrasting the savings or increased revenue with the costs of implementing a given intervention) is a preferred method for making such decisions. To be economically viable, a program must contribute more revenue than it costs.

The budget (see Table 4) prepared for implementation of the basic workplace skills training program is the cost half of the analysis.

Next you must identify and project the measurable monetary impact of correcting the performance problem. This is the benefit half of the analysis.

Then you must compare the costs to the benefits, taking into consideration the nonmonetary as well as the monetary elements.

Table 5 lists items that need to be considered when calculating a cost/benefit analysis. Table 6 describes the steps in conducting a cost/benefit analysis.

Table 7 provides three models that can be used to calculate training benefits. In its simplest form, a benefit forecasting method requires that all increases in performance values (minus the training costs) be determined for training programs under consideration. When the performance value exceeds the costs, the training yields a benefit. If the costs exceed the performance value, no benefits result.

Table

Table 5. Cost/Benefit List of Items for Analysis.

Training Costs

Human Resources
- Consultant expenses
- Salaries and benefits—human resource development personnel
- Salaries and benefits—expert judges
- Salaries and benefits—participants

Travel and Per Diem
- Travel costs
- Per diem expenses

Supplies, Equipment, Facilities
- Office supplies
- Program materials and supplies
- Printing and reproduction costs
- Equipment depreciation costs
- Equipment rental
- Facilities expense allocation
- Facilities rental
- Indirect costs (overhead)

Training Benefits

Productivity Increases
- Units produced
- Forms processed
- Tasks completed
- Items sold

Quality
- Scrap reduction
- Rejects eliminated
- Rework reduced
- Shortages
- Product defects reduced
- Product recall reduced
- Percent of downtime reduced

Work Skills
- Number of promotions
- Lower absenteeism rates
- Lower number of accidents
- Performance appraisal ratings improved
- Reductions in turnover
- Reduced grievances

Table

Table 6. Steps in Conducting a Cost/Benefit Analysis.

1. Identify the specific objectives of the proposed basic workplace skills training program.
    *   What performance problems are to be corrected?
    *   What is the monetary loss to the company caused by the performance problems?

2. Identify alternative solutions to the problem. Consider the following:
    *   New compensation plan.
    *   Restructuring.
    *   New technology.
    *   Job aids.
    *   New staff.
    *   Training (remember, it is important to demonstrate to management that you have considered that the problem might be solved by an intervention other than a formal training program).

3. Estimate the costs of each possible solution to the problem.
    *   What is the immediate cost (one year)?
    *   What is the long-term cost (five years)?
    *   What are the development costs?
    *   What are the implementation and evaluation costs?

4. Project the economic benefits of each of the possible solutions. The benefits might be in one or more of the following areas:
    *   Increased profits or productivity.
    *   Increased sales.
    *   Better service to customers.
    *   Reduction in cost, waste, errors, defects, or complaints.
    *   Reduction in grievances, absenteeism, turnover, and injuries.

5. Compare and rank the costs plus economic returns projected for each possible solution for one year, two years, and five years.

6. Recommend the solution with the highest cost/benefit ranking or give very good reasons why another strategy might be better for the company. (For example, is training as visible to the competition as other strategic levers?)

Table

Table 7. Three Models of Benefit Forecasting.

Model 1: Training Benefit Subtraction

Explanation: Expected training costs are subtracted from anticipated program improvement benefits to determine the estimated bottom-line dollar savings.

Formula: (Performance improvements due to training) – (Training costs) = (Training benefits)

Example: An organization estimates that a 10 percent improvement in turnover rates will save $40,000 a year. A $10,000 training program is proposed to solve the problem.

Calculation: $40,000 – $10,000 = $30,000 training benefits

Model 2: Return on Investment

Explanation: A more technically correct and conservative formula is a return-on-investment (ROI) calculation. An ROI calculation uses a percentile
system for demonstrating whether training has led to benefits for the organization.

Formula: $$\text{ROI} = \frac{\text{Return (benefits)} - \text{Investment (training costs)}}{\text{Investment (costs)}}$$

An ROI greater than 1 indicates that you are getting more than you invested. An ROI equal to 1 shows that your costs and benefits are equal (you are getting in exactly what you put in). An ROI less than 1 means you are investing more than you are receiving.

Example: Use the same example as given in Model 1.

Calculation: $$\text{ROI} = \frac{\$40,000 - \$10,000}{\$10,000} = 3.0$$

An ROI of 3.0 indicates that the training program will lead to significant benefits for the organization.

Model 3: Proportional Model of Responsibility

Explanation: A problem for many training departments when claiming credit for economic returns to the organization is that any success may be partially attributable to other factors. The proportional model of responsibility takes this problem into account. It is used in conjunction with the benefit subtraction model (Model 1).

Once an estimate has been made of the benefits a training program has incurred through increased revenue or reduced costs using the benefit subtraction model, line managers are asked to indicate on a scale of 0.01 to 1.0 (1 to 100 percent) the proportion that they think training is responsible for these improvements. The benefits are then multiplied by this percentile to provide a more realistic assessment of the training program's contribution to the organization.

Formula: (Training benefits) × (Responsibility for training) = (Adjusted benefits)

Example: The example given in Model 1 indicated that the reduction in turnover resulting from training led to $30,000 in savings (training benefits) for the organization. However, skeptics might argue that other forces were partly responsible for reduced turnover, such as improved wages, the labor market, and so on.

To find a more realistic estimate of the value of the training program, the training department asks managers to estimate how responsible they believe the training program is for the decreased turnover. If the consensus is that the training program is 50 percent responsible for the reduced turnover, then the training benefit of $30,000 is multiplied by 0.5. The product of $15,000 is the adjusted benefit from the training program.

Calculations:

1. Training benefits (from Model 1): $40,000 – $10,000 = $30,000
2. Adjusted training benefits: $30,000 × 0.5 = $15,000

Select Training Program Architects

The training proposal needs to include an assessment of whether it is more advantageous to:

1. Contract with an outside provider to design and develop a customized training program or provide an off-the-shelf training program;

2. Design and develop the training program in-house; or

3. Use both in-house and outside resources in a variety of possible configurations from design through program implementation.

Many companies do not have the internal resources or experience to develop and operate a comprehensive basic workplace skills program. Even larger corporations such as General Motors and IBM frequently use specialized outside providers in their training schedules because in-house personnel do not always have the expertise necessary to conduct comprehensive training programs.

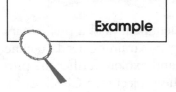

Example

Use of an Outside Provider

In 1986 the education and training department at General Motors (GM) came up with the idea of establishing a long-term preferred relationship with a training provider. This was done in response to conflicting demands for a smaller corporate training staff and more training services in the field. The provider was charged with providing GM with the highest-quality, most competitively priced training products and services available. The arrangement loses the element of competitive bidding, but it gains a close provider-client relationship and a better understanding of corporate needs and culture. The provider obviously enjoys reduced marketing costs and a steady source of business ("Training Today," 1988, pp. 12–14).

Locating Potential Outside Providers

Most communities have training and educational resources that can help. Possible provider sources include local school districts, community colleges and universities, nonprofit literacy groups, for-profit organizations and individuals, private industry councils, and others. See Resource C for a detailed discussion of useful sources for locating outside providers.

Outside providers have differing strengths and weaknesses, and not all will be equally suitable for the job. Advantages to consider when selecting an outside provider include:

- Cost effectiveness,
- Immediate availability,
- Prior experience,
- Positive employee response,
- Better utilization of internal resources, and
- Significant time savings.

Disadvantages to consider include:

- Little experience with training in a particular functional context,
- Reduced control,
- Little knowledge of specific corporate culture, and
- Negative employee response.

Briefing Potential Outside Providers

After potential outside providers have been identified, hold a preliminary meeting with each of them to explain the company's training needs, outline the ground rules of the working relationship, and explore further the provider's ability to deliver what is needed for the project (see Checklist 6). Invite those that you believe are qualified to submit a formal, written proposal.

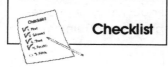 **Checklist**

Checklist 6. Meeting with Potential Outside Providers.

1. Prepare to discuss the corporation's (your) role in the project.
- ☐ Who are the decision makers?
- ☐ Is there a committee or task force involved?
- ☐ Who is the key corporate contact?
- ☐ What roles will be played by the above?

2. How much money is available for the project?
- ☐ How much are you prepared to pay?
- ☐ Is there possible flexibility (willingness to negotiate) on the provider's part?

3. What do you want included in the project?
- ☐ Who are the trainees?
- ☐ What are they to learn?
- ☐ What are their work experience and educational backgrounds?
- ☐ What is the time line for the project?
- ☐ What should be included in the proposal?

4. Does the provider have the expertise the project requires?
- ☐ Who are the key personnel in the outside provider's organization?
- ☐ What is their previous experience in basic workplace skills training?
- ☐ Can you review a previous, completed project?
- ☐ What is their incidence of repeat business?
- ☐ Who are their references?
- ☐ Were projects completed satisfactorily, on time, and within budget?

Source: Adapted with permission from the February 1987 issue of TRAINING, *The Magazine of Human Resources Development.* Copyright 1987, Lakewood Publications, Inc., Minneapolis, MN (612) 333-0471. All rights reserved.

One method for trying to ensure that a provider has the appropriate resources (knowledge, staff expertise, and so on) and can be held accountable is to contract through a competitive bidding process using a standard request for proposals. The request for proposals should be structured to solicit the information shown in Checklist 7.

See Resource D for a detailed sample request for proposals to be given to potential outside providers.

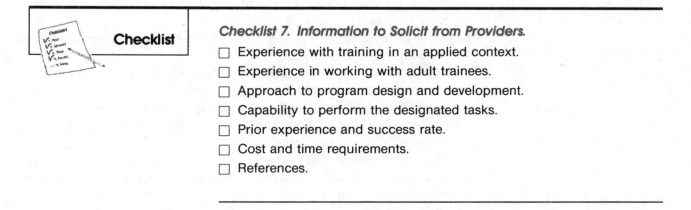

Checklist

Checklist 7. Information to Solicit from Providers.

☐ Experience with training in an applied context.
☐ Experience in working with adult trainees.
☐ Approach to program design and development.
☐ Capability to perform the designated tasks.
☐ Prior experience and success rate.
☐ Cost and time requirements.
☐ References.

Reviewing the Outside Providers' Proposals

When evaluating the various proposals from outside providers look for the following items ("Training Today," 1987, pp. 14–16):

- A summary of the project's background and purpose.
- A list of specific project outcomes.
- A description of activities to be performed.
- A list of items to be delivered.
- Identification of personnel who will actually be working on the project.
- A timetable for completing the work.
- A fee agreement and payment schedule.
- A description of any special arrangements between the parties (for example, access to company information or the work floor), and
- A cancellation clause should the provider fail to perform as contracted.

Many experienced corporate trainers say that the answer often lies in combining in-house staff and outside providers. This allows a company to extend its own subject-matter expertise by taking advantage of a training provider's design and experience in specific subject areas.

For example, an outside provider could be hired who had extensive experience in providing basic academic skills training (reading, writing, computation) for adults in a workplace context, while at the same time in-house staff could be used to develop or obtain material relating to other basic workplace skills such as problem solving, leadership training, team building, career development, or motivation.

Experienced training departments will have used outside providers before and will be aware of both pitfalls and pluses. If this is the first attempt at using an outside source to complement in-house staff efforts, proceed with caution and be clear and exact about what services are required. Figure 2 provides a decision tree for the kind of thinking that needs to go into this decision.

Often when a small business (fewer than 500 employees) decides to implement a basic workplace skills program, it will need to turn to an outside provider for help in design, development, implementation, and evaluation because it cannot afford to maintain a large, multipurpose training department.

Smaller companies will almost always have to rely on outside providers for other services as well, including classroom facilities, audio-visual and other training equipment, and the layout and printing of instructional materials.

There may also be a significant difference between large and small companies regarding how much time the employees can spend away from their jobs and even whether or not the training can be conducted at all during regular working hours.

When assessing community resources, these small businesses should search for larger companies (in related industries) that may have already developed training programs relevant to the needs of the smaller companies.

Figure 2. Go or No Go? Selecting an Outside Provider.

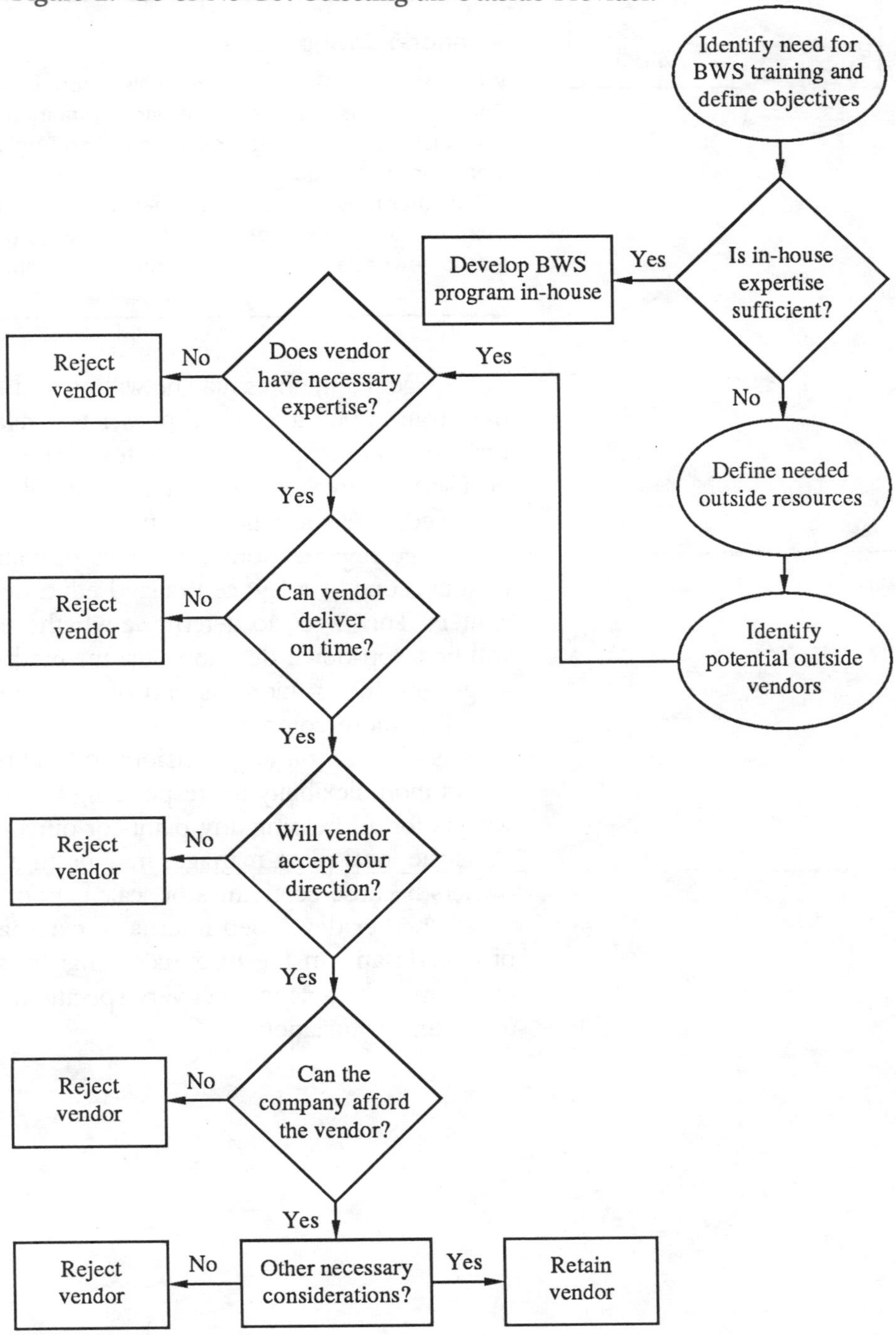

Case Study

American Savings Bank

When American Savings Bank in New York City needed a basic course in English as a first language, the bank combined internal on-the-job materials with the outside subject matter expertise of an English teacher from Bow-Manhattan Community College.

Together they developed a two-day course, but with the two days about a month apart. In the interim, the trainees were given materials to study and written homework assignments (Cothran, 1987, pp. 83–85).

Larger companies may be willing and interested in allowing access to their training for a fee or, if proprietary rights are not an issue, in providing a smaller company with copies of already developed curricula that can be used for free or under a contractual arrangement, and that can be modified to fit the functional needs of the purchasing company.

Large organizations may have operations in multiple locations but maintain one or a few centralized educational resource and development centers. They need to determine whether basic workplace skills training will be a top-down decision implemented throughout the organization at all geographic locations as part of an overall strategic plan.

The more common practice among such large organizations, however, is to leave training decisions to local plant managers. Sometimes this allows more flexibility for responding to local work-force requirements, as well as for addressing any plant- or office-specific needs. In other situations the local plant manager may be in a position similar to local plant owners because economies of scale cannot be achieved.

Whether developed internally, externally, or through a combination of outside and inside resources, what is important is that training programs must be able to meet very specific needs in ways directly appropriate to an organization.

References and Suggested Readings

Berliner, S. "External Consultants." In W. R. Tracy (ed.), *Human Resources Management and Development Handbook*. New York: American Management Association, 1985.

Cothran, T. "Build or Buy?" *Training,* 1987, *24* (5), 83–85.

Krapp, B. O. "Writing a Proposal—No Problem." *Training,* 1988, *25* (3), 55–58.

Lashbrook, V. J. "New Training Programs: To Buy or to Build." *Training,* 1981, *18* (11), 52–55.

Lippit, G. L. "Criteria for Selecting, Evaluating, and Developing Consultants." *Training and Development Journal,* 1981, *35* (6), 24–31.

Lombardo, C. "Cost/Benefit Analysis of Training." In *American Society for Training and Development Handbook for Technical and Skills Training*. Vol. 2. Alexandria, Va.: American Society for Training and Development, 1986.

Phillips, J. J. *Handbook of Training Evaluation and Measurement Methods*. Houston: Gulf Publishing, 1983.

Public/Private Ventures. *Request for Proposals: Guidelines for Solicitation of Educational Providers*. Philadelphia: Public/Private Ventures, 1987.

Silver, M. *Marketing First Handbook*. Washington, D.C.: National Alliance of Business, 1985.

"Training Today." *Training,* 1987, *24* (2), 14–16.

"Training Today." *Training,* 1988, *25* (3), 12–14.

Zawacki, S. J. "Contracting for Support Services." In W. R. Tracy (ed.), *Human Resources Management and Development Handbook*. New York: American Management Association, 1985.

Notes

_____
_____
_____
_____
_____
_____
_____
_____
_____
_____
_____
_____
_____
_____

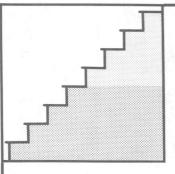

STEP FOUR

Perform a Task Analysis

Learning Objectives

The reader will be able to:

1. Understand the advantages of a good instructional system.

2. Understand the characteristics of a good instructional system.

3. Define the basic terms involved in performing a task analysis: job, duty, task, step.

4. Break a job down into its component duties, a duty into its component tasks, and a task into its component steps.

5. Identify the skills, knowledge, abilities, and attitude required to perform a given task and a given step.

6. List possible sources of information for analyzing a given job.

7. Develop a procedure for validating a job analysis.

8. Write appropriate task descriptions.

9. Develop a procedure for validating a job analysis.

10. Discuss the advantages and disadvantages of the various methods of data collection: questionnaires, interviews, observation, and document analysis.

11. Explain three different approaches to conducting a task analysis.

Introduction

Competencies are the knowledge, skills, abilities, and attitude standards required to succeed in a particular job.

After a plan has been approved, but before curriculum design can begin, the focus of basic workplace skills training must be narrowed to only those **competencies** actually required to perform work on the targeted jobs.

A company will want to expend resources only on the development of learning material for those skills that will result in a significant improvement in worker performance and productivity.

One method that has proved successful in accomplishing this is what is called instructional systems design (ISD). There are many advantages to using ISD or a modification of it to address the performance problems in the workplace. Barbee (1985, pp. 34–35) identifies a few of these:

- It consistently produces the results for which it was designed.

- It does not leave you dependent upon the skills of one person.

- It is replicable.

- It capitalizes on the range of skills and unique talents of various people.

- It places responsibility for learning with the learner and responsibility for the learning environment and management with the instructor.

- It uses what is known about how adults learn.

- It provides a means for adjusting it to better meet present needs.

A good instructional system has specific characteristics. Barbee lists these as the following:

- The curriculum and the instructional program are based on competencies required for a specific job.

- The system lets the trainee know what to expect. It describes both the system's and the trainee's responsibilities.

- It provides the trainee with the occupational context, including a general description of the occupational area, a description of the job, the conditions under which it is generally performed, and the generally accepted standards for its performance.

- It is made up of carefully engineered learning experiences designed to develop the specified competencies in the target trainees.

- The trainee controls the pace, sequence, and strategy of the learning.

- It demonstrates or describes the skill or knowledge to be learned in a way that the trainee understands.

- It is interactive, that is, it actively involves the trainee throughout the training.

- It provides opportunities for the trainee to practice the skill or internalize the knowledge.

- It provides opportunities for the trainee to perform the skill or use the knowledge under conditions closely resembling the job.

- It provides opportunities for trainees to test themselves on the skills and knowledge taught.

- It provides alternative learning strategies to meet the range of individual learning characteristics found in the trainee group(s). This normally requires a variety of media to satisfy the range of such characteristics.

- It measures performance and provides results to the trainee and to the instructor based upon the specific job competencies.

- Competency achievement data is used to improve the effectiveness and efficiency of the system. For example, when trainees fail to achieve a competency within a reasonable time, the training system is examined to see what went wrong and then adjusted accordingly.

Define the Task Analysis

The first undertaking to uncover deficiencies is the **task analysis.**

Task analysis is the process of breaking down a task into smaller units and then sequencing these units in an order of priority based on their importance in performing the job. It is a more in-depth and structured look at the descriptions of job duties that were prepared under Step One (the initial investigation).

At its heart is a validation process that confirms that the competencies identified for training are actually used on the job.

With information thus gained, the basic workplace skills trainer can plan lessons aimed at developing only those skills, knowledge, and behaviors that significantly affect successful job performance.

The purpose of conducting a task analysis is to determine which of the basic workplace skills are necessary to perform a particular job.

Therefore, it is important to recognize that your focus should begin with basic skills problems, not technical problems.

For example, if a company is introducing office automation, the first question it should ask is, Can employees read the computer manuals? not Can employees operate the computers?

Simply put, an accurate task analysis lays the foundation for a sound instructional program.

At this phase of the process in developing a basic workplace skills program, the dominant role is that of the task analyst, who, after describing the tasks, identifies the skills and knowledge necessary to successfully complete the tasks required of the job. The assignment should not, however, be hers or his alone.

Obtain a minimum of one worker and/or supervisor from each job family to be analyzed.

Persons from the advisory committee with expert knowledge of the job or job family to be analyzed should be designated as job-specific review committees. These committees will validate the final task listing for each job or job family in which they have expertise.

Task analysis is the process of breaking down a task into smaller units and then sequencing these units in an order of priority based on their importance in performing the job.

Collect Information Needed to Design the Program

The task analysis will answer certain questions necessary to develop the basic workplace skills instructional program: What is the job? How is the job done? How can job performance be improved? How can the skills and knowledge required for the job be learned? At this time, a basic profile of the worker population to be trained should be developed (see Checklist 8 and Table 8).

It is important to understand the component parts of a job (see Figure 3).

- A *job* is a specific position requiring the performance of specific tasks.

- A *duty* is an arbitrary clustering of related tasks into broad functional areas of responsibility.

- A *task* is a work activity that is discrete, observable, performed within a limited period of time, and leads to a product, service, or decision.

- Two or more *steps* make up a task. Each step alone would not result in a product, service, or decision.

Figure 3. Job Components.

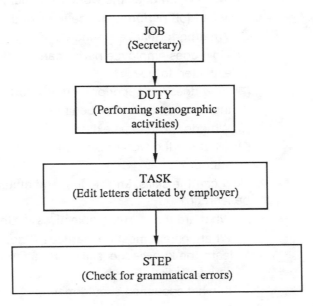

Checklist	

Checklist 8. Collecting the Information.

1. What is the job?
- ☐ What is the job title?
- ☐ What are the major duties of the job?
- ☐ What are the most important outputs of the job?
- ☐ What are the tasks of the job?
- ☐ With what frequency are the various tasks of the job performed?
- ☐ To whom does the worker report?
- ☐ Whom does the worker manage?
- ☐ What important issues, problems, or changes do workers face?

2. How is the job done?
- ☐ What are the steps required to perform the task?
- ☐ What knowledge is required to perform the task?
- ☐ What skills are required to perform the task?
- ☐ What tools or machines are used in performing the task?
- ☐ In what sequence are the steps performed?
- ☐ What safety and health factors are involved in performing the task?
- ☐ How is task performance measured?
- ☐ How much time does it take to perform the task?
- ☐ How difficult, in a relative sense, is it to perform the task?
- ☐ With whom does the worker interact in performing the task?

3. How can job performance be improved?
- ☐ What performance standards, if any, exist for the various tasks?
- ☐ How does employee performance differ from what employees are expected to do?
- ☐ How does the superior worker's performance differ from that of the average worker or beginner?
- ☐ Why do these gaps exist?
- ☐ What are the worker problems in terms of knowledge, skills, and attitude?

4. How can the skills, knowledge, and attitude required for the job best be learned?
- ☐ What are the learning objectives for this job?
- ☐ What content must be learned? (People don't learn a job; they learn the knowledge, skills, and attitude required to perform the various tasks of a job.)
- ☐ In what sequence should material be learned?
- ☐ Can the knowledge, skills, and attitude required for the performance of the various tasks be grouped together in some logical way?
- ☐ What training have these workers already had?
- ☐ What is the educational background of the targeted training population?
- ☐ What is their job experience?
- ☐ What factors may affect efforts to train this group?

Table

Table 8: Sample Job Analysis Work Sheet.

1. The job title of the position being analyzed is: _____ .

2. The experience level of the average jobholder is:

   ☐ 2 years or less   ☐ 3–5 years   ☐ more than 5 years

3. The education level of the average jobholder is:

   ☐ high school   ☐ college   ☐ graduate level

4. The data-gathering methods I will use in my analysis are:

   ☐ Interviews with managers, supervisors, and jobholders

   ☐ Group interviews with supervisors and jobholders

   ☐ Questionnaires

   ☐ Observation

5. Attach job description. List the major duties involved in performing the job:

   _____

   _____

   _____

   _____

6. For each duty, list the major tasks involved:

   _____

   _____

   _____

7. For each task, list the elements involved and the skills or knowledge needed:

   Elements   Skills or knowledge

   _____

   _____

   _____

8. For each element, list the subelements involved together with the skills or knowledge needed:

   Subelements   Skills or knowledge

   _____

   _____

   _____

Source: BLR Handbook of Training Techniques, 1987, pp. 40–41. Used by permission of Business and Legal Reports, Inc.

Identify Sources of Information

There are numerous sources of information, both people and documents, that can be used to help answer the questions in Checklist 8. One should first identify all possible sources and then consider the availability of those sources. The more sources of information one uses, the greater the chance that the task analysis will reflect the actual situation (see Checklists 9 and 10).

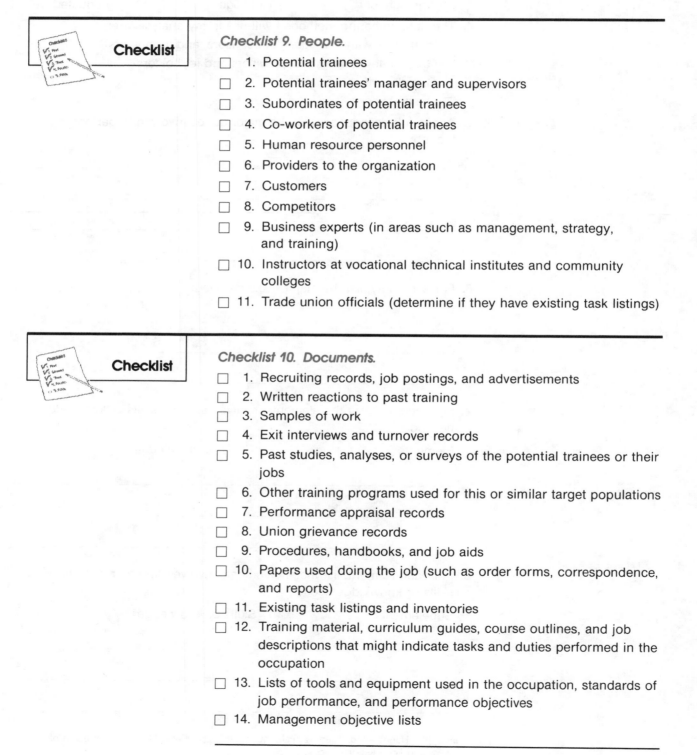

Checklist

Checklist 9. People.

- ☐ 1. Potential trainees
- ☐ 2. Potential trainees' manager and supervisors
- ☐ 3. Subordinates of potential trainees
- ☐ 4. Co-workers of potential trainees
- ☐ 5. Human resource personnel
- ☐ 6. Providers to the organization
- ☐ 7. Customers
- ☐ 8. Competitors
- ☐ 9. Business experts (in areas such as management, strategy, and training)
- ☐ 10. Instructors at vocational technical institutes and community colleges
- ☐ 11. Trade union officials (determine if they have existing task listings)

Checklist

Checklist 10. Documents.

- ☐ 1. Recruiting records, job postings, and advertisements
- ☐ 2. Written reactions to past training
- ☐ 3. Samples of work
- ☐ 4. Exit interviews and turnover records
- ☐ 5. Past studies, analyses, or surveys of the potential trainees or their jobs
- ☐ 6. Other training programs used for this or similar target populations
- ☐ 7. Performance appraisal records
- ☐ 8. Union grievance records
- ☐ 9. Procedures, handbooks, and job aids
- ☐ 10. Papers used doing the job (such as order forms, correspondence, and reports)
- ☐ 11. Existing task listings and inventories
- ☐ 12. Training material, curriculum guides, course outlines, and job descriptions that might indicate tasks and duties performed in the occupation
- ☐ 13. Lists of tools and equipment used in the occupation, standards of job performance, and performance objectives
- ☐ 14. Management objective lists

Plan the Task Analysis

The level of sophistication of task analysis will depend on the budgetary and personnel resources made available to carry it out as well as on the needs of the basic workplace skills program development team.

Limited resources or the desire to conserve abundant resources both require the decision to perform a task analysis only on those jobs (or parts of jobs) most directly related to obtaining the desired results of the basic workplace skills training program.

That might mean those taking the most time, those involving the greatest number of new employees, those with the highest error rate, or those that most directly affect achievement of the company's strategic objectives.

Furthermore, the task analysis should be detailed only to the extent necessary to meet the objectives of the current situation.

If the need is to deal with a relatively short-term issue, such as quality control in a given area, health and safety problems, or increasing customer complaints, the relative urgency of the problem may not allow the trainer time to conduct a full-scale, comprehensive task analysis.

In fact, the job of designing a training program may not require it. The appropriate approach may be quite obvious to the experienced trainer.

On the other hand, the achievement of less urgent but more strategically important objectives, like robotized production or office automation, would warrant a more thorough, time-consuming approach.

Identification of the basic workplace skills problem to be addressed by the training program is the determining factor in deciding the necessary degree of detail.

If all the workers can read, write, and compute at a level of proficiency required to perform the tasks of their jobs, it would be wasteful to continue the task analysis detailing to that extent.

Many experts urge erring on the side of too little detail to avoid wasting resources. If the program development process requires more information, they argue that it is not too difficult to reopen the analysis to meet those needs.

Perform the Task Analysis

In any event, an in-depth task analysis can be time-consuming and costly if some up-to-date materials do not already exist. Unless a job is entirely new, however, there is likely to be substantial material available that can be used as a foundation on which to build a task analysis. This can be accomplished at significantly less cost than starting from scratch.

The first undertakings in the task analysis process should be to review all related literature on the subject and to collect all available task listings, that is, a comprehensive list of tasks performed by workers on a particular job.

There are many excellent published listings of job tasks which can be obtained from such institutions as the National Center for Vocational Education, Ohio State University, the V-TEC, and several state education agencies.

In all instances, but particularly where existing task listings are being adapted, it is crucial for task analyses to be accurate and validated by company employees familiar with the job. This validation process should be used even when an outside provider is collecting the information.

Usually all task listings include basic literacy requirements (reading, writing, and computation) and competency levels necessary to perform a job.

However, few, if any, currently describe other related workplace skills such as goal setting, ethics, and leadership.

Therefore, when adapting task descriptions for use by a particular employer, it will likely be necessary to identify and develop performance measurements for these other basic workplace skills.

The process known as task analysis includes both description and analysis. Description is concerned with stating activities or outcomes of activities and is a necessary first part of the process.

Analysis, the derivation of skill, attitude, and knowledge requirements for successful task performance, is more critical to the development of appropriate training strategies.

The learner must successfully master both to be able to perform the job activity satisfactorily.

The task analysis usually breaks a job into three component parts: task listing, task duty, and task inventory.

Task Listings

Task listings are statements describing the work activities of employees in specific jobs or occupational areas. Tasks are actual units of work performed on a job.

A task is a complete work activity that can be performed independent of other work. It has a definite beginning and ending point, consists of two or more steps, can be observed and measured, and results in a product, service, or decision. The first step is to list all the tasks that are part of the job.

Task listings are statements describing the work activities of employees in specific jobs or occupational areas.

Each duty of a job is comprised of a number of tasks as in the examples of the automobile mechanic and beautician (Maxwell and West, 1980, p. 29).

Prepare a form for the task list. Choose a simple, straightforward format for easy use in recording data. The form should provide space for the task description and any other information necessary for your analysis, such as level of difficulty, degree of importance, and frequency of performance. This information will be useful in developing the training program. Table 9 gives an example of a form that can be used for listing tasks.

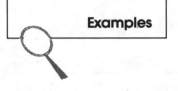

Examples

Task Listing—Automobile Mechanic

Duty: Maintains, repairs, and replaces braking systems

- Repair master cylinder
- Repair and replace brake shoes
- Adjust brake
- Flush brake system
- Repair wheel cylinder

Task Listing—Beautician

Duty: Mixing supplies and sanitizing equipment

- Mix conditioner
- Mix permanent hair colors
- Perform wet sanitizing
- Sanitize equipment with formaldehyde

Task Descriptions

There are a number of key rules for writing task descriptions. They are:

- The subject "I" or "you" is understood. Begin the description with a verb in the present tense.
- Use precise action verbs. Never use words or phrases like "appreciates" or "is responsible for."
- Be succinct.
- Eliminate articles ("the" and "a").
- Describe the same task with consistent language.
- Avoid qualifiers.
- Avoid references to knowledge and attitude needed.
- Avoid references to tools and equipment that merely support task performance.

Table

Table 9. Sample Task Listing Sheet.

Vocation: Electronics Technician

No.	Task	Frequency of Importance	Importance	Learning Difficulty
1.	Troubleshoots and repairs malfunctioning equipment.	Everyday	1	Difficult
2.	Reads electronic schematics.	1 to 10 times a day	2	Moderate
3.	Performs chassis layouts.	Once a week	2	Easy
4.	Uses small hand tools.	Continuously	1	Easy
5.	Checks electronic components.	Frequently	1	Moderate to difficult
6.	Replaces components.	Once in a while	2	Easy to moderate
7.	Solders various components.	Frequently	2	Moderate
8.	Recognizes the applicability of electronic test equipment.	Once in a while	2	Difficult
9.	Interprets test instruments.	Frequently	1	Difficult

Source: Adapted from Mager and Beach, 1967. Used by permission of David S. Lake Publishers.

For examples ot the rules in action, see Table 10.

Table

Table 10. Rules for Writing Task Descriptions.

Poor Task Statement	Rule	Good Task Statement
You repair magnetic drives.	The subject "I" or "you" is understood.	Repair magnetic drives.
Have responsibility for instructors.	Use precise action verbs.	Supervise instructors.
Prepare forms that tell mechanics to perform various jobs.	Be succinct.	Fill out work orders.
Enjoy operating the word processor.	Do not include attitudes.	Operate the word processor.
Use math skills to calculate load limits.	Do not include knowledge.	Calculate load limits.
Operate and maintain vacuum gauges.	Avoid "and" which implies two tasks.	1. Operate vacuum gauges. 2. Maintain vacuum gauges.

Source: Adapted from Carlisle and Arwady, 1986, p. 23. Used by permission of Educational Technology Publications.

Writing a task description is somewhat more complex than it might seem on the surface. "Answer telephone" is a specific task that might be identified for a receptionist. Job performance could be evaluated by whether the worker picks up the telephone when it rings. However, there is obviously more to it than that. The telephone is only a tool that the receptionist uses to perform a number of tasks, such as answering and directing incoming calls, taking clear messages as needed, responding courteously and effectively to customers, and scheduling appointments.

Task Detailing

A **task detailing** is a systematic breakdown of each task to determine the skills, sequencing, knowledge, and attitude an individual needs to know to perform a single task successfully. A task detailing for check cashing would need to include the following information:

- Cues for starting the task (Example: Customer requests that check be cashed);

- Conditions necessary to perform the task (Example: Teller window);

- Major steps of the task (Example: Check signature with signature card);

- Decisions made while performing the task (Example: If check is incorrect, return to customer);

- Safety, technical, and related knowledge necessary to perform the task successfully (Example: Know how to read check register); and

- The degree of desired proficiency or standard (Example: Check written properly; check stamped; proper cash given to customer).

Figure 4 provides an example of a task-detailing flow chart. Table 11 gives an example of a task-detailing sheet.

*A **task detailing** is a systematic breakdown of each task to determine the skills, sequencing, knowledge, and attitude an individual needs to know to perform a single task successfully.*

Step Four

Figure 4. Task-Detailing Flow Chart.

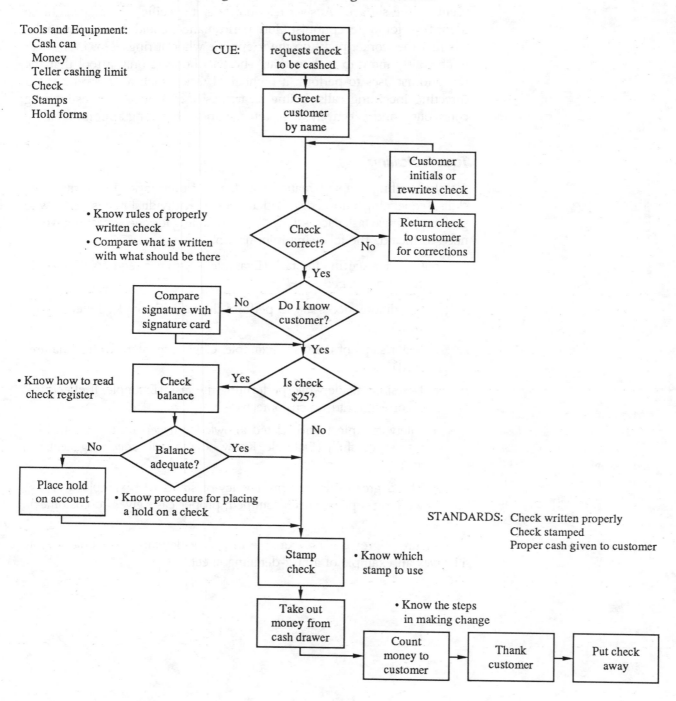

Tools and Equipment:
   Cash can
   Money
   Teller cashing limit
   Check
   Stamps
   Hold forms

CUE: Customer requests check to be cashed

Greet customer by name

Customer initials or rewrites check

• Know rules of properly written check
• Compare what is written with what should be there

Check correct? — No → Return check to customer for corrections

Yes

Do I know customer? — No → Compare signature with signature card

Yes

Is check $25? — Yes → Check balance

• Know how to read check register

No

Balance adequate? — No → Place hold on account

Yes

• Know procedure for placing a hold on a check

STANDARDS: Check written properly
Check stamped
Proper cash given to customer

Stamp check — • Know which stamp to use

Take out money from cash drawer

• Know the steps in making change

Count money to customer → Thank customer → Put check away

Source: Maxwell and West, 1980. Used by permission of the author.

Table

Table 11. Sample Task-Detailing Sheet.

Vocation: X-ray Technician   **Task:** Take an X-ray of the chest

No. of steps in performing the task	Type of performance	Learning difficulty
1. Patient is asked to prepare for the X-ray by removing excess clothing.	Speech	Easy
2. Correctly position the patient, giving special instructions.	Manipulation, speech	Moderately difficult
3. Position and check the distance of the tube with respect to the patient.	Discrimination	Moderately difficult
4. Turn on the X-ray equipment and adjust machine.	Recall	Easy
5. Insert the X-ray film and identification marker into the proper holder.	Manipulation	Easy
6. Expose film and release from examining room.	Manipulation	Moderately difficult
7. Process film.	Manipulation	Difficult
8. Check film for errors.	Discrimination	Very difficult
9. Release patient if film is acceptable.	Recall	Easy

Source: Adapted from Mager and Beach, 1967. Used by permission of David S. Lake Publishers.

Task Inventory

*A **task inventory** is an instrument used to validate the tasks of a job.*

A **task inventory** is an instrument used to validate the tasks of a job.

Validation is the process that confirms that the information gathered in the task analysis process is consistent with the circumstances of actual job performance.

A group of expert workers and supervisors, either in a meeting or in response to a written task inventory, answer certain basic questions about the tasks performed on the targeted job. The task inventory consists of lists of duties and tasks and one or more questions to be asked of incumbent workers about the way a task is performed.

imation gathered in the task analysis process is consistent with the circumstances of actual job performance.

Validation *is the process that confirms that the infor-*

This allows the task analyst to reconcile the information gathered previously to the actual situation. The types of questions asked are:

- How frequently is each task performed?

- How much time is spent performing each task?

- How important is each task for successful performance of the job?

- How difficult is this task to learn?

- Is performance of this task expected of the entry-level worker?

Table 12 gives an example of a task inventory.

Table

Table 12. Sample Task Inventory Sheet.

Job Title: Surgical Technician　　　**Analyst:** Jane Doe

Listed below are a duty and
the tasks it includes. Check
all tasks you perform. Add
any tasks you do that are
not listed, then rate the
tasks you have checked.

Check
if
Done

Time Spent
1. Much below average
2. Below average
3. Slightly below average
4. About average
5. Slightly above average
6. Above average
7. Much above average

Duty: prepares operating
room for surgery.

Inspect operating room
for necessary furniture.

Inspect operating room
for cleanliness.

Scrub for surgery.

Wear required gown
and gloves.

Select instruments and
supplies for each surgery.

Other:

Source: Adapted from Maxwell and West, 1980. Used by permission of the author.

The information in such an inventory will be critical when deciding what instructional techniques to select for teaching a particular task.

Workplace standards for performance of a particular job are obtained by questioning and/or observing at least two expert workers who have been identified by supervisors, management, or performance review, as performing their jobs at a level of competence that meets employer requirements.

Collect Information

There are many different methods for collecting information. Each of the various approaches has advantages and disadvantages.

One might choose an approach or a combination of approaches based on such factors as the type of information required, the sources available, the constraints on time and money, the type of job, and the general makeup of the work force.

For example, it would be inappropriate to use the observation method on a job that is done primarily as mental tasks. It would also be inappropriate to distribute a questionnaire to workers you suspected of having literacy problems.

The following is a description of some of the more common approaches, emphasizing the advantages and disadvantages of each method. Examples are given where appropriate.

Questionnaires

A questionnaire can be used to get workers to provide written answers to questions. It can be distributed to many workers, thereby resulting in the collection of a large amount of data. Because the questionnaire is standardized, it offers an opportunity for comparative analysis. This makes it a relatively cost-effective method.

On the negative side, a questionnaire may yield a low rate of response or be returned by only one type of worker, which could bias the results.

One must make sure the questionnaire is written properly and clearly, because there is no opportunity for in-person clarification.

The questionnaire method may also result in the neglect of issues and/or problems that the designer could not foresee.

Open-ended questionnaires are composed primarily of questions that must be answered with a personalized service. The question is followed by an ample blank space for the response.

Open-ended questionnaires are composed primarily of questions that must be answered with a personalized narrative.

Example

Open-Ended Questions

1. What are the key components of your job?

_____

_____

_____

2. How did you learn your job?

_____

_____

_____

3. In what areas might you benefit from training?

_____

_____

_____

Open-ended questionnaires have several advantages:

- They are easy to construct,
- They allow respondents to introduce new topics,
- They may uncover data not requested, and
- They can be used to encourage respondents to disclose attitudes and perceptions.

Disadvantages of open-ended questionnaires include the following:

- They are difficult for those respondents who cannot express themselves in writing,
- Respondents may be reluctant to commit their responses to paper,
- There is no way to probe further,
- They depend on recall,
- They are poor instruments for data collection, and
- They are difficult to analyze.

Closed questionnaires are composed primarily of questions for which a limited set of responses are provided for the respondent.

Closed questionnaires provide the respondent with a limited set of responses to each question. There are several different types of questions that can be used on this kind of questionnaire. These include the checklist, the two-way question, the multiple-choice question, and ranking scales.

The checklist question gives a list of items, and the respondent is asked to check those that apply to a given situation.

Example

Checklist

In which of these general workplace competency areas do you need the most training in order to be more effective in your current position?

- ☐ Effective writing
- ☐ Effective communication skills
- ☐ Problem-solving techniques
- ☐ Teambuilding, group dynamics, and interpersonal skills

The two-way question has alternate responses, a yes/no or a forced choice between two or more complex statements.

Example

Two-Way Question

How are new employees trained?

a. On the job

b. Seminar

The multiple-choice question gives several choices, and the participant is asked to select the most correct one.

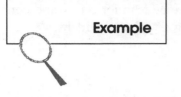

Example

Multiple-Choice Question

How often do you deal directly with clients?

   a. Frequently

   b. Occasionally

   c. Rarely

   d. Never

The ranking scales type of question requires the participant to rank a list of items.

Example

Ranking Scales

In what general workplace competency areas do you most need training in order to be more effective in your current position? Please rank the top three, using 1 for the highest priority and 3 for the lowest.

   ☐ Effective writing

   ☐ Effective communication

   ☐ Effective reading

   ☐ Problem-solving techniques

   ☐ Interpersonal skills

Closed questionnaires have several advantages:

- They are easier to answer,
- They are easier to analyze (computer use reduces time and cost),
- They yield more precise information,
- They are more anonymous, and
- They are less stressful for the respondent.

Among their disadvantages are the following:

- They are more difficult to prepare since two or more plausible, well-stated choices have to be developed for each item,
- They are limited in scope and subtlety,
- They may bias respondents' answers,
- There is no way to probe further, and
- They do not allow for unusual answers.

It is possible and probably desirable to combine both types of questions in a single questionnaire.

The proper method is to begin with closed questions and follow with open-ended questions.

It is also suggested that the questionnaire be read for clarity and content by a worker and supervisor before being distributed widely.

Interviews: Individual or Group

Interviews with master workers, supervisors, subordinates, and so on are obviously a necessary part of the task analysis process. The method involves asking questions of one or more people in a face-to-face meeting.

The **interview** is usually based on a series of questions prepared in advance, but the interviewer introduces, or allows the interviewee(s) to introduce, relevant new topics or questions as the session proceeds.

The interviewer takes notes or tapes the interview. A taped record may seem attractive for any number of reasons, but it can be disruptive, especially in a group situation, and it takes considerable time to analyze.

Interviews have the following advantages:

- Workers become directly involved in the process,
- The process builds commitment in interviewee(s),
- The interview is flexible, allowing the questioner to probe further where needed,
- The interview can clarify and expand on information gathered by other methods,
- The interview is an effective method for learning about mental tasks,
- Group interaction allows on-the-spot verification or clarification, and
- Individual interviews are effective for learning how one worker does a job or performs a task.

Disadvantages of interviews include the following:

- They require skilled interviewers, especially for group sessions,
- They may make people uneasy,
- They may reflect interviewers' biases,
- They are time-consuming,
- They can reach only a relatively small sample of workers,
- They are expensive if travel is necessary,
- They are more difficult to analyze,
- Group interviewees may influence one another,
- The information gathered tends to be subjective, and
- A group interview may not reflect how one worker does the job.

It is best to follow up a group interview with observation.

> **REMEMBER**
>
> Always think beforehand what questions to ask and write them into a guide like the one given in Table 13.
>
> Always leave ample space for notes.
>
> Always take thorough notes and review them immediately after the interview.

 Table

Table 13. Sample Interview Guide.

Interviewee: _____   Position: _____

1. Tell me about your job. *(How time is spent, responsibilities.)*

2. How did you arrive at this job? Is that typical?

3. Tell me about your subordinates. *(Their background, talents, problems, concerns.)* Are they typical?

4. When do you give them feedback? How do you do it?

5. Can you describe a recent feedback meeting with one of your subordinates? What feedback did you give?

6. Did you feel it was a good meeting? Why not?

7. Do you sometimes have to give feedback to an employee whose performance is unsatisfactory?

   If yes, can you describe how you did that?

   If the answer is no, proceed to question 11.

8. What do you think was in that subordinate's mind before that feedback meeting? Did she or he realize what was coming?

9. What would be a typical reason for an employee to perform unsatisfactorily?

10. What approach would you take in a feedback meeting about unsatisfactory performance if you were to hold one? What would you say?

11. Do you have any other thoughts on feedback meetings?

12. Can I call you if I need more information or clarification?

13. Is there anyone else with whom I should speak?

Thank you.

Source: Adapted from K. T. Abella, *Building Successful Training Programs.* Copyright © 1986, Addison-Wesley Publishing Company, Inc., Reading, Massachusetts. Pages 57–59. Reprinted with permission.

Observation

The **observation method** involves a trained person observing workers on the job. Like the interview, this technique requires careful planning and preparation.

Observers must understand what information is sought; they must be trained and given an opportunity to practice.

A form on which each observer can record her or his observations must be designed and tested.

*The **observation method** involves a trained person observing workers on the job.*

The workers, too, must be informed about the purpose of the observation and the use of its results. The effect of the observer's presence on the performance of the worker must also be taken into consideration.

Almost anyone performs differently when watched. To minimize this effect, the observation should take place over a relatively long period of time.

Among its advantages, observation:

- Yields data that are not skewed by recall or interpretation,
- Can bring out subtle things hard to express in interviews or questionnaires,
- Can be a good way to gather data for course materials later on,
- Can build rapport with the target population,
- Is good for a manual job that is not too complex or lengthy, and
- Is a good method for verifying other methods of analysis.

Among its disadvantages are the following:

- It often requires some knowledge of the job,
- It does not always reveal attitudes,
- It can interfere with work,
- It is the most time-consuming technique,
- The observer's presence may influence the work performed,
- It reveals what is, but not necessarily what should be,
- It is useless for mental tasks, and
- Reports will differ, even among skilled observers.

Analysis of Existing Documents

The **analysis of existing documents** involves evaluating manuals and instructions for how work is to be performed. The files of the organization or department should be thoroughly researched to identify any material relevant to the job being analyzed.

*The **analysis of existing documents** involves evaluating manuals and instructions on how work is to be performed.*

Many times, what is written has only a minimal relationship to what actually happens on the job. Existing documents must always be considered in the context of the real day-to-day workplace.

Analysis of existing documents has several advantages. Among them are the following:

- The analyst can get data from several sources in one place, cutting time and cost,
- Doing the analysis seldom involves travel,
- The analyst may be able to use some previous analysis of the data,
- The analysis does not depend on commitment of others, and
- It may greatly reduce the need for initial observation and interviewing, thereby lessening cost.

Among its disadvantages are the following:

- It may produce uneven data, skewing final information received,
- It can consume the analyst's time without producing results,
- It may not cover all areas needed,
- The analyst must be skillful to pick out the right information, and
- The analyst may not be given access to sensitive documents.

Select a Quick Route Through Task Analysis

All of these techniques can be used individually or in conjunction with one another to verify results. Some sophisticated methodologies have been developed combining several of these techniques into integrated systems for performing task analyses.

DACUM

One of the best known and most widely used of these combined systems is DACUM (for *developing a curriculum*), developed by the National Academy for Vocational Education. Basically, **DACUM** is an approach to occupational analysis that brings a committee of experts together under the leadership of a trained facilitator. They use modified brainstorming techniques to specify in detail the tasks that successful workers in their occupation must perform (Norton, 1985).

DACUM is an approach to occupational analysis that specifies in detail the tasks that successful workers must perform in their occupations.

DACUM is a relatively quick (two- to three-day), inexpensive process. Its results are immediately transferrable into course outlines, and it compares favorably in validity with other methods used to identify basic workplace skills.

The basic philosophy behind DACUM is that:

- The best person to describe or define a job is the person who does that job,
- Any job can be described in terms of the tasks that expert workers in that job perform, and
- All tasks require the worker to have certain knowledge and an attitude in order to perform the tasks correctly.

A group of eight to twelve expert workers from the occupation under consideration form the DACUM committee. The ratio of expert workers to immediate supervisors should be about 5:1.

The committee works under the guidance of a facilitator for two to three days to develop the DACUM chart. Modified small-group brainstorming techniques are used to obtain the collective expertise and consensus of the committee. The following are the steps through which the committee goes:

1. Orientation of committee.
2. Review of occupation.
3. Identification of general areas of responsibility.
4. Identification of specific tasks performed.
5. Review and refinement of task and duty statements.
6. Sequencing of task and duty statements.
7. Identification of entry-level tasks.
8. Other options as desired.

The committee usually identifies between eight and twelve duties and 50 to 200 task statements for each occupation. The tasks verified as important become the base for developing instruction for an educational program. Figure 5 gives an example of a completed DACUM chart.

Literacy Task Analysis

Another model, the Literacy Task Analysis (Mikulecky, 1985), is an example of how a traditional task analysis format can be adapted to meet special basic workplace skills needs, in this case to identify job-specific literacy requirements.

The literacy task analysis model is divided into three phases: before, during, and after.

The "before" phase refers to preparing for interviews and observations through:

- Choosing an occupation.
- Identifying frequent and/or highly critical tasks involving basic skills, using J. Greenan's (1984) *The Development of Strategies and Procedures for Assessing the Generalizable Skills of Students in Secondary Vocational Programs*, skills, which identifies approximately 115 skills generalized to more than seventy jobs.

The "during" phase includes:

- Interviewing an experienced worker about the reading, writing, and computation done on the job;
- Interviewing the worker's supervisor about tasks on the job;
- Observing the worker performing reading, writing, and computational tasks on the job; and
- Gathering samples of reading, writing, and computational materials.

The "after" phase focuses on:

- Further analyzing the job tasks using information obtained from observations, interviews, and materials;
- Identifying technical vocabulary; and
- Creating exercises that simulate the job task.

Figure 5. Welder (Entry-Level).

Duties	Tasks									
A Determine Weld-Related Requirements	A-1 Read job method plan	A-2 Verify and upgrade paperwork	A-3 Interpret drawings and blueprints	A-4 Read welding specifications	A-5 Read welding procedures	A-6 Verify welder eligibility				
B Set-up Welding Process(es)	B-1 Gather materials for the job	B-2 Gather welding equipment and tools	B-3 Check welding equipment for safety	B-4 Set-up equipment	B-5 Make test-weld to verify parameters					
C Prepare Joint for Welding	C-1 Prepare joint geometry using oxy fuel	C-2 Prepare joint geometry using carbon arc*	C-3 Prepare joint geometry using plasma arc*	C-4 Prepare joint geometry using mechanical method*	C-5 Clean weld area	C-6 Fit-up joint	C-7 Verify joint preparation			
D Perform Shielded Metal Arc Weld (SMAW)	D-1 Pre-heat joint	D-2 Initiate welding process	D-3 Perform weld sequence	D-4 Control weld technique	D-5 Maintain pre-heat	D-6 Perform inter-pass preparation	D-7 Apply welder's identification	D-8 Control post-weld temperature according to procedures	D-9 Post-clean weld	D-10 Post-finish weld
E Perform Gas Metal Arc Weld (GMAW) — Short Circuit Transfer[1]	E-1 Pre-heat joint	E-2 Initiate welding process	E-3 Perform weld sequence	E-4 Control weld technique	E-5 Maintain pre-heat	E-6 Perform inter-pass preparation	E-7 Apply welder's indentification	E-8 Control post-weld temperature according to procedures	E-9 Post-clean weld	E-10 Post-finish weld
Spray Transfer[2]*	F-1 Pre-heat joint	F-2 Initiate welding process	F-3 Perform weld sequence	F-4 Control weld technique	F-5 Maintain pre-heat	F-6 Perform inter-pass preparation	F-7 Apply welder's indentification	F-8 Control post-weld temperature according to procedures	F-9 Post-clean weld	F-10 Post-finish weld
Pulse Spray Transfer[1]	G-1 Pre-heat joint	G-2 Initiate welding process	G-3 Perform weld sequence	G-4 Control weld technique	G-5 Maintain pre-heat	G-6 Perform inter-pass preparation	G-7 Apply welder's indentification	G-8 Control post-weld temperature according to procedures	G-9 Post-clean weld	G-10 Post-finish weld
H Perform Flux Core Arc Weld (FCAW) — Flux Core Arc: Shielded[1]	H-1 Pre-heat joint	H-2 Initiate welding process	H-3 Perform weld sequence	H-4 Control weld technique	H-5 Maintain pre-heat	H-6 Perform inter-pass preparation	H-7 Apply welder's indentification	H-8 Control post-weld temperature according to procedures	H-9 Post-clean weld	H-10 Post-finish weld
Flux Core Arc: Non-shielded[1]	I-1 Pre-heat joint	I-2 Initiate welding process	I-3 Perform weld sequence	I-4 Control weld technique	I-5 Maintain pre-heat	I-6 Perform inter-pass preparation	I-7 Apply welder's indentification	I-8 Control post-weld temperature according to procedures	I-9 Post-clean weld	I-10 Post-finish weld
J Perform Gas Tungsten Arc Weld (GTAW)[1]	J-1 Pre-heat joint	J-2 Initiate welding process	J-3 Perform weld sequence	J-4 Control weld technique	J-5 Maintain pre-heat	J-6 Perform inter-pass preparation	J-7 Apply welder's indentification	J-8 Control post-weld temperature according to procedures	J-9 Post-clean weld	J-10 Post-finish weld
K Perform Oxy Fuel Welding and Brazing[1]	K-1 Pre-heat joint	K-2 Initiate welding process	K-3 Perform weld sequence	K-4 Control weld technique	K-5 Maintain pre-heat	K-6 Perform inter-pass preparation	K-7 Apply welder's indentification	K-8 Control post-weld temperature according to procedures	K-9 Post-clean weld	K-10 Post-finish weld
L Perform Submerged Arc Weld: Semi-automatic (SAW)[2]*	L-1 Pre-heat joint	L-2 Initiate welding process	L-3 Perform weld sequence	L-4 Control weld technique	L-5 Maintain pre-heat	L-6 Perform inter-pass preparation	L-7 Apply welder's indentification	L-8 Control post-weld temperature according to procedures	L-9 Post-clean weld	L-10 Post-finish weld
M Perform In-process Weld Inspection	M-1 Check weld size	M-2 Perform visual inspection	M-3 Perform in-process magnetic particle test (MT)*	M-4 Perform in-process dye penetrant test (PT)*						
N Perform In-process Rework	N-1 Pre-heat weld (if required)	N-2 Remove weld defect	N-3 Verify defect removal	N-4 Prepare geometry for reweld	N-5 Perform reweld	N-6 Repeat in-process inspection				
O Perform Housekeeping Activities	O-1 Return un-used consumables	O-2 Store tools	O-3 Secure welding equipment	O-4 Secure welding gases	O-5 Clean work area(s)					
P Follow Safety Practices	P-1 Wear personal safety equipment	P-2 Maintain safe work station	P-3 Protect others from ARC flash	P-4 Maintain adequate ventilation	P-5 Mark "hot-work"					

Code: [1] = All positions
[2] = Flat and horizontal only
* = Optional

[For duties D through L, welder uses the process(es) specified in job plan]

Source: Competency Profile of Welder (Entry-Level), The Center on Education and Training for Employment (formerly The National Center for Research in Vocational Education), The Ohio State University. Dr. Robert E. Norton, developer. Reprinted with permission.

Taxonomic Approach

A third very different variation on the traditional task analysis process called the taxonomic approach was developed during a project linking math, reading, and writing skills to jobs (Cooney and Glines, 1978).

In this method, a training interviewer uses a structured questionnaire and guides the respondent, usually an expert employee, through a taxonomy of instructional objectives to identify which basic skills are required on the job.

The questionnaire is based on the Generic Skills Taxonomy of Instructional Objectives developed by Kwala and Smith in 1975 during an extensive study to identify those skills common to seventy-five of Canada's most frequently performed jobs.

The taxonomy presents skill statements that are measurable and easily verifiable. They are stated at a level that is easily perceived and readily understood by the worker, the supervisor, the instructor, the manager, and the CEO.

In preparation for using the questionnaire, to help the respondent picture all the duties and functions of the job, the interviewer and the respondent review company job descriptions or job descriptions from the *Dictionary of Occupational Titles* for the job being analyzed. Once the review is complete, the respondent is asked to walk through the questionnaire step by step with the interviewer.

The process takes approximately one and a half hours and not only specifies the exact skills used on the job but also gathers examples of how these skills are used. The respondent is first asked which broad skill areas are used on the job. Subskills are then identified. Finally, specific measurable objectives are located that match the skill requirements of the job.

REMEMBER

What you should remember about these three composite analytical methodologies is that they are all based on obtaining information from expert or highly skilled workers. Without this type of input, the information on how a job is performed is simply speculation.

Differences in these methods are largely a matter of emphasis. All three approaches begin by breaking the job into its component duties and tasks.

DACUM has the most rigorous analytic approach. The DACUM model analyzes duties and tasks from the inside out. The literacy task analysis and the taxonomic approach study component job skills from the outside in. They begin with a set of skills and match them to the duties and tasks in the job.

For example, the respondent might first consider the computation skill area. The questionnaire presents an array of computation skills that might be needed, such as subtraction, addition, and multiplication of whole numbers, fractions, decimals, and dollars and cents.

For each, the respondent describes when and how the skill is used on the job. Since the skills in the taxonomy are expressed as measurable instructional objectives, the brief interview produces a curriculum of objectives ready to use in a training situation.

The taxonomic interview process is valuable because it asks respondents to supply concrete examples of when the skills are used on the job. This provides a check on the reliability of the responses.

Further, it provides data that will be useful during the development of safe, job-related competency tests. The job-related description of the skill is also useful in instruction because it allows the instructor to describe the skills to be learned in terms of their application on the job and thus capitalize on the motivation of the learner.

The Task Analysis: How to Approach It Generically

Even though there are several different approaches to task analysis, they all share a number of common elements (see Table 14). Understanding these generic procedures can be helpful in selecting the most appropriate system to perform a task analysis. Ultimately, this selection will be determined by the time, resources, and expertise available to carry out these procedures, as well as by the number of jobs for which such an analysis is being considered.

Unless there is considerable in-house expertise available, it may be that reliable information, cost savings, and effective results will be better obtained by using an outside provider to perform the activity or by using specific provider expertise to complement the in-house staff capabilities.

> *REMEMBER*
>
> A task analysis identifies both what employees are actually doing and what they should be doing on the job.
>
> The task analyst should focus on those duties and tasks necessary to accomplish the important goals and objectives of the organization. These may not be those that are most difficult or take the most time.
>
> Use more than one or two methods of data collection to increase the validity of your research.
>
> The essential focus of a task analysis is to identify the underlying skills, knowledge, and attitude necessary to perform the job.

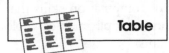 **Table**

Table 14. Generic Elements of Task Analysis.

1. Select the jobs to be analyzed.

2. Develop a preliminary list of duties and tasks performed on the jobs to be analyzed, focusing on basic workplace skills.

   - Search through occupational literature.

   - Interview and observe expert workers and/or supervisors in the occupation.

   - Talk with others who have already performed a task analysis.

   - Check with labor unions and/or the *Dictionary of Occupational Titles* to determine if task and duty lists already exist.

3. Validating the basic workplace skills necessary for the jobs.

   - Use expert committees.

   - Use task inventory survey.

4. Perform a task detailing focused on basic workplace skills for each task to be included in training program.

   - Interview incumbent worker qualified in task.

   - Observe task being performed.

   - Use collective committee knowledge.

   - Use questionnaire.

References and Suggested Readings

Abella, K. T. *Building Successful Training Programs: A Step-by-Step Guide.* Reading, Mass.: Addison-Wesley, 1986.

American Society for Training and Development. "Be a Better Task Analyst." *INFO-LINE,* Mar. 1985.

Armed Forces Staff. *Handbook for Designers of Instructional Development.* Vols. I–VI, Army, Navy, or Air Force, 1978.

Barbee, D. E. *Seminar for Adapting Off-the-Shelf Vocational and Technical Curricula.* Unpublished manuscript, 1985.

Bishop, H. "Accurate Job Descriptions: First Things First." *Performance and Instruction,* Feb. 1988, pp. 15–18.

Butler, E. P., Hahn, A., and Darr, J. *The Literacy-Employment Equation: Education for Tomorrow's Jobs.* San Francisco: Far West Laboratory for Educational Research and Development, 1985.

Carlisle, K., and Arwady, J. P. *Analyzing Jobs and Tasks.* Englewood Cliffs, N.J.: Educational Technology Publications, 1986.

Cooney, J., and Glines, E. *Final Report of the Adult Competency Education Project: An Experimental Adult Basic Education Demonstration Project.* Redwood City, Calif.: Career Preparations Programs, Vocational Education Division, San Mateo County Office of Education, 1978.

Davies, I. K. *Competency Based Learning: Technology, Management, and Design.* New York: McGraw-Hill, 1973.

District of Columbia Department of Personnel. *Task Analysis Handbook.* Washington: District of Columbia Department of Personnel, 1973.

Duffy, T. M. *Literacy Instruction in the Military.* Pittsburgh, Penn.: Communications Design Center, Carnegie Mellon University, 1983.

Eitington, J. E. *The Winning Trainer.* Houston, Tex.: Gulf Publishing, 1984.

Esseff, P. J., and Esseff, M. S. *Behavioral Task Analysis.* Columbia, Md.: Educational Systems for the Future, 1974.

Gossman, J. R., and Martinetz, C. "The Missing Link, a Bridge Between Task Analysis and Training Strategy." *Performance and Instruction,* Feb. 1988, pp. 26–28.

Greenan, J. P. *The Development of Strategies and Procedures for Assessing the Generalizable Skills of Students in Secondary Vocational Programs.* Springfield, Ill.: State Board of Education, Dept. of Adult, Vocational, and Technical Education, 1984.

Mager, R. F., and Beach, K. M., Jr. *Developing Vocational Instruction.* Belmont, Calif.: David S. Lake Publishers, 1967.

Maxwell, G. W., and West, L. N. *Handbook for Developing Competency-Based Curricula for New and Emerging Occupations: A Handbook for California Vocational Educators.* Unpublished manuscript, San Jose State University, 1980.

Mikulecky, L. "Job Literacy: The Relationship Between School Preparation and Workplace Actuality." *Reading Research Quarterly,* 1982, *17* (3), 400–419.

Mikulecky, L. "Literacy Task Analysis: Defining and Measuring Occupational Literacy Demands." Paper presented at American Education Research Association Convention, Mar. 1985.

Mikulecky, L., Ehlinger, J., and Meehan, A. L. *Training for Job Literacy Demands: What Research Applies to Practice.* University Park: Institute for the Study of Adult Literacy, College of Education, Pennsylvania State University, 1987.

Norton, R. E. *DACUM Handbook.* Leadership Training Series, no. 67. Columbus: National Center for Research in Vocational Education, Ohio State University, 1985.

Notes

_____

_____

_____

_____

_____

_____

_____

_____

_____

_____

_____

_____

_____

_____

_____

_____

_____

_____

_____

_____

_____

_____

_____

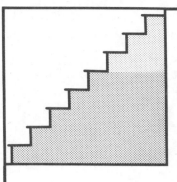

STEP FIVE

Design the Curriculum

Learning Objectives

The reader will be able to:

1. Understand how to construct a good instructional system built on performance-based training concepts and job-specific learning.

2. Understand how to develop:
   - Performance objectives,
   - Criterion-referenced tests,
   - Evaluation procedures, and
   - Documentation and record keeping.

3. Understand and be able to develop an accurate learning center budget.

Introduction

This step involves actually designing the curriculum. What happens here is that the job situation is transformed into valid learning situations that simulate the pressures or conditions on the job under which an individual must work. This involves the design of performance objectives, which in turn form the basis for the criterion-referenced tests that signify competence. It also includes the design of evaluation and record-keeping instruments to provide feedback on how successful the training strategy has been as it relates to the needs of the organization. To ensure continuity between the program design, development, and implementation phases, the position of program manager should be filled no later than the design stage, and earlier if desired.

Other key personnel may also be hired at this point or even earlier, depending on the internal needs of the organization. These key personnel should play an integral role throughout the evolution of the program. (See Step Seven for an in-depth discussion of staff selection procedures.)

What Is Performance-Based Training?

Most state-of-the-art training designs today are developed using a performance-based formula. **Performance-based training** is a systematic way of organizing instruction to ensure that learners become competent in tasks that have been designated as essential for successful performance and that they do not spend time on unrelated skills.

Specifically, a performance-based curriculum includes the following (Stiles, Tibbetts, and Westby-Gibson, 1984):

Performance-based training is a systematic format of instruction in which skills to be learned are clearly identified for the trainee and designed to reflect the skills required to achieve and/or retain employment. The skill mastery requirements for each task are clearly stated prior to the beginning of instruction in each module.

- Success is demonstrated by measurable knowledge gained rather than by time put in. Learners progress through instructional sequences at their own rate and not according to fixed schedules.

- The specified competency is carefully identified, verified, and made known in advance to all concerned.

- The standards for successful performance are clearly stated and openly shared with all parties so they will know what degree or level of learning must be demonstrated for certification.

- Prior learning or achievement is measured and accounted for in developing each learner's training program.

Work-related performance-based training leads trainees toward demonstrated mastery of skills necessary to function proficiently on the job.

Table 15 illustrates some of the differences between conventional and performance-based programs. In performance-based programs, the emphasis is on being able to achieve goals at an individual pace without having to sit through instruction of material already known.

Therefore, performance-based education is especially attractive to adults. Often for the first time they see learning as real, specific, and attainable.

Performance-based training rests on the following assumptions:

- The specific behavior needed for successful job performance can be learned.
- Once successful performance has been identified, training based on this performance will succeed.
- The knowledge, skills, and attitude acquired by the learner can be measured.

Table

Table 15. Characteristics of conventional and performance-based programs.

Program characteristics	Conventional adult programs	Performance-based adult programs
1. Desired outcomes	Nonspecific, not necessarily measurable; typically goal-level statements	Specific, measurable, statements; typically at an objective level
2. Instructional content	Subject-matter based	Outcome or competency based
3. Amount of time provided for instruction	Fixed units of time (semester, term)	Continued until trainee demonstrates mastery
4. Mode of instruction	Emphasis on instructor presentation	Emphasis on instructor as facilitator of trainee performance
5. Basis of instruction	What the instructor is able to or likes to teach	What the trainee wants or needs to learn
6. Instructional materials	Single sources of materials	Multiple texts and media
7. Reporting performance results	Delayed feedback	Immediate feedback
8. Pacing of instruction	Instructor or group paced	Individually paced
9. Testing	Norm referenced	Criterion referenced
10. Exit criteria	Final tests and grades	Trainee demonstration of competence

Source: Adapted from Stiles, Tibbetts, and Westby-Gibson, 1984.

In fact, performance-based training serves particularly well when the skill or knowledge problem is clear. Learners who take expertly designed performance-based training courses often succeed in mastering the skill, knowledge, or behavior with which they had problems.

The element most crucial to success may be the fact that an employee receives information about the program *before* enrollment—information about the goals of the program, who the participants will be, the content to be covered, and what a typical learning session will be like.

This preview helps alleviate discrepancies between learner expectations and actual experiences, which is the major cause of program dropout for adult learners (Darkenwald and Valentine, 1985).

It is also important that employees view the program's goals as relevant to their jobs and to their employer's priorities and as attainable within a reasonably brief period of instructional time. These considerations eliminate the main barriers to program participation.

What Is Functional Context Learning?

In order to provide successful adult training in the workplace, it is recommended that the concepts of **functional context learning** (Sticht, 1987) be integrated into the performance-based system.

Functional context learning uses the concepts of performance-based training but adds the following steps to ensure that learning outcomes mirror the needs of both individuals and institutions:

Functional context learning is an approach to training in which instruction is taught contextually (in ways that reflect actual use on the job). It is designed to produce the quickest, most effective results in the area of improved employee performance.

- Integrating instruction in basic workplace skills into job-related training so that learners can better negotiate the requirements for these skills in the program and more readily transfer the acquired skills to the job,

- Preparing course objectives by analyzing the knowledge and skill demands of the job, and

- Making every effort to utilize contexts, tasks, materials, and procedures that have been taken from the job the training addresses.

A workplace basics curriculum that uses a functional context approach will, for example, teach problem solving to workers using the materials in a job-related manner. This way, students build an understanding of how to solve problems that is based on a familiar and usable context. They see the immediate practical value of what they are learning. "The more similar the basic skills training tasks are to the actual job tasks, the greater will be the likelihood that the training will pay off in improved performance of job . . . tasks. Thus, for youth and adults aiming at work in a given industry or organization, the use of job-related materials serves two purposes. On the one hand, it provides a functional context for the learner—that is, he or she can see that the materials are relevant to the employment goal—and hence motivation to use the material is elevated. On the other hand, the organization can see that the training is relevant to its needs and that there is some likelihood of the trainees actually becoming competent in the performance of job-relevant skills. Thus organizational motivation to participate in the training is gained" (Sticht and Mikulecky, 1984, p. 33).

The major point to understand in developing a functional context training program for adults is that the human mind should be thought of as an information-processing system that develops new capabilities over time using prior knowledge and skills to acquire new knowledge and skills.

From the employer's perspective, the advantage of a functional context approach to training is that it is more likely to achieve the objective of upgrading a work force at a fraction of the cost of academic model programs. Overall this cost-effective and performance-based method of achieving a productive work force contributes to the strategic goals of the organization.

Design Performance Objectives

*A **performance objective** is a description of the performance you want the learner to be able to exhibit before you consider her or him competent.*

The first step in developing a functional competency curriculum is to write **performance objectives** for each task selected for training. A performance objective is a description of the performance you want the learner to be able to exhibit before you consider her or him competent. It describes the result of instruction rather than the process.

The goals of a particular program can be defined in terms of three kinds of performance outcomes as demonstrated by:

- Changes in knowledge,
- Changes in attitude, and
- Changes in behavior.

It can have one of these purposes or all three.

Definition of Performance Objective

Performance objectives are important because they provide a sound basis for:

- Selection or design of instructional content and techniques;
- Organizing the learner's own efforts and activities; and
- Evaluating or assessing the success of instruction.

A performance objective is a clear, concise, and measurable statement of:

- Performance (what the learner is able to do),
- Conditions (important conditions under which the performance is expected to occur, including necessary tools and equipment), and
- Criterion (the standard or level of performance that will be considered acceptable).

Writing Performance Objectives

The performance part of the objective is based on an action verb that precisely specifies what the learner must demonstrate an ability to do. Verbs such as to know, to learn, to understand, or to increase are statements of general learning goals and are virtually impossible to measure.

Performance objectives require specific action verbs such as to list, to identify, to name, to classify, to diagram, to repair, to adjust, to make, and so on. These describe learner behavior that can be observed and measured.

Table 16 contains a partial list of action verbs that can be used for writing performance objectives.

Table

Table 16. Verbs for Writing Performance Objectives.

Acceptable

To list	To display	To translate	To classify
To compare	To select	To write	To solve
To order	To quote	To demonstrate	To name
To operate	To locate	To inject	To blend
To multiply	To clean	To illustrate	To measure
To alter	To subtract	To fabricate	To match
To perform	To observe	To assemble	To solder
To calculate	To prepare	To practice	To differentiate
To state	To deliver	To load	To combine
To add	To identify	To synchronize	

Unacceptable

To know	To understand	To improve	To develop
To appreciate	To know how	To learn	To increase
To feel	To believe	To be better	To become

The conditions part of the objective outlines the circumstances under which the learner will be required to perform the activity. It describes:

- Tools and materials with which the learner must work,
- The setting in which the learner will be required to perform,
- Information with which the learner will be provided, or
- Any combination of these.

The criterion part of the performance objective defines how well the learner must be able to perform the activity. It includes specifications of accuracy, speed, percentage or number to be achieved, maximum number of errors allowed, degree of excellence, or combinations of these.

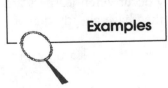

Examples

Flat Tire

Given a car with a flat tire, a jack, a spare tire, and a lug wrench (conditions), change the flat tire (performance) according to the manufacturer's instructions and specifications in fifteen minutes without injury or damage (standard) (Maxwell and West, 1980).

Correspondence

Given a sample of correspondence (conditions), find and correct 95 percent (standard) of the errors in grammar and spelling (performance) (Maxwell and West, 1980).

Math

Using only pencil and paper (conditions), calculate ten math questions (performance) in thirty minutes without error (standard) (Maxwell and West, 1980).

Checklist 11 may be used in developing performance objectives to ensure that they are correct.

 **Checklist**

Checklist 11. Guidelines for Developing Performance Objectives.

A well-written performance objective should meet the following standards:

- ☐ It is clear.
- ☐ It is relevant.
- ☐ The learner can do it.
- ☐ It improves performance.
- ☐ It is measurable.
- ☐ It is necessary.
- ☐ It states terminal behavior (performance), conditions, and criteria.

Table 17 shows a completely developed task statement, including a correct performance objective.

In a performance-based system a learner learns only the skills and knowledge that she or he needs to successfully carry out a specific task.

The instructor provides the learner with a series of instructional materials individualized to her or his needs.

These needs have been identified during a pretest process that has pinpointed learner problems that pertain only to the job for which the learner is being prepared.

Performance-based instruction goes a long way toward eliminating the problems related to boredom that frequently occur when learners are forced to repeat information or tasks in which they have already demonstrated competency.

Using a performance-based approach accelerates the learning process and enhances learner retention.

For example, an individual who is working as a machinist but already knows how to change fractions into decimals would not be required to relearn this skill during training. She or he would move on to new learning areas.

Table

Table 17. Sample Task Statement with Performance Objective.

Program: Automotive   **Task No.** 315.000

Task Statement: Change a flat tire (performance)

Conditions under which task is performed: any (conditions)

Cue: Car has a flat tire.

Tools, equipment, materials, references, aids used:
    Spare tire, jack, lug wrench (conditions)

Key Steps *List sequentially the key steps and decisions that lead to the completion of the task.*	Essential Knowledge *For each key step, list (if any) what an individual has to know (technical safety and related knowledge) to complete each step*
1. Set emergency brake and block wheel.	1. Block front and rear of wheels.
2. Remove hub cap.	
3. Loosen nuts with lug wrench.	3. Do not remove nuts before raising car.
4. Raise car with jack.	4. Know how to operate jack.
5. Remove nuts and remove flat tire.	
6. Install spare tire.	6. Know how to lift wheel on hub.
7. Tighten nuts.	7. Tighten securely.
8. Lower car with jack.	8. Lower jack slowly.
9. Replace hub.	
10. Put tools away.	

Student Performance Objective: Given a car with a flat tire, a jack, a spare tire, and a lug wrench, change flat tire according to manufacturer's instructions and specifications in fifteen minutes without injury.

Student performance objective based on steps and/or knowledge:
    Operate a jack.

Standards: (acceptable level of performance for entry-level worker):

Quality: Without injury or damage   **Time Limit:** 15 minutes

Amount: (Does not apply)   **Content:** According to manufacturer's specifications

Source: Maxwell and West, 1980, p. 53. Used by permission of the author.

Design Criterion-Referenced Tests

Criterion-referenced tests are designed to measure learner ability to perform specifically stated performance objectives. This assessment is not concerned with how quickly trainees learn or how they perform compared to one another.

Successful learning of the skill is defined in terms of some predetermined performance standard—knowledge is measured by the number of questions that must be answered correctly, skill by the time in which a task must be performed, and so on.

Criterion-referenced tests are designed to measure the exact objective and the specific behavior required to accomplish a particular task.

Functions of Criterion-Referenced Tests

During the course of the performance-based instructional program, criterion-referenced tests are used at three different points to perform three important functions: the pretest for diagnosis, the test during instruction for feedback, and the post-test for results.

Pretests should give employees the opportunity to perform representative samples of each of the task behaviors they are required to perform on the job. Testing trainees before the program begins:

- Identifies those tasks in which the individual worker is deficient.

- Serves as a screening device to indicate which workers are functioning at nonliterate or marginally literate levels and will need special instruction in beginning reading skills,

- Assures learners that they are not being exposed to instruction they do not really need, and

- Assures learners that they are not placed in a learning situation for which they lack the required skills.

Assessment during the course of instruction ensures that a trainee is successfully learning the material, and allows the instructor to make appropriate adjustments in the materials, methods, or pace of the program.

Learner mastery in the basic workplace skills training program is measured by comparing performance on post-tests with the learners' pretest results.

Construction of Criterion-Referenced Tests

The tests should be constructed using actual or simulated job situations and materials.

Pretests should give employees the opportunity to perform representative samples of each of the tasks they are required to perform on the job. Post-tests should be of identical length and format but should test only those task behaviors treated during the instructional program.

Construction of relevant, functional pretests and post-tests is most effectively accomplished after performance objectives have been written and the actual materials to be used for instruction have been developed.

Typically, a separate criterion-referenced test is written for each performance objective. The type of objective being measured determines the form of test to be used.

- Written tests measure knowledge.

- Performance tests measure skill development.

- Checklists can be used to ascertain changes in attitude.

Choose what is best to assess, regardless of whether the particular performance objective has been met.

Criterion-referenced testing has particular usefulness and appeal to management. As Ivor Davies (1973) explained, criterion-referenced tests can be customized to validate training outcomes preestablished by employers. The training then takes on a legitimacy it might not otherwise have, because the tests clearly profile workplace needs.

The results of this type of assessment are very easy to interpret in that the trainee demonstrates that she or he either has or has not learned the knowledge, skill, or attitude defined in the performance objectives and accordingly is or is not ready to perform a given task up to company standards. (See Table 18 for an example of a criterion-referenced test.)

 Table

Table 18. Sample Criterion-Referenced Test.

Objective: Given a car with a flat tire, a jack, a spare tire, and a lug wrench, change the flat tire according to manufacturer's instructions in fifteen minutes without injury or damage.

Activity	Rating Acceptable	Unacceptable
1. Unaffected wheels were blocked front and rear.	☐	☐
2. Emergency brakes were applied.	☐	☐
3. Jack was correctly positioned.	☐	☐
4. Lugs were loosened before wheel was completely raised.	☐	☐
5. Tire was lifted onto hub correctly.	☐	☐
6. Lugs and replacement wheel were sufficiently secured.	☐	☐
7. Removed wheel and tools were returned to appropriate place in trunk of car.	☐	☐
8. Tire was changed within fifteen minutes.	☐	☐

Source: Maxwell and West, 1980, p. 64. Used by permission of the author.

Design Evaluation Instruments

Without good training program evaluation, accomplishments must rely on the perceptions of management that training is valuable and successful. However, as cost pressures increase within organizations, training will need to demonstrate its value in more substantive ways if it is to successfully compete for scarce resources.

A training evaluation, to be worth anything, must be able to determine which is the most appropriate (rather than the best) program and which program will best further organizational objectives.

Evaluation plans are developed in consultation with the client. The term *client* can refer to anyone who has a vested interest in the training program, such as participants, instructors, supervisors, managers, the training department, and customers. However, the primary client group is usually the individual or group sponsoring and financing the training.

The design and development of training will need input from the line managers and supervisors so that they will be knowledgeable about how to evaluate the effectiveness of training.

In a job-related program, success is measured by behavior changes back on the job. The more groundwork that is done early in the design and development process, the more successful the program will be, especially if the program is staffed largely by part-time instructors or by an outside provider.

A successful evaluation design must be able to demonstrate that a training program bears some responsibility for changes that take place in both the trainees and the organization.

For example, without an evaluation design that quantifies that impact of nontraining factors, it would be hard to prove that a training program in improving customer service is actually responsible for improved sales.

An evaluation design:

- Identifies program procedures for collecting, interpreting, and reporting data;

- Dictates when and from whom program data will be collected; and

- Helps the evaluator draw conclusions by having information available to compare preprogram and postprogram behavior. (See Step Eight for a more detailed discussion of evaluation.)

Design and Develop a Documentation and Record-Keeping System

Other tasks that should be initiated at this point include designing and developing a record-keeping system that includes employee learning contracts (goals statements signed by employees and supervisors) and other types of backup documentation.

Documentation is a formal and coordinated process to collect, record, analyze, and report accurate data on the progress and performance of individual learners.

The documentation process as a whole provides written proof that the training occurred and furnishes evidence as to whether it was successful. Over time this type of documentation can be used very effectively as part of an employee's career development plan.

Decisions on how record keeping will be done (manually or by computer) and by whom, as well as how extensive it will be, will determine the design of the forms to be developed.

Only data directly related to the training should be included, such as attendance, hours of instruction, literacy placement pretests, workplace basic test results, employee educational background, and so on.

Also among the records to be kept is the performance-based competency profile that tracks learner progress in acquiring skill mastery.

Tables 19 and 20 illustrate two different types of documentation that might be found in an employee's training or personnel file.

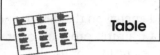

Table

Table 19. Sample Effectiveness Data Table.

	Model N:	Passed Pretest %	Passed Post-test %	Failed/ Incomplete %	Training Effectiveness %
Table of contents	710	19	67	14	83
Index	710	16	56	28	67
Table and graphics	710	20	53	27	66
Body of manual	710	3	49	48	48
Procedural Directions	710	9	30	61	33

Source: Adapted from Sticht, T. G. and Mikulecky, L. *Job-Related Basic Skills: Cases and Conclusions,* p. 23. Copyright © 1984 by the National Center for Research in Vocational Education, The Ohio State University. Used with permission.

Table

Table 20. Sample Learner Competency Profile.

Name: _____   **Date:** _____

Instructor: _____   **School:** _____   **Program:** _____

Rating scale:

4-Outstanding   3-Skilled   2-Satisfactory   1-Satisfactory with supervision

Competencies	4	3	2	1
Process communications	☐	☐	☐	☐
Type memo or unarranged copy	☐	☐	☐	☐
Type unarranged business letter	☐	☐	☐	☐
Use telephone service	☐	☐	☐	☐
Type manuscript	☐	☐	☐	☐
Select duplication process	☐	☐	☐	☐
Type table	☐	☐	☐	☐
Type invoice	☐	☐	☐	☐
Receive or place calls	☐	☐	☐	☐

Source: Adapted from Sticht, T. G. and Mikulecky, L. *Job-Related Basic Skills: Cases and Conclusions,* p. 23. Copyright © 1984 by the National Center for Research in Vocational Education, The Ohio State University. Used with permission.

Obtain Final Budget Approval to Implement

At this point, before spending extensive time and energy on the design and development of curriculum materials, prepare a training program operations budget and proposal to present to management for approval.

A part of this budgetary exercise should be a determination of whether outside providers will be used to perform any or all of the actual training. The decision should be based on:

- Cost effectiveness;

- The expertise of in-house personnel;

- The volume of work required versus the size of the training and education staff;

- A preliminary determination of the level of instructional technology to be employed; and

- The complexity of the program design.

Even the larger companies such as General Motors and IBM frequently use specialized outside providers in their training schedules because in-house staff does not always have the expertise necessary to actually conduct the comprehensive training.

The same procedures detailed in Step Three for selecting outside providers should be used here and, where appropriate, throughout the process for creating the complete training program.

Table 21 shows an example of a budget to set up and operate a basic workplace skills learning center using a combination of computer-assisted and written materials.

The center would provide individualized instruction for up to twenty learners per two-hour session. Operating at full capacity, it could serve sixty participants a day.

Since the cost of learner replacement time is such a variable, no provision for that is included in the budget.

The budget also does not calculate the costs of basic workplace skills program management and administration, which could be handled by staff from the company's human resource department as a regular part of their job.

Table

Table 21. Sample Budget for a Workplace Basics Learning Center.

Setup Costs

1. Computer Hardware (four learner stations, one management information system)	$ 8,000
2. Printed courseware	5,000
3. Comprehensive Competencies Program (CCP) implementation package	5,000
4. Computer-assisted instruction software	5,000
5. Furniture	2,500
6. Facilities improvement and restoration	2,000
Total setup costs	**$27,500**

Operating Costs

1. Full-time instructor (salary and fringes)	$29,250
2. One half-time aide	12,675
3. Rent ($1,500 per month)	18,000
4. Supplies	900
5. Duplication costs ($50 per month)	600
6. Insurance (liability, bonding, equipment)	3,000
7. User fee CCP	1,000
8. Technical assistance (outside consultant)	2,500
9. Telephone	1,800
10. Printing materials	1,000
11. Postage	750
Total operating costs	**$71,475**

References and Suggested Readings

Austin, K. J., and Titus, A. A. "Beyond Performance-Based Training." *Training,* 1988, *25* (1), 53–55.

Barbee, D. E. *Seminar for Adapting Off-the-Shelf Vocational and Technical Curricula.* Unpublished manuscript, 1985.

Berk, R. A. (ed.). *Criterion-Referenced Measurement: The State to the Art.* Baltimore, Md.: Johns Hopkins University Press, 1980.

Bishop, H. "Accurate Job Descriptions: First Things First." *Performance and Instruction,* Feb. 1988, pp. 15–18.

Business Council for Effective Literacy. *Job-Related Basic Skills: A Guide for Planners of Employee Programs.* New York: Business Council for Effective Literacy, 1987.

Chapados, J. T., Rentfrow, D., and Hochheiser, L. I. "Four Principles of Training." *Training and Development Journal,* 1987, *41* (12), 63–66.

Darkenwald, G. G., and Gavin, W. J. "Dropout as a Function of Discrepancies Between Expectations and Actual Experience of the Classroom Social Environment." *Adult Education Quarterly,* 1987, *37* (3), 152–163.

Darkenwald, G. G., and Valentine, T. "Factor Structure of Deterrents to Public Participation in Adult Education." *Adult Education Quarterly,* 1985, *35* (4), 177–193.

Davies, I. K. *Competency-Based Learning: Technology, Management, and Design.* New York: McGraw-Hill, 1973.

District of Columbia Department of Personnel. *Task Analysis Handbook.* Washington: District of Columbia Department of Personnel, 1973.

Eitington, J. E. *The Winning Trainer.* Houston, Tex.: Gulf Publishing, 1984.

Glines, E., and Cooney, J. *Final Report of the Adult Competency Education Project: An Experimental Adult Basic Education Demonstration Project.* Redwood City, Calif.: Career Preparations Programs, Vocational Education Division, San Mateo County Office of Education, 1978.

Golde, R. A. "Management Training? Get Serious!" *New Management,* 1987, *4* (3), 30–33.

Knox, A. B. *Helping Adults Learn.* San Francisco: Jossey-Bass, 1986.

Lawrie, J. "Training: Are Employees Using What They Learn?" *Personnel Journal,* 1988, *67* (4), 95–97.

Lee, C. "Basic Training in the Corporate Schoolhouse." *Training,* 1988, *25* (4), 27–36.

Lerche, R. S. *Effective Adult Literacy Programs: A Practitioner's Guide.* New York: Cambridge Book Company, 1985.

Mager, R. F. *Preparing Instructional Objectives.* Belmont, Calif.: Pitman Learning, 1984.

Maxwell, G. W., and West, L. N. *Handbook for Developing Competency-Based Curricula for New and Emerging Occupations: A Handbook for California Vocational Educators.* Unpublished manuscript, San Jose State University, San Jose, Calif., 1980.

Morris, R., Strumpf, L., and Curnan, S. *Using Basic Skills Testing to Improve the Effectiveness of Remediation in Employment and Training Programs for Youth.* Washington, D.C.: Center for Remediation Design, 1988.

Peterson, L. J. "Thirteen Powerful Principles for Training Success." *Performance and Instruction,* Feb. 1988, pp. 47–55.

Phillips, J. J. *Handbook of Training Evaluation and Measurement Methods.* Houston, Tex.: Gulf Publishing, 1983.

Sticht, T. G. *Functional Context Education.* San Diego, Calif.: Applied Behavioral and Cognitive Sciences, 1987.

Sticht, T. G., and Mikulecky, L. *Job-Related Basic Skills: Cases and Conclusions.* Columbus: National Center for Research in Vocational Education, Ohio State University, 1984.

Stiles, R., Tibbetts, J., and Westby-Gibson, D. *Why CBAE?* Unpublished manuscript, Center for Adult Education, San Francisco State University, 1984.

Stoker, R. "Literacy in the Workplace." In R. Craig (ed.), *Training and Development Handbook.* (3rd ed.) New York: McGraw-Hill, 1987.

Teague, W., and Faulkner, T. L. *Developing Performance Objectives and Criterion-Refer-enced Measures for Performance-Based Instruction in Vocational Education.* Montgomery, Ala.: Division of Vocational Education, Alabama State Department of Education, 1977–78.

Zemke, R. "Job Competencies: Can They Help You Design Better Training?" *Training,* 1982, *19* (5), 28–31.

Notes

_____

_____

_____

_____

_____

_____

_____

_____

_____

_____

_____

_____

_____

_____

_____

_____

_____

_____

_____

_____

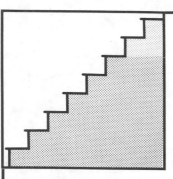

STEP SIX

Develop the Program

Learning Objectives

The reader will be able to:

1. List the components of a course outline.

2. Write a clear course objective.

3. Explain various ways of sequencing instructional material appropriate to the preferred learning styles of adults.

4. Develop a lesson plan.

5. Write a clear learning objective for a lesson.

6. Identify materials necessary for the lesson.

7. Provide for an evaluation of the degree of learner achievement.

8. List the steps involved in developing instructional material.

9. List key principles of adult learning theory.

10. Discuss the appropriate use of various training delivery systems.

11. Discuss the appropriate use of various training methodologies.

12. List the considerations for designing an appropriate learning facility.

13. Outline evaluation and monitoring needs for the program.

Introduction

The next step involves translating the curriculum design into instructional materials: course outlines, lesson plans, instructor and participant (trainer and trainee) manuals, audio-visual materials, computer-assisted instructional programs, and so on.

Prepare the Course Outline

*A **course outline** is a description of the structure and sequence of the instructional program.*

First, the developer prepares a **course outline**: a description of the structure and sequence of the instructional program.

This involves designing and sequencing instructional units (lessons) in a way that is most meaningful to the student, to enable the student to master the skills, knowledge, and attitude necessary for improved job performance.

Sequencing Instructional Material

There are many important considerations to keep in mind when sequencing instructional material:

- Begin with the objective of the course, module, or lesson. A clearly defined learning objective assures that the methodology and materials are directly related to the purpose of instruction.

- Provide an overview of the course, module, or lesson. Adults like to get an understanding of the big picture before moving on to details.

- Progress from easy to difficult and from simple to complex. Trainees need to find the material both challenging and achievable to avoid being bored or overwhelmed. Keeping early activities easier will allow the trainees to experience success and build confidence in their ability to learn.

- Use the trainees' experience. When introducing new material, combine unfamiliar content with familiar methods and unfamiliar methods with familiar content. That way learners will always be able to use some aspect of their experience and present ability in the learning situation.

- Move from general to specific. The initial introduction of general material helps learners apply their current level of knowledge and skill to the situation. This serves to make new material more meaningful and easier to remember.

- Begin with basic "how to" questions (the performance itself) and move on to more detailed considerations, like "why," "unusual applications," and "next steps" only after the basics have been mastered.

- Be aware of logical order. Sometimes one piece of material must be learned first because it forms a necessary basis for the next.

Of all of these, the most important consideration in sequencing, of course, is to help the trainees progress in the achievement of their learning objectives. The interests and preferences of the instructor must be of secondary importance.

Structure of Instructional Materials

The structure of instructional materials must also be appropriate to the adult learner (Knox, 1986). Important factors include:

- Choice. Alternative materials that differ in emphasis and complexity allow learners to select materials that are interesting and challenging to them as well as to proceed at their own pace.

- Relevance. Learner interest is maintained through working with materials that are drawn from the trainees' own work or personal experience.

- Preferred Learning Styles. Many adults with reading problems, for example, have learned to acquire information and knowledge by listening or observing. Varied instructional materials allow these trainees to use their presently preferred learning style while acquiring new ones.

- Questions. The use of questions can introduce problems to be solved, encourage trainees to challenge content, and lead them to figure out how to use or apply their newly learned concepts or procedures to their own situations.

- Application. Materials should be designed so that the trainees can immediately apply their new knowledge. Clarify use of the content, encourage application by offering suggestions and guidelines, and provide immediate opportunities for practice while learners are still in the instructional situation.

- Review. Throughout the program, materials should include constant repetition and review of what has been learned to provide feedback to the trainees and reinforce the new knowledge being acquired.

Table 22 gives an example of a lesson incorporating several of these factors.

Table

Table 22. Sample Trainer's Outline.

A Lesson in Shared Decision Making

Time: Three hours

Intent: This lesson focuses on the idea of shared leadership within work groups that regularly meet to make and implement decisions. It begins with a discussion on decision making and group dynamics. The lesson continues with two decision-making simulations intended to enable the learners to identify specific behaviors and understand their effect on the decision-making process and the cohesiveness of the work group. It concludes with a wrap-up during which participants suggest how the lesson can be applied to their own work situations.

Materials and Equipment: Flip chart, pen, and masking tape. Overhead projector and shared-leadership slides. Shared-leadership observation handouts for distribution to the learners. Role sheets for the two simulations. Remember: Prepare two problems appropriate to the participants' work situations for use in the simulations.

Instructions:

1. Arrange the room, preferably using a horseshoe or U arrangement with a small head table for the instructor and materials at the open end. Place five chairs to be used in the simulations in a circle in the center of the U or at the front of the room.

2. Using the instructor's guide, open the lesson by explaining its purpose and process.

3. Using the overhead projection and slides, lead the learners through a discussion of the shared-leadership concept, task functions, group maintenance functions, and antigroup behavior.

   - Ask the learners to suggest examples from their experience for each of the functions introduced.

   - Lead a general discussion of the shared-leadership concept and the individual responsibility of each member of the work group.

   - Record on a flip chart the main points of the discussion.

Take a fifteen-minute break.

4. Simulation no. 1
   a. Select five role players and give each a role sheet and directions.
   b. Select five observers, give them observer sheets, and assign each to concentrate on one of the role players.
   c. Announce the problem assigned to the group and instruct them to begin.
   d. Intervene after a period of time and thank the role players.
   e. Ask each observer in turn to analyze the behavior of the role player she or he observed.
   f. Ask each role player in turn to read her or his assigned role.
   g. Lead the group in a discussion of the dynamics demonstrated in the simulation.

5. Simulation no. 2 (same procedure as simulation no. 1)

6. Ask the participants to contrast the effectiveness of group leadership and participation in shared decision making as demonstrated in the two simulations.

7. To conclude the session, ask each participant to suggest how what she or he learned could be applied to the decision-making process of the work situation.

Develop Lesson Plans

*A **lesson** is a cohesive unit of instruction with a specific learning objective: the acquisition by the learner of defined knowledge or skills.*

Next is the development of a lesson plan for each task identified for training in the course outline. A **lesson** is a cohesive unit of instruction with a specific learning objective: the acquisition by the learner of defined knowledge or skills.

The **lesson plan** defines the learning objective, describes the activities (learning experiences) and instructional materials, and provide an evaluation of the degree to which the objective was achieved by the trainee.

*The **lesson plan** defines the learning objective, describes the activities (learning experiences) and instructional materials, and provides an evaluation of the degree to which the objective was achieved by the trainee.*

There is no fixed format for lesson plans, but they must be designed to make the most effective use of available resources (time, materials, and personnel) in engaging the trainees in activities that will help them achieve their learning objective.

A rule of thumb is to use a format that will identify what the student will be doing rather than what an instructor wants to do.

Use the following guidelines (Mager and Beach, 1967) to develop a lesson plan:

1. Write the **lesson objective**: what the trainee will be able to do at the end of the lesson. (See Step Five for how to write performance objectives.)

2. Determine the knowledge and skills the trainee must learn to accomplish the objective. This enables the developer to determine the subtopics of the lesson.

3. Put the subtopics of the lesson in a preliminary sequence, applying the principles described in the course outline section.

4. Identify the content of the various subtopics of the lesson. Answer the question: What must the trainee know or be able to do for satisfactory performance of each lesson subtopic?

5. Select instructional procedures appropriate to the learning of each lesson subtopic. Identify materials and equipment needed.

*The **lesson objective** is what the trainee will be able to do at the end of the lesson.*

6. Review the instructional sequence. Adjust as necessary to provide variety and movement for the learners.

7. Provide a means of instructional monitoring and learner feedback.

8. An appropriate criterion-referenced test should be prepared to evaluate the degree to which the trainees have achieved the learning objective of the lesson.

Table 23 provides a sample training plan.

Table

Table 23. Sample Training Plan.

Unit: The problem-solving process.

Training topic: Identifying and selecting the problem.

Objective: The trainee, working as part of a group, develops a statement of the problem that is clearly understood by all members. In addition, the group may develop a statement of the desired state to be achieved by solving the problem.

Introduction: Start with an awareness that something isn't right; there is a discrepancy between what is and what ought to be.

Method: Brainstorming discussion: "What are the possible reasons for the problem?"

- Break the problem down into smaller problems, then review, combine, eliminate, and rank the problems.

- Clarify and write problem statements.

- Select one problem statement.

Resources: Problem-solving case study based on actual work situation.

Evaluation: Through consensus, group will use a checklist to determine if a satisfactory conclusion has been reached before moving on to the next step.

Develop Instructional Materials

The following steps should be followed when developing or adapting material for the program:

1. Define the need for the lesson.

   a. What information or knowledge (content) is to be learned?

   b. What skills are to be learned? (Use how-to guides or other materials to help answer this question.)

   c. What practice exercises or application opportunities are required?

   d. What test or evaluation materials are needed?

2. Define the interests, needs, and abilities of the training population.

3. Gather all relevant job-related material.

4. Investigate outside sources for appropriate material.

5. Develop or adapt material as needed.

6. Evaluate material for instructional effectiveness and trainee appropriateness.

Evaluate Training Materials

When considering potential material for the instructional program, ask these questions:

- Does the content fit the lesson objective?
- Is it up-to-date?
- Will it work with planned instructional methodologies?
- Is the material appropriate for the trainees' learning level?
- Is the material of interest to the trainees?
- Is the material attractive and well produced?

The material a learner actually uses on the job, which was collected during the task analysis, should be integrated into the program whenever possible because this provides a link with the learner's job experience.

Only material that will help the learner satisfy the performance objectives should be selected for each task. Material should be at (or move toward) a level the learner will use on the job.

Use Concepts of Adult Learning

Research has demonstrated that adults learn differently from children. Therefore, care should be taken to avoid materials that have been developed specifically for children.

Some of the key findings (Knowles, 1987) are as follows:

- Adults need to know why they should learn something. They learn best when they understand how the new knowledge will be immediately useful in their work or personal lives.

- Adults need to be self-directed in their learning. They want to be in charge of their lives and responsible for the decisions they make. They need to be quickly shown that "learner" and "dependent" are not synonymous. They need to participate in choosing and planning their own learning activities.

- Adults need to have their experience respected and considered a resource for the learning process. There should be emphasis on hands-on techniques that draw on the learner's accumulated skills and knowledge (such as problem solving, case studies, or discussion) or techniques that provide learners with experiences from which they can learn (such as simulation or field experiences).

- Adults make a voluntary commitment to learn when they experience a real need to know or to be able to do something. They do not respond to an authority figure saying it will be good for them.

- Adults have a task-centered or problem-centered approach to learning. For children, learning is organized around subject matter. For adults, learning should be organized around real tasks. "Composition" becomes "How to Write Effective Business Letters."

- Adults are motivated to learn. They respond to extrinsic motivators like higher wages and promotional possibilities, but even more to intrinsic motivation like the need for self-esteem, recognition, broader responsibilities, and achievement.

- Adults need to have the process of learning considered carefully. The focus is not on the instructor transmitting the content but on the learner acquiring it.

- Adults need to have feedback regarding their learning. They want clear learning objectives, and they want to know regularly the extent to which their objectives have been achieved.

Consider Learning Styles

Most people do not consciously think about how they learn best, but they do know which kinds of learning activities they like or dislike. Becoming aware of one's own dominant learning style or method can greatly accelerate the ability to learn from a given situation. In the workplace, however, an individual's first choice for learning is not always available. For example, an employee might prefer to learn a new technique from reading a manual. But there may not be a manual, or the technique may better lend itself to training through other means.

Maturity and mastery in the ability to acquire new information is demonstrated by being willing and able to use the training tools available to improve personal job performance, even if they are not the most personally satisfying or efficient. According to recent studies (James and Galbraith, 1985), there are several primary learning styles, which include:

- *Print:* the preference of the reader or writer who learns well from traditional texts and pencil and paper exercises;
- *Visual:* the preference of the observer who likes to look at slides, films, videos, exhibits, demonstrations, and charts;
- *Aural:* the preference of the listener who enjoys lectures and who also learns well from tapes and records;
- *Interactive:* the preference of the talker who learns best from discussions and question-and-answer sessions;
- *Tactile:* the preference of the toucher or handler who wants hands-on activities and who also learns well from model building or sketching;
- *Kinesthetic:* the preference of the mover who likes role playing and physical games and activities; and
- *Olfactory:* the preference of the smeller or taster who associates learning with smells and tastes.

Learners can also be characterized by their attitude to learning; that is, the degree of dependence or independence with which they approach new material. Several years ago Ronne Toker Jacobs and Barbara Schneider Fuhrman developed a learner-trainer style analysis from this perspective (see Table 24).

Table

Table 24. The Implications of Learning Styles for Training.

Learner Style	Learner Needs	Trainer Role	Trainer Behavior
Dependent: May occur with introductory courses, new work situations, languages, and some sciences when learner has little prior information.	Structure Direction External reinforcement Encouragement Esteem from authority	Director Expert Authority	Lecturing Demonstrating Assigning Checking Encouraging Testing Reinforcing Transmitting content Grading
Collaborative: May occur if the learner has some knowledge or ideas and would like to share them or try them out.	Interaction Practice Probe of self or others Observations Participation Peer challenge Peer esteem Experimentation	Collaborative Co-learner Environment setter	Interacting Questioning Providing feedback Coordinating Evaluating Managing Grading
Independent: May occur when the learner has knowledge or skill on entering the course and wants to continue to search on her or his own.	Internal awareness Experimentation Time Nonjudgmental support	Delegator Facilitator	Allowing Providing requested feedback Providing resources Consulting Listening Negotiating Evaluating Delegating

Source: Reprinted from J. William Pfeiffer and Leonard D. Goodstein (eds.), *The 1984 Annual: Developing Human Resources.* San Diego, Calif.: University Associates, Inc., 1984. Used with permission.

Select Audio-Visual Materials

The use of audio-visual materials can add interest and variety to any lesson. The following (adapted from Gallup and Beauchemin, 1987, p. 89) are different tools that a trainer may use to assist the learners:

- Overhead transparencies can be used effectively to support a classroom presentation made by the instructor. The transparencies can be prepared in advance, or the instructor can write on a blank.

- Slide-tape programs can be used to support a classroom presentation or as a self-directed instructional program accompanied by a learner's workbook.

- Films or videotapes can be used to introduce new material or to reinforce material that is also presented in another way. They are effective in showing how something can be done or how people interact. Because they are expensive to produce, look first for appropriate commercially available films or tapes.

- Video playback is a very useful device for providing learner feedback, a critical element in adult learning. Because the learners can see and hear their own performance, extensive critique by the instructor is seldom needed.

- Computer-assisted training is excellent for learner-directed and self-instructional programs. Learners get instant feedback, assistance when needed and proceed through the lessons at their own pace.

Integrate Instructional Techniques

A great deal of discussion has taken place on utilizing a variety of instructional techniques to improve the delivery of information to the learner and to take advantage of individual learning styles. Although the type of instructional technique selected can improve the presentation of the material and simulate more exactly the job to be performed, the two factors that appear to give the best results in training are time on task (that is, the greatest amount of time possible spent actively engaged in a learning task) and instructor feedback (Sticht and Mikulecky, 1984).

In performance-based instruction, the emphasis usually is on providing individuals or small groups of trainees with high-quality learning material that provides a major part of the instruction on an individualized basis.

The instructor becomes the manager of the learning process, asking and answering questions, giving mini-lectures and demonstrations, checking learner progress, and giving feedback.

Of major importance to an organization planning a large training program is selecting instructional techniques that will minimize costs without affecting the quality of results. The techniques used will determine the type of facility, the number of instructional personnel, the cost of producing original materials, and so on. All of these factors, plus the impact on individual learning, must be taken into consideration.

REMEMBER

People generally recall:

- 10 percent of what they *read,*
- 20 percent of what they *hear,*
- 30 percent of what they *see,*
- 50 percent of what they *hear and see,*
- 70 percent of what they *say or write, and*
- 90 percent of what they *say as they do it.*

Case Study

IBM

IBM, a leader in the use of a systems approach in training, claims that despite new technology, "about 75–80 percent of all education at IBM today is still conducted within the traditional classroom." However, IBM believes that over the next ten years at least half its training will be delivered by "student-driven, learning-center-based systems—mainly computer-based training, interactive videodisc with personal computer, or other self-study methods, using either workbooks or videos."

For IBM a key strategy to reduce costs has been to off-load large-volume classroom courses to self-study, computer-based training, or interactive videodisc training. Although there are large up-front costs associated with these instructional choices, IBM reports that it has cut total costs by 25–50 percent. A further advantage of these new delivery systems is that the same amount of learning can occur with equal effectiveness with as much as a 50 percent reduction in time (Casner-Lotto, 1988, pp. 255–270).

Classroom Training

Classroom training, usually in conjunction with other delivery techniques, is still the staple of training. Where traditional classroom training is the selected instructional strategy, it lends itself to many well-known techniques such as lecture; study; group discussion; presentation; use of film, video and audio tapes; and so on.

The guiding principles for selecting the right instructional techniques for the classroom are:

1. Be clear about the desired performance.
2. Identify the procedures most appropriate for achieving the desired performance.
3. Select those that are most practical and job related.

4. Be clear about the skill level of the learners. For example, computer-assisted learning may not be practical for those with little or no computer exposure.

There are several delivery systems that can be used to present instructional material, all of which have differing strengths and weaknesses. They include traditional classroom, multimedia classroom, tutored video classroom, interactive TV classroom, self-study, guided learning center, computer-based training, and interactive videodisc with personal computer.

Traditional Classroom

The **traditional classroom** is a situation where the learners are seated individually behind desks or tables facing the front of the room, where the instructor operates behind a desk or lectern with a blackboard, overhead projector, flip chart, and other audio-visual aids.

*The **traditional classroom** is a situation where the learners are seated individually behind desks or tables facing the front of the room, where the instructor operates behind a desk or lectern with a blackboard, overhead projector, flip chart, and other audio-visual aids.*

The main advantages of the traditional classroom are as follows:

- It is a good setup for lectures and presentations because there are few distractions for learners and all participants can see and hear what the instructor does,

- It establishes the superiority and authority of the instructor, and

- It is a familiar, traditional setting for learning.

Among its disadvantages, it:

- Discourages learner participation,

- Stifles interaction among learners, and

- Allows little freedom of movement and limits access to learning materials other than those directly in the learner's possession.

As you can see, traditional classroom training, like other instructional techniques, has both advantages and disadvantages. Its primary disadvantage is that frequently adults carry unpleasant memories of this type of training from when they were in a traditional school setting. It is important to remember, however, that a training technique that is inappropriate in one instance may be the right method under other circumstances.

Using the same basic furniture and equipment, the instructor can create a classroom configuration that sends a clear message to the adult learner: "This experience will be different."

Figure 6 shows examples of how a classroom can be set up to facilitate many instructional methods and encourage learner participation and learner interaction.

Figure 6. Layouts That Improve Learning.

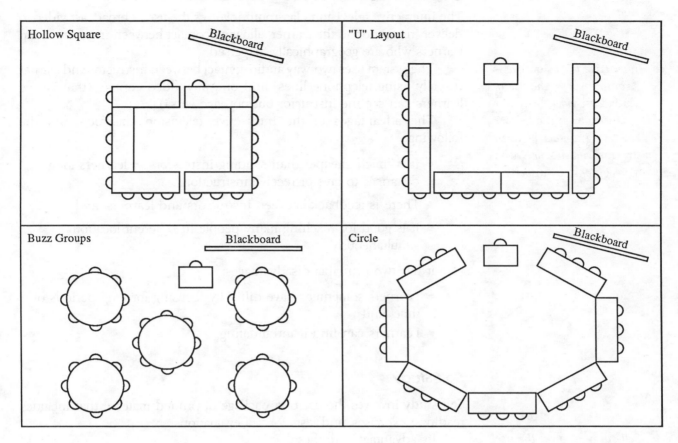

Multimedia Classroom

The **multimedia classroom** is set up so that learners have opportunities to use a variety of learning media such as films, tapes (audio or visual), slides, print, radio, and so on.

*The **multimedia classroom** is set up so that learners have opportunities to use a variety of learning media such as films, tapes (audio or video), slides, print, and radio.*

The multimedia classroom has these advantages:

- It is more interesting and varied,
- It works well with learners who learn best through visual methods,
- It works well with learners with reading difficulties, and
- There is less dependence on the instructor.

Its disadvantages are these:

- It may be distracting,
- The equipment requires maintenance and setup, and
- It can be costly.

Interactive Television Classroom

The **interactive television classroom** involves the use of broadcast video to deliver instruction to the learner, allowing contact between instructors and learners who are geographically dispersed.

Interactive television class-room involves the use of broadcast video to deliver instruction to the learner allowing contact between instructors and learners who are geographically dispersed.

The system uses two-way audio contact between instructor and learner (usually using telephone lines) and one-way video contact (that is, the learners can see the instructor but not vice versa).

The advantages of the interactive television classroom are the following:

- It is much cheaper than sending instructors or learners long distances to give or receive instruction,
- There is feedback between instructors and learners, and
- It is good for reaching many people in different locations simultaneously.

It has two principal disadvantages:

- Learners sometimes have difficulty focusing for long periods of time, and
- Learners can find it intimidating.

Self-Study

Self-study involves the use of a package of printed material that includes readings, exercises, and tests for self-evaluation.

Self-study involves the use of a package of printed material that includes read-ings, exercises, and tests for self-evaluation.

Its advantages are these:

- It is individualized,
- It requires learner activity,
- It provides evaluation of learner progress, and
- The process is under student control.

Its disadvantages are these:

- Feedback is limited,
- It assumes an employee can read well enough to comprehend material,
- It requires learner interest and initiative, and
- The learner must depend upon the instructor or other learners for assistance (*Principles of Instructional Design*, 1983, pp. 7–12).

Guided Learning Center

A **guided learning center** is designed so that instruction is individualized and self-paced. Instructors and/or aides are used at particular points, but learners should be able to go through the educational process by themselves. A range of instructional materials are used, such as print, audiovisual aids, and computer.

The advantages of a guided learning center are as follows:

*A **guided learning center** is designed so that instruction is individualized and self-paced. Instructors and/or aides are used at particular points, but learners should be able to go through the educational process by themselves. A range of instructional materials are used such as print, audiovisual aids, and computer.*

- It allows learners to work at their own pace,
- It gives learners a sense of being an active participant in their education, and
- It allows learners of different abilities and subjects to be taught in the same room.

It has two main disadvantages:

- It can be expensive, and
- It can be inappropriate and/or frustrating for learners below a fourth-grade level.

Computer-Based Training

During **computer-based training**, the learner interacts with a computer program that presents subject matter, allows for practice exercises, gives feedback, analyzes performance, and provides assistance as needed.

Among the advantages, computer-based training:

*During **computer-based training**, the learner interacts with a computer program that presents subject matter, allows for practice exercises, gives feedback, analyzes performance, and provides assistance as needed.*

- Allows for a varied presentation combining text, graphics, animation, and sound,
- Is highly interactive and individualized,
- Stimulates interest through the use of good visuals,
- Is responsive to learner control, and
- Provides instant feedback and assistance as needed.

Its disadvantages include the following:

- The equipment is costly,
- It is complex and expensive to produce, and
- It is somewhat complicated for learners to operate, although that too is valuable learning. (*Principles of Instructional Design*, 1983, pp. 7–22).

Figure 7 gives an example of how a room can be set up to facilitate computer-based training.

Figure 7. Facility Rearranged for Computer-Based Training.

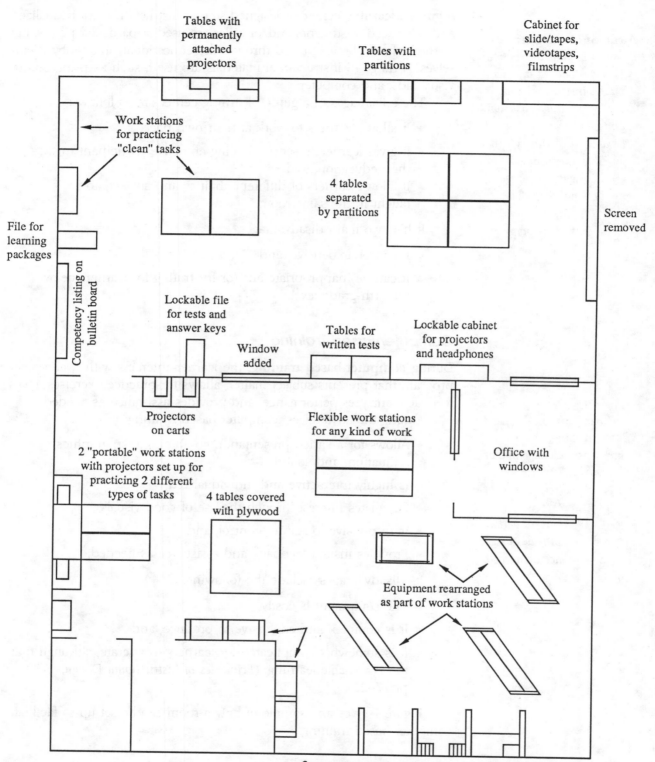

Tables with permanently attached projectors

Tables with partitions

Cabinet for slide/tapes, videotapes, filmstrips

Work stations for practicing "clean" tasks

4 tables separated by partitions

Screen removed

File for learning packages

Competency listing on bulletin board

Lockable file for tests and answer keys

Window added

Tables for written tests

Lockable cabinet for projectors and headphones

Projectors on carts

Flexible work stations for any kind of work

Office with windows

2 "portable" work stations with projectors set up for practicing 2 different types of tasks

4 tables covered with plywood

Equipment rearranged as part of work stations

3 permanent work stations for viewing media about and then practicing 3 distinct kinds of competencies; included are all needed tools, manuals, etc., in lockable cabinets

Interactive Videodisc

Interactive videodisc is the use of a video delivery system designed to respond to choices made by the individual user.

Interactive videodisc technology, combining the advantages of video and computer-assisted training, has great promise as a training tool.

Interactive videodisc is the use of a video delivery system designed to respond to choices made by the individual user. These choices may be spontaneous on the part of the user or they may be prompted by the system (Smith, 1987).

The advantages of interactive videodisc are as follows:

- It can simulate real work experiences,

- It is highly interactive and individualized,

- It provides excellent and varied visuals combining video and the computer screen,

- The random access capability of disc technology permits maximum flexibility in program design and operation, and

- It is highly responsive to learner control.

Its main disadvantages are as follows:

- The equipment is costly,

- It is complex and expensive to produce, and

- It is somewhat complicated for learners to operate (Beausey, 1988).

Choose an Effective Training Methodology

There are a number of different training methodologies that instructors can choose from in designing a program or lesson. Among the most useful are task force exercises, case studies, simulations and games, role playing, group discussion, individual exercises, presentations and lectures, behavior modeling, and written exercises.

Task Force Exercise

A **task force exercise** takes place when a group of three to eight trainees work together on a problem and present their solution to the class.

*A **task force exercise** is a method of training in which three to eight trainees work together on a problem and present their solution to the class.*

The task force exercise is used when the learning objective is to:

- Encourage group interaction in problem-solving situations,
- Acknowledge and use the experience and expertise of the learners,
- Practical analytical skills,
- Test trainees' understanding and application of a concept or process, and
- Generate a plan to be used back on the job.

To be effective, task force exercises:

- Require the meaningful application of the process or concept being learned,
- Must be realistic and related to the learners' work situations,
- Must be challenging but not too complex for the time allowed, and
- Must provide enough information for the learners to do the task well.

Case Studies

A **case study** is a description of a situation in writing or on audio or videotape that the trainees study and discuss under the guidance of the instructor.

*A **case study** is a description of a situation in writing or on audio or videotape that the trainees study and discuss under the guidance of the instructor.*

Discussion of a case study is used when the objective is to:

- Encourage learners to participate,
- Teach analytical skills rather than the right answer,
- Simulate a real situation in a limited amount of time, or
- Demonstrate how the program content is related to the learner's actual situation.

To be effective, the case discussion must be constructed so that:

- The problem is realistic,
- The answer or decision is not obvious, and
- The case study offers enough information for a spirited discussion.

Simulations and Games

A **simulation** is an exercise that represents a real job situation and allows the learners to practice skills and application of knowledge within a limited time frame and in a risk-free environment (the classroom).

Games have the same intent—to provide nonthreatening opportunities for the application of learning—but the situation is contrived and unrelated to the learners' world.

Simulations and games are used to:

- Encourage participation,
- Give learners realistic, job-related experience,
- Elicit the learners' natural tendencies and provide feedback, and
- Test the learners' application of complex skills or knowledge.

To be effective, simulations and games must:

- Be realistic (simulations) or relevant (games),
- Be clear and understandable but not so simple as to be boring,
- Not emphasize winning to the extent that the competition detracts from the learning,
- Encourage the behavior that is the objective of the lesson, and
- Allow for meaningful discussion of the experience.

Role Playing

Role playing is an exercise in which learners simulate a real or hypothetical interactive situation. A discussion and analysis follow to determine what happened and why.

Role playing can be used to analyze the learners' customary ways of dealing with the situation, but more often it is used to allow the learners to apply newly learned procedures or skills.

A role-playing exercise is used:

- When the objective is hard to understand through discussion and analysis,
- To allow participants to practice skills or procedures needed in the given situation,
- To build learners' confidence to handle the situation, and
- To give nonparticipating learners an opportunity to practice observational skills.

*A **simulation** is an exercise that represents a real job situation and allows the learners to practice skills and application of knowledge within a limited time frame and in a risk-free environment (the classroom).*

Role playing is an exercise in which learners simulate a real or hypothetical interactive situation. A discussion and analysis follow to determine what happened and why. Role playing can be used to analyze the learners' customary ways of dealing with the situation, but more often it is used to allow the learners to experience the application of newly learned procedures or skills.

To be effective, the role-playing exercise:

- Must be constructed so that the various roles are clearly defined yet allow the players some freedom to act and use the newly learned skills,

- Must put some pressure on the players to resolve the problem with which they are confronted, and

- Must be clearly structured so that players understand what they are to do, the process to use, the timing of various actions, and the end result.

Much of the learning occurs in the analysis phase. For that to work well, the observers must know what they are looking for. In fact, the points to be learned must have actually been demonstrated.

The success of the role-playing exercise depends upon careful preparation of the materials, effective orientation of the players, and feedback tied clearly to the objective of the lesson.

Group Discussions

A **group discussion** is a planned opportunity for participants to freely exchange ideas or opinions in a large group or in subgroups.

Group discussion can be an effective training methodology when:

*A **group discussion** is a planned opportunity for participants to freely exchange ideas or opinions in a large group or in subgroups.*

- The subject is of much interest,

- Members of the group are knowledgeable or hold differing ideas about the subject,

- The subject is rarely discussed, and

- The objective is to encourage group interaction in solving real problems or creating an action plan.

More than anything else, the success of group discussions depends on the leader's ability to:

- Make the purpose or subject clear,

- Keep the discussion on track,

- Prevent domination by eager learners and encourage participation by shy members, and

- Bring the discussion to a timely and satisfactory conclusion (by agreement or by understanding and acceptance of disagreement).

Individual Exercises

Individual exercises allow learners to apply the lesson objectives to their own situations or to test their understanding.

Individual exercises allow learners to apply the lesson objectives to their own situations or to test their understanding.

Individual exercises are used to:

- Test learners' understanding of the lesson content,
- Show learners and instructors where learning has been insufficient,
- Prepare learners to use their new learning back on the job, and
- Build commitment to do so.

Individual exercises work most effectively when:

- The learners' individual work situations are different (if they were the same, a group activity would be more appropriate),
- The task is clearly explained and relevant to each learner,
- The learners feel a need for confidentiality, and
- The task is not too difficult to complete in the time allotted.

Presentations and Lectures

Presentations and lectures are structured one-way communications from the instructor to the learners.

Presentations and lectures are structured one-way communications from the instructor to the learners.

They can be used effectively to:

- Introduce new material and
- Impart information quickly to a large group of people.

They are most effective when:

- The presenter is known and credible and
- No other method is usable.

To be effective, lectures and presentations must be:

- Well-prepared and organized,
- As short as possible, and
- To the point.

Behavior Modeling

Behavior modeling involves giving learners a step-by-step model for handling a given interactive situation, followed by a demonstration of the steps, usually on video. There are opportunities for the learners to practice using the steps and to get feedback on their performance.

Behavior modeling involves giving learners a step-by-step model for handling a given interactive situation, followed by a demonstration of the steps, usually on video.

This provides learners with a specific, proven way to deal with an interactive situation and gives them an opportunity to practice new behavior so that they feel confident of their ability to handle the targeted situation.

Behavior modeling is used when the objective is:

- To have the learner develop a skill,
- To have the learner learn a specific sequence of steps to follow, or
- To limit the number of ways a situation is handled.

To be effective, behavior modeling must:

- Present a learnable number of clearly defined steps,
- Be based on a video or demonstration that effectively represents the desired behavior,
- Provide the learners with a realistic and challenging opportunity for practice, and
- Give the learners positive feedback on their performance.

Written Exercises

Written exercises involve giving learners written materials that they respond to in writing.

Written exercises involve giving learners written materials that they respond to in writing.

To be effective, written exercises must:

- Be presented in the context of the total lesson,
- Include all the information the learners need to complete the activity,
- Have meaning to the learners in the context of their personal experiences,
- Be completable within the allowed time limits, and
- Have clear written instructions.

Exercise instructions are given to:

- Present information learners need to participate in the exercise,
- Be used as a reference,
- Guide the exercise in the intended direction, and
- Ensure consistency in the exercise process and results.

When to Use Which Method

Choose an instructional method by identifying the kind of learner performance to be developed.

Using presentation techniques such as lectures, panel presentations, film, videotape, slide-tape shows, or readings if you want learners to get new facts or information they do not have, get an overview of a problem or issue, or hear a logical point of view.

However, presentation methods should be followed quickly by methods that involve learners.

Use hands-on techniques that emphasize practice, projects, exercises, simulations, and video if you want learners to build skills, put their learning to work, or experience doing a task.

The instructor must provide introductory guidelines and meaningful feedback during the course of this kind of activity.

Use group-building techniques such as pairs, share groups, team projects, and open group discussion if you want learners to get to know one another, build group unity and commitment, or share ideas and experiences.

Figure 8 provides an indication of which techniques lead to the greatest participant involvement. It is usually best to intersperse low-involvement techniques with those that will engage the trainee and refocus attention.

The instructor should clearly articulate the value of knowing and working together for the organization's goals.

When selecting instructional methods, choose the one that:

- Most closely approximates the conditions called for in the performance objective for the job task related to the lesson,

- Causes the learner to perform in a manner approximating the performance on the job, or

- Allows the learner to make the largest number of relevant responses (repetitions) in a given time frame (Mager and Beach, 1967, pp. 55–56).

Figure 8. Participant Involvement Continuum.

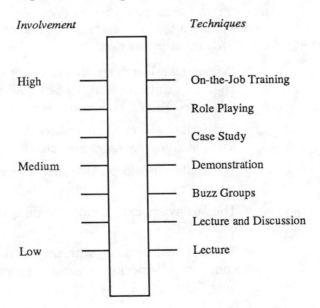

Involvement	Techniques
High	On-the-Job Training
	Role Playing
	Case Study
Medium	Demonstration
	Buzz Groups
	Lecture and Discussion
Low	Lecture

Select Facilities and Equipment

The selection of appropriate facilities and training equipment will depend on a number of variables including:

- The type of learning required (heavy equipment, production line, office),
- The instructional strategies selected (traditional classroom, self-study),
- The location (on-site or off-site),
- The number of learners (few or many),
- Any budgetary restrictions,
- The time available for training,
- The training presenter (in-house or provider), and
- The curriculum.

This is a decision that a company will live with for a long time since it is likely to entail significant capital outlay. It should, therefore, involve a team effort that includes the program director, selected instructional staff, job experts, and perhaps an outside facilities design specialist.

Facilities Design for Individualized Instruction

The traditional classroom is not required, nor is it desirable for individualized performance-based instruction.

There are a few important considerations when designing a facility for individualized instruction:

- Different work stations should be set up at which trainees could engage in different learning tasks. All or most of the material they need should be found there.

- The facility will need specialized furniture for storing and using learning packages and auxiliary media and equipment.

- The facility should provide the learners with freedom of movement.

- The facility should provide several quiet spots within the classroom.

- There should be tables with partitions where learners can complete self-checks on learning progress in private (*Organize Your Class* . . . , 1986).

Figure 9 gives an example of a typical facility layout for individualized instruction.

Figure 9. Typical Facility Layout for Individualized Instruction.

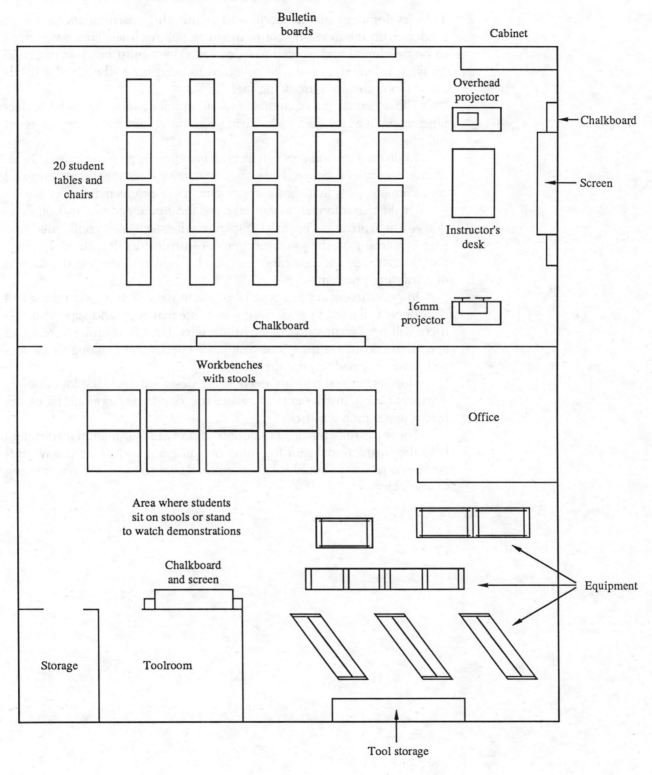

Develop Evaluation and Monitoring Instruments

The development of evaluation and monitoring instruments moves in tandem with the development of instructional materials. Forms will need to be developed and procedures detailed. There must be clear direction on what information must be collected to determine whether the needs of everyone involved are being met.

The accumulation of credible evaluation information will provide documentation at a later date for justifying continued company expenditure on the program.

Evaluation instruments can be both quantitative and qualitative. Quantitative data can be gathered by using accurate post-testing instruments and measurement tools that clarify improvements in productivity.

Qualitative information can take the form of anecdotes and observations in such areas as improved employee self-esteem, self-confidence, and ease of learning on the job. Measurement instruments that show improvements in attitude and demeanor can also be used to determine the success of a training program.

In order to collect this type of program data, training designers and developers will need to work closely with line managers and supervisors so there will be a common perspective on what kind of training is required and what constitutes improved workplace effectiveness among employees who have returned to jobs after training.

Monitoring instruments need to be designed and developed along with evaluation instruments to reflect the day-to-day operations of the instructional program itself.

These instruments need to be able to provide information feedback to help the instructional staff fine-tune the program and develop any mid-course corrections should it be determined that trainees are not meeting course objectives.

References and Suggested Readings

American Society for Training and Development. "Training and Learning Styles." *INFO-LINE,* Apr. 1988.

Anderson, R. J. *Selecting and Developing Media for Instruction.* New York: Van Nostrand Reinhold, 1976.

Beausey, M. "Videodisc Development: No Lone Ranger, Please." *Training,* 1988, 25 (2), 65–68.

Casner-Lotto, J. "Achieving Cost Savings and Quality Through Education: IBM's Systems Approach." In J. Casner-Lotto and Associates, *Successful Training Strategies: Twenty-Six Innovative Corporate Models.* San Francisco: Jossey-Bass, 1988.

Cooney, J. *Final Report of the Adult Competency Education Project: An Experimental Adult Basic Education Demonstration Project.* Redwood City, Calif.: Career Preparation Programs, Vocational Education Division, San Mateo County Office of Education, 1978.

Darkenwald, G. G., and Valentine, T. "Factor Structure of Deterrents to Public Participation in Adult Education." *Adult Education Quarterly,* 1985, 35 (4), 177–193.

Duggan, P. *Literacy at Work: Developing Adult Basic Skills for Employment.* Washington, D.C.: Northeast-Midwest Institute, Center for Regional Policy, 1985.

Fields, D. L., Hull, L., and Sechler, J. A. *Adult Literacy: Industry-Based Training Programs.* Columbus: National Center for Research in Vocational Education, Ohio State University, 1987.

Gallup, D. A., and Beauchemin, K. V. *Business and Legal Reports (BLR) Handbook of Training Techniques.* Madison, Conn.: Bureau of Law and Business, 1987.

Jacobs, R. T., and Fuhrman, B. "The Concept of Learning Style." In J. W. Pfeiffer and L. D. Goodstein (eds.), *The 1984 Annual: Developing Human Resources.* San Diego, Calif.: University Associates, 1984.

James, W. B., and Galbraith, M. W. "Perceptual Learning Styles: Implications and Techniques for the Practitioner." *Lifelong Learning,* Jan. 1985, pp. 20–23.

Knowles, M. S. *The Modern Practice of Adult Education.* (2nd ed.) New York: Cambridge Book Company, 1980.

Knowles, M. S. "Adult Learning." In R. L. Craig (ed.), *Training and Development Handbook.* (3rd ed.) New York: McGraw-Hill, 1987.

Knox, A. B. *Helping Adults Learn.* San Francisco: Jossey-Bass, 1986.

Lerche, R. S. *Effective Adult Literacy Programs: A Practitioner's Guide.* Cambridge, Mass.: Adult Education Company, 1985.

Mager, R. F., and Beach, K. M., Jr. *Developing Vocational Instruction.* Belmont, Calif.: David S. Lake Publishers, 1967.

Manage the Adult Instructional Process. Module N-5 of Category N (Teaching Adults), Professional Teacher Education Module Series. Columbus: National Center for Research in Vocational Education, Ohio State University, 1986.

Organize Your Class and Lab to Install Competency-Based Education. Module K-3 of Category K (Implementing Competency-Based Education), Professional Teacher Education Module Series. Columbus: National Center for Research in Vocational Education, Ohio State University, 1986.

Plan Instruction for Adults. Module N-4 of Category N (Teaching Adults), Professional Teacher Education Module Series. Columbus: National Center for Research in Vocational Education, Ohio State University, 1987.

Principles of Instructional Design. Columbia, Md.: GP Courseware, 1983.

Provide Instructional Materials for Competency-Based Education. Module K-4 of Category K (Implementing Competency-Based Education), Professional Teacher Education Module Series. Columbus: National Center for Research in Vocational Education, Ohio State University, 1986.

Select Student Instructional Materials. Module B-5 of Category B (Instructional Planning), Professional Teacher Education Module Series. Columbus: National Center for Research in Vocational Education, Ohio State University, 1977.

Smith, E. E. "Interactive Video: An Examination of Use and Effectiveness." *Journal of Instructional Development,* 1987, *10,* 2–10.

Songer, T. *Learning Styles Survey.* Charlotte, N.C.: Central Piedmont Community College, 1987.

Sticht, T. G., and Mikulecky, L. *Job-Related Basic Skills: Cases and Conclusions.* Columbus: National Center for Research in Vocational Education, Ohio State University, 1984.

Notes

_____

_____

_____

_____

_____

_____

_____

_____

_____

_____

_____

_____

_____

_____

_____

_____

_____

_____

_____

_____

_____

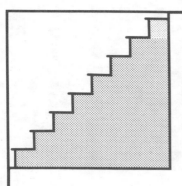

STEP SEVEN

Implement the Program

Learning Objectives

The reader will be able to:

1. Discuss the role of the program manager, her or his major duties and responsibilities, the skills and abilities required, and the education and experience required.

2. Discuss the role of the program administrator, her or his major duties and responsibilities, the skills and abilities required, and the education and experience required.

3. Discuss the role of the instructional staff, their major duties and responsibilities, the skills and abilities required, and the education and experience required.

4. Conduct a train-the-trainer workshop.

5. Discuss the advantages and disadvantages of peer training and the buddy system.

6. Discuss the role of counseling and possible resources.

7. Develop a learning contract.

8. Decide whether to pilot test the training program.

9. Conduct a pilot test of the training program.

Introduction

Once management has given the go-ahead, the training program implementation should begin simultaneously with the design and development phases.

The most important activity during the early implementation period should be moving the employee awareness campaign into high gear to talk up the new training program.

A significant part of this campaign should address the issue of how this training will affect individual employees as well as management.

Meetings should be scheduled to answer all employee questions, and employees should be encouraged to attend. Outside organizations that may be used as support networks should be informed of the impending start-up and their input solicited on potential problems and procedures that may need to be followed.

If an outside provider is to be selected to operate the actual program, the selection process should be activated using previously determined criteria. (See Step Three for a more detailed discussion on selecting training providers.)

Although the discussion of staff has been reserved for the implementation phase, the program manager should be on board early enough to actively participate in the development of the training program design.

Selecting the Program Manager

The training program manager will play a crucial role and will need to be chosen very carefully. A review board composed of members from the advisory committee should have responsibility for selecting the individual who will fill the position of manager.

The program manager is responsible for developing all project objectives. She or he has the role of planning, organizing, staffing, and controlling the training project and linking the training project operations with other organizational activities.

The manager is the key link back to the production line, and her or his evaluation role is vital. For example, the program manager can use evaluation sessions as a means to educate managers on how the program serves their purposes and what role they need to play to ensure program success.

Accordingly, a manager should be expected to:

- Participate in program design and development,
- Develop and evaluate staff,
- Develop and monitor the program budget,
- Develop project standards, policies, and procedures,
- Hire, evaluate, and develop staff,
- Coordinate and evaluate outside providers,
- Exchange information with department heads and supervisors,
- Establish a positive work climate,
- Develop solutions to project problems,

- Communicate with other organizational entities, internal and external, and
- Help to develop and provide feedback on program evaluation (American Society for Training and Development, 1983).

A major selection criterion for filling the position ought to be substantial knowledge of company practices and the corporate culture. This person should also possess a background in education and training with a heavy emphasis on evaluation.

Table 25 gives a sample job description for a program manager.

Table

Table 25. Sample Program Manager Job Description.

Job Title: Program manager.

Broad Scope of Position: Overall managerial responsibility for basic workplace skills training program.

Reports to: Director, human resource development.

Major Duties and Responsibilities:

1. Be responsible for program design and development.
2. Chair program advisory committee.
3. Develop and monitor program budget.
4. Negotiate and administer agreements with outside providers.
5. Develop program standards, policies, and procedures.
6. Ensure program complies with company policy and procedures.
7. Be responsible for selection, development, and evaluation of all program staff.
8. Monitor program implementation and provide feedback to human resource development director and other company management.
9. Meet regularly with outside provider and/or project administrator.
10. Meet regularly with union representatives and appropriate company personnel.
11. Evaluate program effectiveness and report to management.

Personal Characteristics:

1. Is dynamic, innovative, and energetic.
2. Accepts responsibility.
3. Establishes a positive work climate.
4. Relates well with people ranging from top company management to union leadership.

Skills and Abilities Required:

1. Demonstrate leadership and managerial skills.
2. Demonstrate negotiation and administrative skills.
3. Demonstrate written and verbal communications skills.
4. Demonstrate ability to lead work team (advisory committee).

Education and Experience:

1. Demonstrated experience in project management.
2. Demonstrated experience in contract negotiations and administration.
3. Demonstrated experience in adult basic skills training.
4. Demonstrated experience in training program design and development.
5. Demonstrated experience in staff development.
6. Demonstrated experience in program evaluation.
7. Education includes adult learning theory and practice.

Source: Adapted from *Job-Related Basic Skills: A Guide for Planners of Employee Programs,* June 1987, New York: Business Council for Effective Literacy.

Selecting the Program Administrator

The second most important staff position is that of the program administrator. The program administrator works in close cooperation with the manager to ensure the program's success.

While the manager's role involves acting as a link between management, department heads, supervisors, outside providers, and the union, the program administrator's responsibilities are focused almost entirely on the program itself. She or he is primarily responsible for facilitating the instructional activities of the project. An administrator should be expected to:

- Evaluate instructional staff performance with respect to utilization of instructional techniques, working with adults, and achieving program objectives;
- Select and schedule facilities and equipment;
- Secure participant attendance records;
- Schedule instructional staff;
- Ensure course material is prepared and available;
- Maintain physical environment;
- Establish contingency plans for backups and emergencies; and
- Ensure program follow-up is accomplished (American Society for Training and Development, 1983).

This individual should have a strong background in project management and instructional technology, some background and experience in working with adults, and some experience using evaluation techniques. The administrator will also need to have a comfortable working knowledge of corporate policies and procedures.

Table 26 gives a sample job description for a program administrator.

Table

Table 26. Sample Program Administrator Job Description.

Job Title: Program administrator.

Broad Scope of Position: Administrative responsibility for implementation of basic workplace skills program.

Reports to: Program manager.

Major Duties and Responsibilities:

1. Be responsible for program implementation and administration.
2. Serve on program advisory committee.
3. Assist in design and development of program.
4. Ensure compliance with company and program policies and procedures.
5. Assist manager in selection of instructional staff.
6. Conduct and/or arrange training for staff as needed.
7. Schedule instructional staff.
8. Select and schedule facilities and equipment.
9. Ensure course material is prepared and available when needed.
10. Take an active part in learning about the curriculum and observe it being used.
11. Initiate meetings and otherwise establish procedures for instructors to discuss problems and concerns.
12. Ensure implementation of procedures for monitoring and evaluating the program.
13. Evaluate instructional staff performance.
14. Maintain necessary program and learner records.
15. Maintain physical environment.
16. Establish contingency plans for backups and emergencies.

Personal Characteristics:

1. Creates positive work climate.
2. Is dynamic, innovative, and energetic.
3. Is open and supportive with subordinates.
4. Is confident when dealing with superiors.

Skills and Abilities Required:

1. Demonstrate leadership and administrative skills.
2. Demonstrate written and verbal communications skills.
3. Demonstrate ability to relate to and lead diverse work groups.
4. Demonstrate ability to identify and solve project problems.

Education and Experience:

1. Demonstrated experience in project administration.
2. Demonstrated experience in adult basic skills training.
3. Demonstrated knowledge of adult learning theory and practice in an applied context.
4. Demonstrated experience in staff development, supervision, and evaluation.

Source: Adapted from *Job-Related Basic Skills: A Guide for Planners of Employee Programs,* June 1987, New York: Business Council for Effective Literacy.

Selecting the Instructional Staff

The program manager and the project administrator together should select the instructional staff. Successful instructors in job-related basic workplace training programs must have special skills. Some questions to keep in mind when selecting instructional staff are:

- Is the person familiar with adult learning and the psychology of learning?

- Has the person a history of actually working with adults, and what kind of evaluation feedback is available on performance?

- What is the level of subject expertise?

- Will the person be comfortable using new subject curricula and instructional approaches that are not school based?

- Does the person have experience teaching basic workplace skills in a job-related context?

- Will the person be responsive to company requirements and working with company personnel?

Many instructors do not have an understanding of the differences between working with children and working with adult learners. Knowledge of adult learning theory as well as hands-on experience in working with adults should weigh heavily in the selection process.

This knowledge and experience may make the crucial difference between a program with a positive image that gains increasing employee support and a program that dies as a result of bad publicity.

Table 27 gives a sample description of an instructor's job.

Table

Table 27. Sample Instructor Job Description.

Job Title: Instructor.

Broad Scope of the Position: Instruct workers using basic workplace skills training program curriculum.

Reports to: Program administrator.

Major Duties and Responsibilities:
1. Instruct adult learners using basic workplace skills training program curriculum and materials.
2. Diagnose individual learner problems and help select appropriate instructional program and materials.
3. Monitor learner progress.
4. Support learners in their efforts and recommend counseling services when appropriate.
5. Administer tests.
6. Keep records of attendance and progress.
7. Assist and cooperate with other program personnel.
8. Bring concerns and problems to attention of program administrator.

Personal Characteristics:
1. Is dynamic and energetic.
2. Is flexible and open to cooperation.
3. Is patient and supportive.

Skills and Abilities Required:
1. Demonstrated knowledge of adult education theory and practice.
2. Demonstrated knowledge of basic skills subject matter.
3. Successful experience teaching basic skills to adults.
4. Direct work experience or demonstrated awareness of knowledge, skills, and attitudes required in trainees' jobs.
5. Demonstrated knowledge of company policies, procedures, and culture.

Train-the-Trainer Workshop

Once selected, staff must be adequately prepared for the job ahead. The train-the-trainer workshop should be separated into three phases: institutional orientation, training program familiarization, and human relations training.

Institutional Orientation

Phase one is orientation to the institution. This orientation should be conducted by the human resource development department.

It should cover such areas as corporate mission and philosophy, employment regulations, compensations, benefits, performance reviews, disciplinary action, termination, and appeals procedures.

Union representatives should have an opportunity to present the union point of view.

This orientation should be presented even to an outside provider's instructional staff so they will share a common frame of reference with program participants.

Training Program Familiarization

This effort involves familiarizing the instructional staff with the training program itself.

Program orientation should be conducted by in-house staff, expert employees, and training providers who have worked directly on the development of the training program.

The information used to train the instructional staff should include:

- Review of applied learning perspectives,
- Review of curricula with hands-on practice,
- Familiarization with course objectives,
- Familiarization with course procedures and accountability requirements,
- Case studies in counseling and human relations,
- Familiarization with record-keeping and documentation requirements, and
- One week observing or working on actual jobs for which training is being provided.

Human Relations Training

Trainers may not be familiar with the characteristics of the potential training population or know how to relate to them.

The instructors should be given human relations training to help them relate to trainees of different races, different cultural backgrounds, both sexes, different educational levels, different socioeconomic backgrounds, and different ages.

The program might include some of the following subjects:

- Knowledge of human relations tendencies,
- Understanding of self in group relations,
- Help in developing working relationships,
- Articulating feelings,
- Understanding the dynamics of exclusion, and
- Understanding the educationally and economically disadvantaged.

It would be desirable to have a representative group of the training population involved in the human relations course to contribute realism and aid in evaluating the potential instructors' ability to relate to them.

Peer Trainers

Few companies can afford to hire full-time instructors for training in basic workplace skills. In some situations, it may be beneficial to train experienced employees and managers to become trainers on a part-time or full-time basis.

Potential candidates include employees who have an interest in taking on a different responsibility because they have mastered their jobs and want a new challenge or because they want a break in their work routine. Such individuals may view becoming a trainer as a way to increase their status within the company. Particularly in union companies, using these employees can generate a level of confidence that cannot be obtained any other way.

It is better to use these peer instructors full-time, because otherwise the employee must consider her or his original job as the principal assignment. Also, if the person is transferred to another job, it can mean the sudden loss of an instructor (Stoker, 1987, p. 736).

The decision to use peer trainers must be carefully thought out and implemented. One of the most sensitive questions to be worked out in advance between union and management is how to maintain seniority rights for employees who transfer out of their old jobs to work full-time as trainers.

Most of the employees who show an interest in becoming trainers will want the option to return to their old positions in case the new job does not work out.

Holding seniority rights on the old job is essential, particularly where the seniority roster is departmental, location-specific, or geographic rather than company-wide. The number who will be interested in teaching will probably be small, and developing a procedure for maintaining seniority should not be very disruptive.

The employees who express an interest in becoming trainers will need to have special training in instructional techniques. They should also be provided with support counseling because most will be facing a totally new and exciting experience—and also a frightening one.

Using the Buddy System

One means for ensuring that interested employees actually have the capability to teach basic workplace skills is to pilot test the program using those employees who have expressed an interest in becoming peer trainers.

One benefit of pilot testing is that experienced employees can offer suggestions and ideas for program improvement. After the employees have successfully pilot tested the new training program and participated in a train-the-trainer workshop, they are observed by experienced instructors and staff for a probationary period. As new trainer positions open up, successful peer trainers who are certified as qualified would fill them.

This screening and selection process can be ongoing as staff members identify outstanding employees in the basic workplace skills training program who express an interest in becoming trainers.

In this way, new trainers will always be available to fill positions vacated by senior peer trainers who leave or retire. A 1:1 ratio of peer instructors to professional trainers provides a high-quality instructional staff.

After the initial staff assessment, monitoring, and evaluation, accepted peer trainers should continue to be observed for the first several cycles of training.

One effective method for accomplishing this is through a buddy system in which a peer trainer is paired with a professional instructor.

The objective is for each to critique the other formally using written evaluation instruments that rate performance in terms of ability to communicate information, relationship with learners, substantive knowledge, use of instructional techniques, and so on.

If there are any problems with either the professional instructor or the peer trainer, it becomes the responsibility of the buddy to determine what corrective action should be taken.

Checklist 12 gives a form for rating an instructor's performance.

The performance evaluations of both the peer trainer and the professional instructor will include a rating for efforts with the buddy. This activity should take place under the direction of a supervising instructor. Such an exercise inmutual accountability is an excellent team-building mechanism and ensures that each buddy has a stake in the success of the other. It acts as a booster to unify two diverse groups into one effective staff with common goals and objectives.

Using these two different types of instructional staffs can lead to an enormously effective program and facilitate company-wide employee buy-in in a manner that cannot be replicated in any other way.

The opportunity for on-board employees to become trainers acts as a real motivator. The up-front costs of using peer trainers may appear to be high, but mixing peer with professional instructors more than pays off in generating high morale, program credibility, and high-quality outcomes.

Another approach to finding instructors is to hire outside on a part-time basis. This allows for more flexible scheduling. The program manager has the task of integrating staff with varying schedules into a functioning team, but the payoff in flexibility and solid programming is high.

A third option is to contract with an outside provider, as described in Step Three.

Checklist

Checklist 12. Rating Sheet for Overall Instructor Performance.

	Level of Performance				
	N/A	Poor	Fair	Good	Excellent
1. The instructor was prepared for class.	☐	☐	☐	☐	☐
2. The instructor's presentation was well organized.	☐	☐	☐	☐	☐
3. Lesson objectives were made clear.	☐	☐	☐	☐	☐
4. The instructor was interesting and enthusiastic.	☐	☐	☐	☐	☐
5. The instructor's voice was audible.	☐	☐	☐	☐	☐
6. The instructor could communicate the subject matter to the students.	☐	☐	☐	☐	☐
7. The instructor answered questions clearly.	☐	☐	☐	☐	☐
8. The instructor made sure students were given feedback on their achievement of lesson objectives.	☐	☐	☐	☐	☐

Source: Adapted from *Evaluate Your Instructional Effectiveness,* Second Edition, Module D-6 of Category D—Instructional Evaluation, "Professional Teacher Education Module Series." Copyright © 1986, The National Center for Research in Vocational Education, The Ohio State University. All rights reserved. Used with permission.

Counselors

It is important to consider counseling an integral part of a successful training program. Many employees will not have been in a formal learning situation for some time and will be fearful of failure. Some will also have had negative experiences when they were in school and will be anxious about whether they will perform well in this new program.

Providing a counselor to communicate the message that the company's commitment is to see the employees succeed at learning is a necessary reinforcement mechanism.

In designing the counseling functions of the program it is necessary to answer three questions:

- What support will the program and students require?
- Who will be responsible for providing it?
- What in-service training in counseling technique should be provided for all program personnel?

The counseling function begins before instruction and continues during and after the instruction is completed.

Preinstruction counseling focuses on:

- Orientation to the training program,
- Diagnostic testing, and
- Learner placement.

The counselor can be a prime source of learner motivation and commitment to basic skills training as the program is broken down into learnable tasks (Cooney and Glines, 1978, p. 18).

During the course of the instructional program, counselors, teachers, and others initiate informal and formal counseling opportunities to elicit the learners' views on the program and their progress in it.

Timely counseling can help trainees overcome difficulties they may be experiencing and prevent them from dropping out of the program.

Following completion of instruction, counseling is involved in assessing the program's effectiveness in meeting the individual learner's needs.

It can also be helpful in encouraging trainees to apply what they have learned to their job situations (Lerche, 1985, p. 68).

In many programs it is the classroom trainers who handle the tasks normally reserved for counselors. They routinely counsel students while diagnosing the basic skills problems of trainees, assessing their progress through the instructional program, and making final evaluation of their achievement.

Teachers should make appropriate referrals for services a learner may require beyond those they are able to provide (Lerche, 1985, p. 78).

It may be a more effective use of time and training to hire a separate counseling staff. Professionals with training in adult counseling techniques can be used on a full- or part-time basis, as the situation dictates.

It may be that counseling can be contracted with local human service agencies, which are geared to providing such services.

Counselors, both internal and external, should also be provided with orientation to company goals, objectives, and procedures governing employee behavior, as well as to the criteria for successful course completion.

Procedures should be developed for referral to counselors, confidentiality, access to employees, accountability, and establishment of a reporting hierarchy. The areas in which employees might need counseling include health and child care, transportation, family and personal difficulties, education, financial emergencies, and job training and placement.

Possible sources of counseling for employees include community colleges, community service programs, youth employment and training programs, social service agencies, health care institutions, community action organizations, community centers, religious institutions, vocational and technical institutes, civil rights organizations, private counseling centers, and the AFL-CIO's community services department.

Develop a Learning Contract—Yes or No?

During the program implementation period, employees are being selected for training. One useful tool that is frequently used to help an employee understand what the training experience will involve is a **learning contract**. Learning contracts set out the following information:

*The **learning contract** is a mutually agreed upon written document between the program operator (the employer) and the learner (the employee).*

- Where the learner is now, based on criterion-referenced pretests,
- Where the learner needs to be to meet company standards,
- What barriers may exist to learning,
- A plan for action to overcome obstacles,
- The time frame within which learning will take place, and
- Company commitments.

A learning contract is useful in both voluntary and required training situations because there is up-front clarification of employee training needs, the probable time frame to achieve positive results, the process to be used, and the learning objectives.

A learning contract is not a required part of the training program, but it is recommended as a good tool to help learners and staff keep training on track. It is also a mechanism by which management can monitor how well the program is going.

The learning contract is a mutually agreed upon written document between the program operator (the employer) and the learner (the employee). The training plan (competencies to be achieved) is a part of the learning contract. The contract is updated as competencies are mastered and is reviewed on a regular basis. (For an example of a learning contract, see Table 28.)

In contract learning, the role of the instructor shifts from that of a transmitter of information and controller of learners to that of a facilitator of self-directed learning and content resource. The roles of the employee, the instructor, and the employer can be clearly defined (Knowles, 1986, pp. 43–45).

The role of the employee is to:

- Propose a written learning contract of what and how she or he wants to learn,
- Establish a time line or schedule,
- Take the initiative to seek assistance from the instructor when required, and
- Meet with the instructor regularly to discuss progress.

The role of the instructor is to:

- Assist in developing the trainee's learning contract,
- Recommend appropriate learning resources,
- Be an available and interested resource, and
- Make a final report of learner accomplishment.

The role of the employer is to:

- Refrain from using training evaluation results in a disciplinary way,
- Hold training evaluation results in confidence,
- Understand that individuals learn at their own pace and in their own way,
- Allow time on the job to learn,
- Give support before, during, and after training, and
- Support application of new learning on the job.

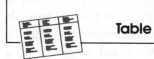 **Table**

Table 28. Sample Learning Contract.

Competency-Based Evaluation Contract

Base Assignment: Business Communications Letter Writing

Objectives	Strategies	Evidence
At the end of the course the participant will be able to:		
1. Define a writing objective (define a primary objective).	The participant will read and study the definitions of a primary objective until she or he understands them and is able to recall the definitions' meanings and intentions.	1. The participant will write the definitions. 2. The participant will define a writing objective and/or a primary objective at given times.
2. Recognize the primary writing objective.	The participant will be given at least ten unfamiliar letters and will be asked to pick out the primary writing objective in each.	The participant will have correctly identified the primary writing objective in all of the letters given.
3. State a basic plan (method) in outline form.	The participant will read about making a plan.	The participant will write a basic information block. The participant will verbally state the three basic blocks and the purpose of each in one of the following ways: in front of the class; to the instructor alone; and in a small discussion group.
4. Use the block effectively for a letter of complaint.	The participant will write a complaint letter according to the outline given in class.	The participant's letter will give the summary statement first, the complaint in the second paragraph, and the action in the concluding paragraph. The letter will be effective according to the instructor's evaluation criteria.
5. Organize thoughts into formats for at least three types of letters used by the participant at work, or according to her or his need or choice.	The participant will design a format for each type of letter chosen and design at least one letter for each.	The participant will submit the designs for the letter types chosen to the instructor for evaluation, or present the design formats to the class (in writing or orally) for evaluation, or use another method chosen by the participant and accepted by the instructor.
6. Write a good business letter without prior knowledge of the topic, given a time limit.	The participant will be given three unfamiliar topics for reply.	The participant will write a reply for each of the three topics within a stated time limit.

This is a contract. The objectives are not renegotiable. Strategies and evidence are renegotiable subject to approval by the instructor. If you wish to try and meet the objectives, please sign below.

Employee: _____   **Instructor:** _____

Employer: _____   **Date:** _____

Source: Adapted from Knowles, 1986, pp. 144–145. Used by permission of the author.

Should the Program Be Pilot Tested?

After guidelines have been established for administration and paperwork, it is often useful to operate a small pilot program to validate the training and change any material that is not suitable. This could be done using employees who have indicated an interest in becoming peer trainers, but it can be done just as effectively with a group of employees who have been identified as needing learning enhancement. A pilot test might serve the following purposes:

- Check the flow of the training program,
- Help work out any bugs in the program design,
- Develop the instructor's notes,
- Provide an opportunity for instructor exposure to the programming,
- Build credibility by demonstrating the program developers' flexibility and openness to input from program instructors and participants,
- Provide an opportunity for publicity and demonstration of management support, and
- Provide an opportunity to test expensive instructional materials before final production, using written scripts and thus avoiding the cost of possible remakes (Abella, 1986).

If the decision is made to conduct a pilot test, the procedures in Table 29 would be appropriate.

Table

Table 29. How to Conduct a Pilot Test.

1. Preparation of Session
   a. Finalize materials.
   b. Choose participants.
   c. Decide on evaluation process.
   d. Choose and brief instructors.
   e. Select other nonparticipant observers.

2. Conduct the program
   a. Downplay the fact that it is only a pilot session.
   b. Hold regular instructor briefing sessions.
   c. Collect as much data as possible.

3. After the pilot test
   a. Resolve any problems that emerged during the test.
   b. Revise training material.
   c. Finalize instructor notes.
   d. Publicize the pilot results.
   e. Inform design team of pilot test results.

References and Suggested Readings

Abella, K. T. *Building Successful Training Programs: A Step-by-Step Guide.* Reading, Mass.: Addison-Wesley, 1986.

American Society for Training and Development. *Models for Excellence.* Alexandria, Va.: American Society for Training and Development, 1983.

Business Council for Effective Literacy. *Job-Related Basic Skills: A Guide for Planners of Employee Programs.* New York: Business Council for Effective Literacy, 1987.

Cooney, J., and Glines, E. *Final Report of the Adult Competency Education Project: An Experimental Adult Basic Education Demonstration Project.* Redwood City, Calif.: Career Preparation Programs, Vocational Education Division, San Mateo County Office of Education, 1978.

Evaluate Your Instructional Effectiveness. (2nd ed.) Module D-6 of Category D (Instructional Evaluation), Professional Teacher Education Module Series. Columbus: National Center for Research in Vocational Education, Ohio State University, 1986.

Knowles, M. S. *Using Learning Contracts: Practical Approaches to Individualizing and Structuring Learning.* San Francisco: Jossey-Bass, 1986.

Lerche, R. S. *Effective Adult Literacy Programs: A Practitioner's Guide.* Cambridge, Mass.: Adult Education Company, 1985.

Stoker, R. "Literacy in the Workplace." In R. L. Craig (ed.), *Training and Development Handbook.* (3rd ed.) New York: McGraw-Hill, 1987.

Notes

_____

_____

_____

_____

_____

_____

_____

_____

_____

_____

_____

_____

_____

_____

_____

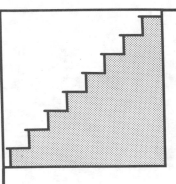

STEP EIGHT

Evaluate and Monitor the Program

Learning Objectives

The reader will be able to:

1. List the reasons for undertaking an evaluation.

2. Define and give examples of the four primary levels of data used to evaluate training effectiveness.

3. Design an evaluation system.

4. Define the purpose of program monitoring.

5. Design appropriate forms and procedures to meet the monitoring needs of a given program.

Introduction

Training has become big business in this country, but employers and training professionals are plagued by the question, How do you measure and evaluate the results of training? Although evaluation of training has increased over the past ten years, the problem of identifying assumptions about training and the methodology for evaluating these assumptions still remains up in the air.

According to evaluation expert Donald Kirkpatrick, the basic assumption that should underlie all evaluation efforts is composed of two parts:

1. A training program must have an ultimate objective that spells out what changes should take place in behavior; and

2. The training program must be designed to provide each trainee with a series of carefully selected and executed learning experiences that contribute in a specific way to the desired change (1975, p. 188).

If this assumption is taken as a given in preparing all training programs, then we see that measurement and evaluation should be an integral part of the training business and not an optional feature or an afterthought.

Checklist 13 contains a sample evaluation system checklist that gives some indication of the scope of what must be considered when developing both a training program and the evaluation that accompanies it.

The evaluation process really begins when the learning objectives are first established. Initial plans for evaluation begin with meetings between the client and the evaluator to determine measurement plans. These meetings should be conducted before the training program ever begins. Once a training program has completed at least one cycle and employees have returned to their work stations, the evaluation mechanisms swing into operation.

Checklist

Checklist 13. Evaluation System Checklist.

	Yes	No	Uncertain

1. Do you have your evaluation process written up? ☐ ☐ ☐
Does it include: (check all that apply)

☐ A determination of who needs what kind of data for what purpose?

☐ An evaluation of all training programs on a periodic basis (for example, six weeks, six months, and one year following training)?

☐ A description of ties to needs assessment and other elements in the training process (how evaluation is fed by them and how they are fed by evaluation)?

☐ An assessment of changes in clients on a continuing basis?

2. Do you have a management information system that ☐ ☐ ☐
tracks a client description, client movement in conditions of life, activity of the helper(s), and costs?

3. Do you have a formalized way of providing evaluative ☐ ☐ ☐
data to those who need it? (check all that apply)

☐ Do you have a way of determining who needs what kinds of data?

☐ Do you design formats for providing the data that each group needs?

☐ Do you determine beforehand the types of questions that they are likely to ask and prepare to answer them?

4. Do you actually design your evaluations as outlined ☐ ☐ ☐
in no. 1 above? For each training program do you: (check all that apply)

☐ Determine acceptable on-the-job evidence that training provided relevant behaviors that were then used on the job for each training program.

☐ Design or identify instrument(s) to determine the degree to which the skills and knowledge acquired through training are utilized on the job.

☐ Name person(s) to conduct the evaluation and orient them to your process and provide them with guidelines.

☐ Plan evaluation schedule (six weeks, six months, and one year).

☐ Conduct six-week follow-up.
  • Mail out follow-up questionnaire.
  • Follow up on return.
  • Tabulate and analyze results.
  • Provide management with preliminary relevant data and recommendations.
  • Merge needs discovered with other needs assessment data.
  • Develop specific recommendations for immediate changes to be made, if any.

☐ Conduct six-month follow-up.
  • Mail out follow-up questionnaire.
  • Follow up on return.
  • Tabulate and analyze results.
  • Provide management with relevant data and recommendations.
  • Merge needs discovered with other needs assessment data.
  • Develop specific recommendations for changes in training program.

☐ Develop quarterly summaries of client movement data from assessments.

☐ Conduct one-year follow-up.
  • Mail out follow-up questionnaire.
  • Follow up on return.
  • Tabulate and analyze results.
  • Provide management with relevant data and recommendations.
  • Merge needs discovered with other needs assessment data.
  • Develop specific recommendations for changes in training program.
  • Merge with other evaluative data from client assessments.

5. Do you review the evaluation data and needs assess-   ☐   ☐   ☐
   ment data annually to formulate recommendations for
   new training programs or major modifications in existing ones? (The annual plan would be developed at this
   time.)

6. Do you review the evaluation process itself (at least   ☐   ☐   ☐
   annually) and make necessary modifications?

Source: Barbee, 1985. Used by permission.

Reasons to Evaluate

There are several very good reasons why the human resource development department should include evaluation as an integral part of its design for the basic workplace skills training program.

- There is increasing pressure from top executives for such programs to prove their effectiveness in measurable terms, showing how they contribute to the profitability of the organization and achievement of its strategic goals.

- There is increasing pressure from the training managers and trainees themselves to obtain better measures of the effects of the training.

- A system of evaluation protects the program from the inadequate judgments of people who have no solid information about results.

- Organizations want to know about the relative effectiveness of their various departments, programs, and services.

- Specific measurements of a past program's success build credibility and can help secure funds for future projects.

- It is reasonable that evaluation should be required of an activity that represents a significant expenditure from the organization.

- Finally, including an evaluation system in the proposal to management shows you are confident that you can demonstrate the success of the program in meeting its stated objectives.

Purposes and Uses of Evaluation

Evaluation is undertaken for several purposes. Generally, evaluations fall into two categories: to improve the human resource development process, or to decide whether to continue it.

When the goal is to improve the process, the following objectives should be kept in mind:

- *Identify the strengths and weaknesses in the training program.* This is probably the most common purpose of evaluation. Things to look at include methods of presentation, learning environment, program content, training aids, faculty, schedule, and the instructor.

- *Identify which participants benefited the most or the least from the program.*

- *Gather data to assist in marketing future programs.* Ask questions like: Why did you attend this program? Who made the decision for you to attend? How did you find out about the program? Would you recommend it to others?

- *Establish a data base that can assist management in making future decisions.*

When the goal is to decide whether to continue the program, the following objectives should be kept in mind:

- *Determine whether a program is accomplishing its objective.* As the job provides the context for learning and instruction, so it serves as the main test of program effectiveness. If employees can better perform their jobs, the employee and company objectives are being met.

- *Decide who should participate in future programs.* Sometimes a follow-up evaluation simply determines the benefits of the program to the participants. Communicating these benefits to prospective participants can help meet their needs.

- *Determine the cost/benefit ratio of the program.* An increasing reason for evaluation is to determine whether a training program justifies its cost. This aspect of evaluation compares the cost of the program to its usefulness or value.

- *Reinforce the major points to the participants.* A follow-up evaluation serves as a review to reinforce the information covered in a program for its participants.

- *Determine if the program was appropriate.* Evaluation can help determine whether the original problem was indeed a training problem. In this case, the purpose is not to determine if it was the best program but rather if it was the most appropriate solution to the problem.

Types of Evaluation

Four primary levels of data are used to evaluate training effectiveness:

1. Reaction, or post-training surveys—to determine reaction of learners;

2. Learning, or pretests and post-tests—to determine what learning has taken place;

3. Behavior, or interviews and job observation with learners and supervisors—to determine whether training has produced any behavioral changes; and

4. Results, or impact on business—to determine if the company has benefited overall.

Table 30 illustrates the various characteristics of these different types of evaluation.

Table

Table 30. Characteristics of Evaluation Criteria.

Criteria	Reaction	Learning	Behavior	Results
Value of Information	Lowest	$\rightarrow$	$\rightarrow$	Highest
Frequency of Use	Relatively Frequent	$\leftarrow$	$\leftarrow$	Relatively Infrequent
Difficulty of Assessment	Relatively Easy	$\rightarrow$	$\rightarrow$	Relatively Difficult

Source: From *Handbook of Training Evaluation and Measurement Methods,* by Jack J. Phillips. Copyright © 1983 by Gulf Publishing Company, Houston, Tex. Used with permission. All rights reserved.

Reaction

The most common step in evaluation is to determine the reactions of those taking the training.

Courses are sometimes changed on the basis of one or two comments that make their way up the chain of command.

It is important that participants like the training in order to obtain maximum benefits from it.

To measure reaction adequately, it is necessary to do it in an organized fashion with written comment sheets designed to obtain the desired results.

It is also important that the program coordinator or another trained observer make an appraisal of the training in order to obtain a more meaningful, objective result.

For lengthy programs, an end-of-the-program evaluation may be a mistake because participants may be unable to remember what was covered. To deal with this problem, an ongoing evaluation should be distributed at the beginning of the program, and participants should be asked to react to each segment of the program as it is completed (Phillips, 1983).

Table 31 gives a sample form for rating the usefulness of a program.

Table

Table 31. Sample Rating Form—Course Usefulness.

Key	Programs
A	Modern Leadership for Middle Management
B	Supervisors' Leadership in Cost Control
C	Developing Supervisory Skills
D	Human Relations for Foremen and Supervisors
E	Leadership and Growth
F	Creative Thinking for Supervisors
G	Human Relations for New Foremen
T	Totals

	A	B	C	D	E	F	G	T
Questionnaires returned:	3	3	5	11	5	1	1	29
1. I thought the program was:								
a. Very well organized and helpful	3	3	5	11	5	1	1	29
b. Of some value								
c. Poorly organized and a waste of time								
2. In reference to the subject content:								
a. It was all theory and of little practical value								
b. It was both theory and practical	3	2	2	3	1			11
c. It was very practical	0	1	3	9	4	1	1	19
3. Concerning the quality of instruction:								
a. The instruction was excellent	2	3	4	11	4	1	1	26
b. The instruction was average			1		1			2
c. The instruction was poor								

Source: Adapted from Kirkpatrick, 1975, p. 4.

Table 32 gives a sample form for rating instructor performance.

Table

Table 32. Sample Rating Form—Instructor Performance.

Leader: _____

Subject: _____

Date: _____

1. Was the subject pertinent to your needs and interests?

   ☐ No   ☐ To some extent   ☐ Very much so

2. How was the ratio of lecture to discussion?

   ☐ Too much lecture   ☐ OK   ☐ Too much discussion

3. How about the leader?   *Excellent   Good   Fair   Poor*

   a. How well did she or he state objectives?

   b. How well did she or he keep the session alive and interesting?

   c. How well did she or he use the blackboard, charts, and other aids?

   d. How well did she or he summarize during the session?

   e. How well did she or he maintain a friendly or helpful manner?

   f. How well did she or he illustrate and clarify the points?

   g. How was her or his summary of the close of the session?

   h. What is your overall rating of the leader?

4. What would have made the session more effective?

   _____

   _____

   _____

   _____

Source: Adapted from Kirkpatrick, 1975, p. 2.

Table 33 gives a sample form for rating course content.

Table

Table 33. Sample Rating Form—Course Content.

Course Title: _____   Date: _____

Location: _____   Instructors: _____

To guide us in planning future seminars and workshops, please answer the questions below. You need not sign the sheet unless you so desire.

How would you rate the following?   *Excellent   Satisfactory   Unsatisfactory*

Quality of presentation

Adequacy of course content

Length of course

Adequacy of course materials

Conduct of workshops

Adequacy of facilities

If any factor is rated "unsatisfactory," please provide explanation:

_____

_____

_____

What was of most value to you in this seminar?

_____

_____

What was of least value in this seminar?

_____

_____

Additional comments would be appreciated.

_____

_____

_____

Signature (optional): _____

Source: Kirkpatrick, 1975, p. 49.

Learning

A great deal of effort is required to measure whether learning has taken place in a program. It involves planning the evaluation procedure, analyzing the data, and interpreting the results.

However, documentable learning gains can significantly enhance the status of training within the organization.

See Table 34 for a sample questionnaire intended to test participants' learning gains in a seminar to improve decision-making skills.

 Table

Table 34. Sample Form for Testing Participant Learning.

For each question, check all that apply:

1. If my boss handed back to me a well-done piece of work and asked me to make changes on it, I would:

   ☐ Prove to her or him that the job is better without changes.

   ☐ Do what she or he says and point out where she or he is wrong.

   ☐ Complete the changes without comment.

   ☐ Request a transfer from the department.

2. If I were the office manager and one of the best clerks kept complaining about working conditions, I would:

   ☐ Try to determine the basis for the complaints.

   ☐ Transfer her or him to some other section.

   ☐ Point out to her or him that complaining is bad for morale.

   ☐ Ask her or him to write out the complaints to my superior.

3. If my supervisor criticized my work, I would:

   ☐ Compare my record with co-workers for her or him.

   ☐ Explain the reason for my poor performance.

   ☐ Ask her or him why I was selected for criticism.

   ☐ Ask her or him for suggestions about how to improve.

4. If I were setting up a new procedure in an office, I would:

   ☐ Do it on my own without enlisting anyone's aid.

   ☐ Ask my superiors for suggestions.

   ☐ Ask the people who work under me for suggestions.

   ☐ Discuss it with my friends who are outside the company.

Source: Adapted from Kirkpatrick, 1975, pp. 8–9.

Aetna Life Insurance Company

Aetna Life Insurance Company instituted a claims-processing training program for new employees and used a pretest, post-test design to evaluate its effectiveness. The pretest revealed that the new employees had little knowledge of claims processing. Shortly after completion of the training program, participants were given a post-test that revealed significant learning gains. It is unlikely that any factors other than the training were responsible for the performance improvement.

   Sometimes when it can be assumed the participants have little or no knowledge of the subject matter, the pretest can be dispensed with. For instance, when IBM offered a training program in basic Japanese to its international sales representatives, no pretest was given because of the participants' lack of prior exposure to the language.

General Electric

General Electric reported on a before-and-after evaluation of one of its safety programs. The purpose of the program was both to reduce the number of accidents and to increase the regularity with which accidents were reported. The training program consisted of rather traditional presentations, discussions, and movies describing industrial accidents and their implications. The post-training evaluations indicated no significant change in employee behavior, so a new approach focusing on the relationship between worker and supervisor was tried. An evaluation of this program indicated the desired change in behavior had been achieved.

Behavior

Several guidelines need to be followed in measuring change in terms of behavior:

- A systematic appraisal needs to be made of on-the-job performance on a before-and-after basis.

- Appraisal needs to be made by one or more of the following groups: the learner, the supervisor or department head, subordinates, and peers.

- A statistical analysis should be made to compare before-and-after performance and related changes to the training program.

- Post-training appraisals should be made no sooner than three months after training so learners have a chance to put into practice what they have learned.

- It is recommended that a control group of employees not receiving training be used.

Case Study

AT&T

AT&T used a special evaluation staff to rate the effectiveness of supervisors who had participated in supervisory relationships training and those who had not. Each supervisor handled three simulated problem discussions.

The improvement in those who had been trained was marked. Eighty-four percent of the trained employees performed exceptionally well, and only 16 percent were average or below average. By contrast, only 33 percent of the untrained employees performed exceptionally well, while 67 percent were average or below average (Phillips, 1983).

Results

This is the most difficult evaluation to make because even when improvement appears to be the result of training, it is usually difficult to separate how much improvement is due to training alone as compared to other factors.

Some measure of results can be seen in such areas as:

- Improved productivity,
- Reduction of costs,
- Reduction of turnover and absenteeism, and
- Increase in quantity and quality of production.

Case Study

An Electronics Firm

In an effort to reverse shrinking profits, an electronics firm instituted an in-house training program to alter leadership approaches from traditional management-by-crisis and win-lose styles to participative, people-oriented, team management styles. Following the application of behavioral science theories and training, improved performance occurred. This was evidenced by (1) increased efficiency and quality (monthly shipping dollars went up by 128 percent); (2) a decrease in absenteeism by 72 percent and in turnover by 50 percent; and (3) a 10 percent reduction in cost (Bartlett, 1967, pp. 381–403).

What is apparent is that using all four factors to evaluate the effectiveness of training builds a more credible case for training's effectiveness. No one factor alone will provide accurate feedback.

Feasibility of the Evaluation System

Clarifying the purposes, audiences, and issues of evaluation helps to decide not only how much evaluation is warranted but also when data collection should occur and when reports should be made.

It is also important to consider what is feasible given the available money, commitment, time, and expertise. Like any other project, the evaluation should be planned so that the benefits exceed the time and money spent.

Case Study

Xerox Corporation

Xerox used four sources of data to evaluate the effectiveness of a training program to improve the job performance of sales representatives. First, a survey was distributed to determine the participants' reactions.

Second, participants were observed to determine what product knowledge gains they had made during the training.

Third, managers were interviewed regarding their employees' job performance after training.

Fourth, sales records were compared before and after the training.

The use of several data collection methods gave a more credible evaluation of the training program's effectiveness.

Feasibility is partly a matter of the intended scope of the evaluation effort. Trainers seldom conduct a thorough and comprehensive evaluation of either a single program or the total human resource development program. To do so would cost more than to provide the program. One way to reduce scope is to emphasize planning, improvement, or justification as the main purpose of the evaluation.

For the purpose of the proposal to management, it makes sense to tie the evaluation design to the initial needs assessment. Answer the question: To what extent did the training program solve the problem it addressed?

When discussing the subject of evaluation, a clear distinction needs to be drawn between evaluation, which is performed periodically to determine whether program goals are being met, and monitoring, which is a continual process.

Provide Program Monitoring

Program monitoring is an ongoing process that provides feedback on whether program instruction is working well from day to day.

Program evaluation is usually carried out by personnel specially trained in evaluation techniques or by an independent evaluation specialist, but program monitoring falls within the domain of the program manager, project administrator, and instructional staff.

Program monitoring enables the staff to:

Program monitoring is an ongoing process that channels information back to program operators on how effectively the instructional process is operating. Where program efficiency and effectiveness are determined to be less than optimal, changes are made to improve performance.

- Measure the competence of participants in terms of whether they have achieved the stated objectives,

- Determine which objectives have not been realized in order to take appropriate remedial action,

- Keep the instructor informed of the effectiveness of the teaching strategy so corrective action can be taken, and

- Devise procedures to improve course design.

In other words, program monitoring channels information back to program operators on how effectively the instructional process is operating. Where program efficiency and effectiveness are determined to be less than optimal, changes are made to improve performance.

Tables 35–40 indicate some of the monitoring activity that goes on in a typical training program.

Table 35 can be used by the instructor to monitor an individual employee's progress while in training. It is completed after problem identification has been conducted and key areas for action have been identified.

Table

Table 35. Sample Employee Action Plan Worksheet

Name: _____ **Dept./Sect.:** _____ **Date:** _____

Overall Objective: _____

_____

No.	Learning Objective	Action to Be Taken	Person Responsible	Target Date	Completion Date

Source: From *Handbook of Training Evaluation and Measurement Methods*, by Jack J. Phillips. Copyright © 1983 by Gulf Publishing Company, Houston, Tex. Used with permission. All rights reserved.

Table 36 gives an example of a form that the individual employee can use to monitor his or her progress in a basic workplace skills training program. The cards can be kept in a central location and updated by the learners themselves as each segment of the program is completed satisfactorily. Notice the column "Recycled" for students who require special assistance or another try to achieve the desired competency in a given part of the program before proceeding further.

Together, then, monitoring and evaluation provide the information feedback that closes the circle of the systematic method for providing practical training in a workplace context.

Table

Table 36. Sample Employee Daily Progress Record.

Basic Workplace Skills Training Program: _____

Name: _____ **Date:** _____

Program Start-Up Date: _____ **Completion:** _____

Instructor: _____

Guide No./Title	Started	Recycled	Achieved
A-1			
A-2			
A-3			
B-1			
B-2			
B-3			

Table 37 shows a class progress chart, which can help the instructor monitor the progress of a group of learners through the modules or lessons in a basic workplace skills training program. It is essentially a compilation of the individualized records listed in Table 36.

Table

Table 37. Sample Class Progress Chart.

Group: _____ **Date:** _____

Program Start-Up Date: _____ **Completion:** _____

Name	Module or Learning Guide Numbers					
	A-1	A-2	A-3	B-1	B-2	B-3

Computers can be very useful in charting student progress. The students themselves can be taught to update their individual records, and the computer can be programmed to combine these into a record for the learners as a group. This reduction of paperwork can be very helpful in freeing up the instructor's time to work directly with the learners.

The program administrator and instructors must develop a system to keep track of the program materials and equipment. Forms such as the ones in Tables 38, 39, and 40 would be useful for this function.

Table

Table 38. Sample Inventory Record: Learning Package Check-out.

Learning Package Number: _____

Learning Package Title: _____

Date of Check-out	Time	Name	Date of Check-in	Time

Source: Module K-5, *Manage the Daily Routines of Your CBE Program,* of "Professional Teacher Education, Category K—Implementing Competency-Based Education Module Series." Copyright © 1986 by The National Center for Research in Vocational Education, The Ohio State University. All rights reserved. Used with permission.

Table

Table 39. Sample Inventory Record: Equipment Sign-Up Sheet.

Equipment/Work Station: _____

Name	Program	Date Needed	Hours Needed

Source: Module K-5, *Manage the Daily Routines of Your CBE Program,* of "Professional Teacher Education, Category K—Implementing Competency-Based Education Module Series." Copyright © 1986 by The National Center for Research in Vocational Education, The Ohio State University. All rights reserved. Used with permission.

Table

Table 40. Sample Inventory Sheet: Supplies Check-out.

Description	Name of User	Time/Date of Check-out	Time/Date of Check-in	Condition

Source: Module K-5, *Manage the Daily Routines of Your CBE Program,* of "Professional Teacher Education, Category K—Implementing Competency-Based Education Module Series." Copyright © 1986 by The National Center for Research in Vocational Education, The Ohio State University. All rights reserved. Used with permission.

Connect Back to Management

When an evaluation model can demonstrate accomplishment and success, it makes it much easier to convince management that training is an appropriate option. Involving managers in program design and evaluation early in the training development process provides them with a sense of ownership.

Lombardo (1986) notes that an explanation to management about economic improvements due to training should include the following:

- Description of original problems,

- Discussion of cost,

- Discussion of how training costs and training benefits were estimated,

- Description of how return-on-investment figures were derived, and

- Final examination of the economic benefits to the organization.

References and Suggested Readings

Barbee, D. E. *Seminar for Adapting Off-the-Shelf Vocational and Technical Curricula.* Unpublished manuscript, 1985.

Bartlett, A. C. "Changing Behavior as a Means to Increased Efficiency." *Journal of Applied Behavioral Science,* 1967, 3 (3), 381–411.

Kelley, A. I., Orgel, R. F., and Baer, D. M. "Evaluation: The Bottom Line Is Closer Than You Think." *Training and Development Journal,* 1984, 38 (8), 32–37.

Kirkpatrick, D. L. (ed.). *Evaluating Training Programs.* Alexandria, Va.: American Society for Training and Development, 1975.

Lombardo, C. "Cost/Benefit Analysis of Training." In *American Society for Training and Development Handbook for Technical and Skills Training.* Vol. 2. Alexandria, Va.: American Society for Training and Development, 1986.

Manage the Daily Routines of Your Competency-Based Education Program. Module K-5 of Category K (Implementing Competency-Based Education), Professional Teacher Education Module Series. Columbus: National Center for Research in Vocational Education, Ohio State University, 1986.

Phillips, J. J. *Handbook of Training Evaluation and Measurement Methods.* Houston, Tex.: Gulf Publishing, 1983.

Notes

_____

_____

_____

_____

_____

_____

_____

_____

_____

_____

_____

_____

_____

_____

_____

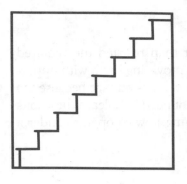

Resource A:
A New Plant Perspective:
Case Study from Mazda
(The Applied Approach)

Mazda: A Program for a New Plant

The approach to skills training described in this book provides a flexible framework that can be adapted by any kind of organization. This case study demonstrates how Mazda Motor Manufacturing (USA) Corporation makes good use of this applied approach.

As you review the Mazda story, think about the challenges facing your organization. You will uncover both similarities and differences, but most importantly, you will see in the Mazda experience a realistic point of reference that can help you plan how to make this approach work for you.

In 1986, sales topped $10 billion for Mazda, a Japanese manufacturer that has produced automobiles since 1931. In late 1987, in Flat Rock, Mich., the corporation opened its first U.S. plant—a thriving operation employing 3,500 people, of whom more than 3,000 are nonsupervisory personnel.

Before the plant opened, Mazda prepared a detailed training plan for every new employee. Phase One of the plan focused on the basic workplace skills essential for successful plant start-up. It included courses in company orientation, Japanese life, job-specific off-line training, and on-the-job training. Each employee level had its own common training track with a special combination of courses on topics such as *kaizen* (constant improvement), group processes (how to work in groups), problem solving and decision making, safety and health, creative thinking, interpersonal skills, and statistical process control. (See Figure 10 for an illustration of Mazda training design concepts.)

The following describes step by step how Mazda built a training program.

Step One: Identify Job Problems or Changes

Because Mazda's Michigan plant was new, it had no problems or job changes that required investigation. But to avoid possible future problems, the company took a proactive stance. From the outset, Mazda sought to instill its corporate culture in new employees through an effective, comprehensive training program. To ensure that employees would be prepared to meet the new plant's technological and cultural demands, most phase one training was required, although several courses were voluntary.

Virtually all employees welcomed rather than resisted the required training because they realized that Mazda was providing them with opportunities to learn valuable skills. Again, Mazda had an advantage because the plant was new: managers and employees did not need to unlearn the habits and procedures of an old system before learning how to operate under a new one.

Figure 10. Training Design Concepts.

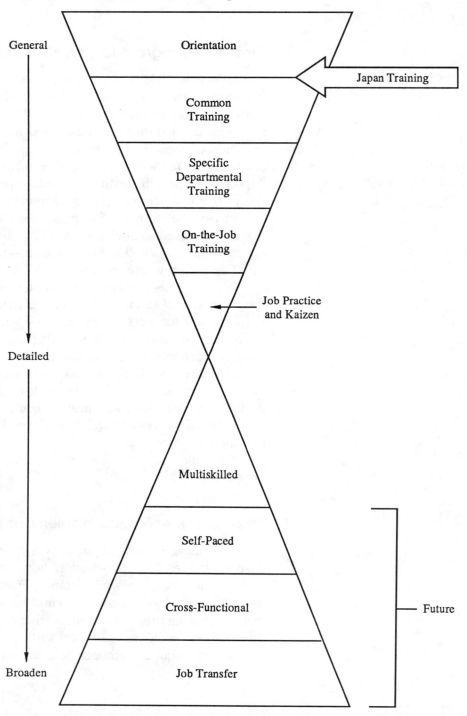

Source: Mazda Motor Manufacturing (USA) Corporation. Used with permission.

To hold down costs, Mazda conducted job and task analyses concurrently. Job and task analyses were done for every position because all positions were new and unstaffed. In Step One, each identified job was broken down into major tasks, but a description of the training a person needed to achieve optimal task performance was left for the program design phase of Step Six.

Together Mazda's vice presidents for personnel and manufacturing coordinated job and task analyses. To carry out the analyses, cooperation was vital—from training and development staff, department managers, labor relations department staff, personnel administration staff, and advisers sent from Mazda in Japan. But at the time the training plan was developed and implemented, gaining union support was not pertinent because plant employees were not unionized. A year and a half after training program development began, employees voted to unionize. By then, the program was established and running smoothly, and the union had little concern with its direction, devoting only a brief section of the union contract to reinforcement and clarification of expectations regarding training. Since then the union has become actively involved with the training program and has a training representative to assist and advise on Mazda's training programs.

In Michigan, analysts interviewed each manager, executive, and resident Japanese adviser individually to learn their expectations and opinions about skill requirements for the new plant's work force. In addition, a delegation went to observe Japanese employees in a Mazda plant similar to the one that was to open in the United States. The delegation also interviewed the sister plant's managers and advisers and got copies of its job descriptions to use in developing their American counterparts.

The interviews and job and task analyses indicated that training in measurable, technical skills (the so-called hard skills) was required and that managers and executives also considered training in soft skills essential. Soft skills related to such matters as mutual respect among co-workers, striving for constant improvement of the production process (*kaizen*), open communications, pride, caring, and putting forth an extra effort. Because soft skills are relatively difficult to measure, clear-cut information about skill levels required for them was difficult to obtain.

Step One was accomplished by a training and development staff of only three employees, with no outside assistance.

Using data gathered in this step, the training and development staff, with help from a newly formed steering committee, drafted a preliminary action plan.

Step Two: Build Management and Union Support

Japanese corporations traditionally have a strong commitment to employee development. So gaining general support from Mazda's top managers was not difficult, although the training and development staff had to promote the specific training plan and process that they proposed to use.

Mazda's managers in Michigan demonstrate support of training through their involvement in all aspects of training program development and implementation. (See Figure 11 for an illustration of the relationship between functional areas and training.) For example, each supervisor plays a training and coaching role, taking responsibility for development of the employees in his or her area. But because support for Mazda's training program originally came from the top, formal coalitions were organized to build and maintain support throughout the organization.

One of the coalitions is a steering committee that was established after jobs and tasks were analyzed. During the training program's initial planning, development, and implementation, this committee met every week. Since then it has met approximately twice a year to provide leadership by giving guidance, trouble-shooting, and solving problems. Its role is to help with training plan development and to keep all employees involved in and informed about the training program's progress.

The twelve steering committee members, each from a different plant area, are chosen by their division heads. Although most committee members are managers, nonsupervisory employees are also represented. The training and development staff specifically requested that the committee include employees at various levels so that all employees could feel ownership of the training program.

There are other coalitions, namely, the training coordinators' group and the instructor leadership groups. The number of people in the training coordinators' group varies, but is typically fifteen of the employees designated as training coordinators for their work groups. Coordinators are responsible for implementation and coordination of training within their work groups. The training coordinators' group was formed when the curriculum was being developed and met at least once a week during that phase to provide guidance.

Each instructor leadership group is composed of approximately five internal trainers from a given program. These trainers become a task team with responsibility for the content and structure of the particular program, making all of the day-to-day decisions about it. Together, the instructor leadership groups provide support and generate new ideas for the effective implementation of training.

To ensure that the training program will not suffer or disappear as staff changes are made, all aspects of training are carefully documented. For example, lesson plans are consistently designed so any instructor can review them and be prepared to teach a course.

Figure 11. Relationship Between Functional Areas and Training and Development Department.

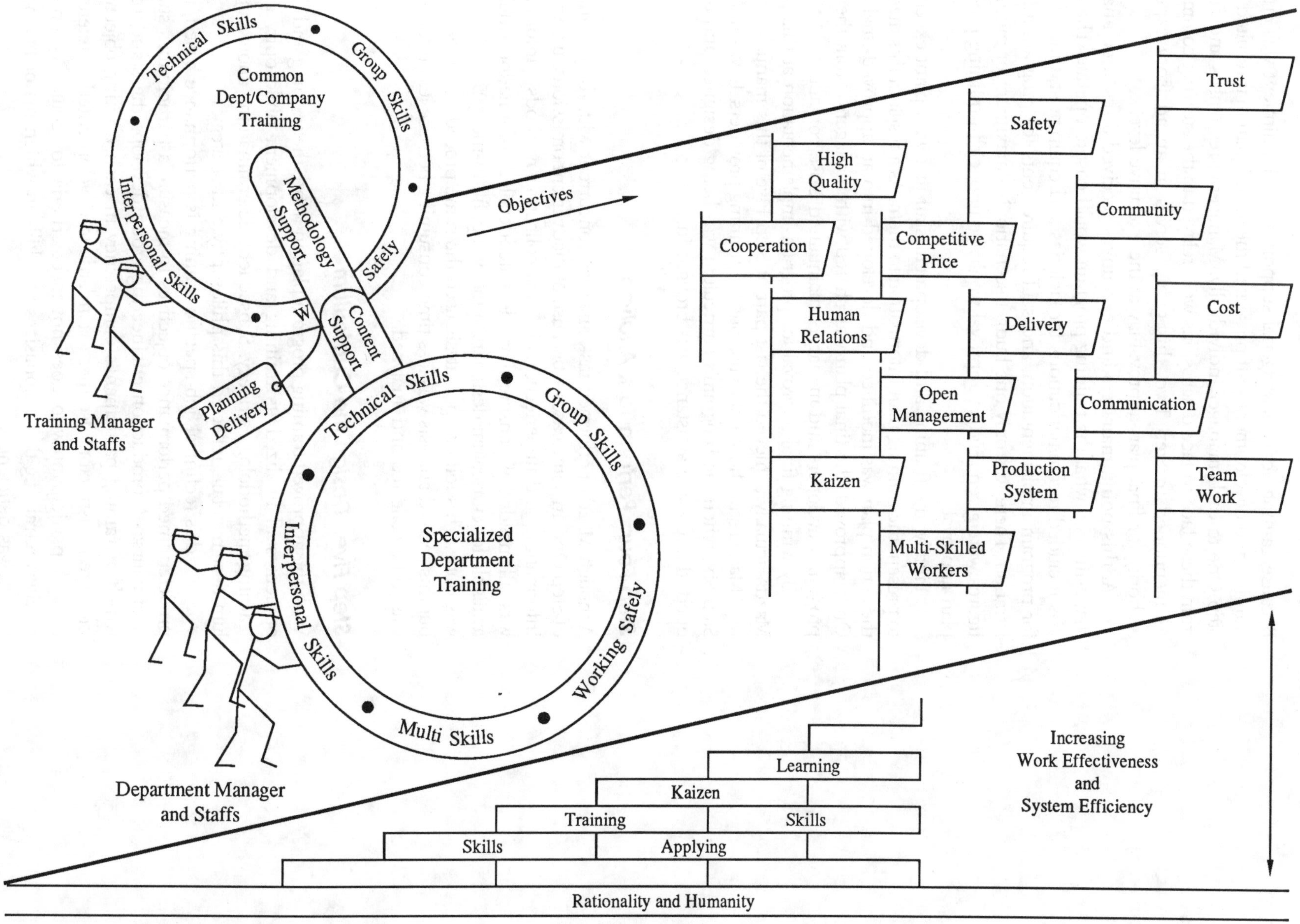

Source: Mazda Motor Manufacturing (USA) Corporation. Used with permission.

Step Three: Present Strategy and Action Plan

Because gaining active managerial support and commitment was crucial, training and development staff presented the action plan that resulted from Step One to each manager individually. Managerial responses and advice from these face-to-face discussions were relayed to the steering committee. As mentioned in Step Two, this group serves in an advisory capacity; authority for final plan approval lay at the executive level.

At this point, managers and executives received a resource analysis that estimated what the training program would cost to operate. The analysis included recommendations for facilities and equipment, time needed for program implementation, and staff requirements for program administration. There was only one budget scenario: No maximum or minimum figures were given. Budget approval would be implicit in training program plan approval.

Finally, the training and development staff met with plant executives to present the training plan information to them. As a result of this meeting, the action plan was modified and developed into an approved final plan. Once approved, the final plan was shared with managers. From then on, program developers and managers maintained close contact.

By winning final approval for program implementation at this point, Mazda actually achieved the last part of Step Five of this manual's model.

Mazda still chose not to use outside training providers. It was not until Step Six, when the program's curriculum was being designed and developed, that outside assistance was brought in.

Step Four: Perform Task Analysis

Although Mazda performed task analyses concurrent with the job analysis of Step One, in some cases—because of inadvertent omissions, unavailable information, and imperfections in data collection methods—information was still needed. To ensure that adequate, detailed information would be available for curriculum designers, a follow-up, fill-in-the-gaps task analysis was done. This follow-up analysis used the same procedures as Step One, but this second analysis was less time-consuming because less information was to be collected and analyzed.

Step Five: Design the Curriculum

With the approved training program plan in hand, the training and development staff finalized its training and development philosophy and a learning methodology strategy. Subsequent determinations about curriculum design details reflected this philosophy and strategy.

Mazda's technical, job-specific training is performance based, using predetermined performance objectives to measure a participant's success in a course. A production engineering group develops the standards by which a training participant's competency in each training objective is measured. Instructors use these standards to develop criterion-referenced tests. A participant who does not meet criteria for course completion receives retraining that emphasizes the skills in which his or her performance was deficient.

Soft skill training—in team building, interpersonal relations, problem solving, and so on—is not performance-based because it is difficult to isolate specific, measurable criteria for demonstration of these skills' mastery. Rather, participants are required to complete activities as a group to demonstrate the skills and techniques and to provide each other with support and less intimidating observation of actual skill practice. Objectives for this training are set by course instructors, and participants are observed; if they cannot meet soft skills criteria, they are individually counseled to determine an appropriate corrective action. These skills are taught through techniques such as interactive learning and behavior modeling, which allow participants to practice skill application. For example, in the team-building course, participants divide into groups to practice concepts the instructor has presented. To some extent, an instructor can assess participants' understanding by observing these practice sessions or by assessing participants' responses in discussions or on tests. But hard and fast measurement of these skills is not possible.

Mazda emphasizes training in a functional context; that is, training is expected to be relevant to participants' jobs. By definition, most technical skills training is directly related to an employee's current or upcoming job. In soft skills training, job-relevant or industry-relevant information and examples are incorporated into teaching material as much as possible. For example, in a team-building course, problems likely to be encountered in the auto-manufacturing industry are chosen when participants use role playing to practice application of team concepts. At times, however, direct job tie-in is not possible, and generic examples are then used.

Mazda uses a learn-apply-verify method in all its training programs. "Learn" refers to the procedures by which knowledge is transferred from the instructor to the learner, such as lectures or learning by doing. "Apply" refers to trainees' ability to use a skill in a normal job situation. "Verify" refers to the process by which a trainer, coach, or someone else with expertise certifies that a trainee has learned skills introduced in training and is able to apply them. This three-part method reflects the philosophical intent for all training although, in reality, formal verification does not always take place.

At first, Mazda kept track of employees' training through a manual record-keeping system. The training department currently uses computerized record keeping. With the new system, various kinds of information can be combined and printed. For example, the employees who have completed training in a specific skill can be listed, or the training each employee has had can be identified. The computerized system will be easier to update, giving trainers quick and easy access to current information.

The start-up training budget was $43 million, which included $19 million in state funds that came from the Governor's Office for Job Training and from the General Purpose General Fund appropriated for the Michigan Training Fund and the Michigan Business and Industrial Training Fund. Early resource requirements analysis and approval of a final training plan precluded the need for developing a specific operational budget at this point. Management was firmly committed to the program.

Step Six: Develop the Curriculum

Training curriculum design and development, which Mazda did concurrently, took approximately a year. In the development stage, Mazda began to consider and evaluate outside training providers. Up to this point, Mazda was confident that in-house expertise was sufficient for performing necessary training functions. However, for curriculum development, Mazda wanted the best expertise available, whether from in-house or outside. Mazda conducts thorough searches for expert outside providers who share its philosophy of training and development. Mazda expects excellent, up-to-date course content and instructional design as they relate both to technical training and to the workplace basics skills, so it looks both inside and outside of its ranks for the most cost-effective combination of course developers. Many times, the work of a technical expert is coupled with that of an instructional design expert.

Mazda joins forces with a variety of training providers, primarily independent consultants. A request-for-proposals system is used to determine which qualified providers are available in the workplace basics areas and can meet Mazda's needs best. Everyone who is hired as a consultant has submitted a proposal.

To help determine which provider is best able to provide what Mazda wants, the training and development department also uses a formal evaluation sheet. The sheet lists criteria such as price, content flexibility, follow-up, ability to run evaluation pilot programs, and so on. Each criterion is weighted and may be awarded from one to ten points. The points are multiplied by the weight given the criterion, then points for all criteria are totaled. The provider with the most points comes closest to matching Mazda's preferred criteria. For example, the weight for the price a provider will charge for the program is twenty, so the top score of ten results in a total of 200 points. However, if there is a low value, such as a weight of one for geographic proximity, the criterion score would result in a total of ten points.

A variety of instructional techniques are used in Mazda's training programs. The traditional classroom lecture is common, but other techniques (such as interactive instruction, including role playing, behavior modeling, and videotaping) are also used extensively. Mazda plans to add computer-based training and self-paced learning centers to its curriculum.

Mazda has a central training center in a revamped building that came with the Michigan site, and operational units have dedicated training areas at each manufacturing location.

Step Seven: Implement the Program

Because Mazda had decided that the first phase of training would be required for all new hires, in-house marketing to ensure participant attendance was not necessary—although it was important to advertise when and where training would be. Recently, a course catalogue was compiled for the second phase of training—a continuation of training for employees already on board. For this second phase, vigorous in-house marketing will encourage employees to attend voluntary courses.

For phase one, training delivery staff were chosen and began work in time to be involved in curriculum design as well as delivery. Mazda has four in-house instructors, augmented by an outside staff of eighteen instructors. The in-house staffers were chosen for their professional training and instructional expertise.

More than 300 in-house employees also serve as part-time trainers in technical and workplace basics skills. Employees from the team leader on up can serve in trainer positions, but first they must complete a train-the-trainer course that emphasizes training processes and instructional technology. These content experts do stand-up training, but before they teach alone, they learn teaching techniques through team teaching with a professional trainer. Content-expert trainers are taken away from their usual jobs just long enough to conduct particular courses (which may last from a few hours to a few days).

Outside trainers usually come from a training and education background. They are chosen based on their work experience with the particular skill they will be teaching, their presentation skills, and their understanding of how people work in groups. These trainers must participate in a train-the-trainer course with an emphasis opposite that of the course for in-house content-expert trainers: For outside trainers, the focus is on content rather than on how to train.

Mazda offers employee guidance. Supervisors help each employee develop a training plan and also provide on-the-job coaching. Mazda also has a formal employee assistance program that has two representatives, one union-appointed and one from the company. This program is aimed at helping employees with any type of problem at work or outside the company.

Mazda does not use learning contracts to keep track of employee training except in very unusual circumstances. But the employee development plan that employees and their supervisors develop together is similar to a learning contract. Its development process becomes an inherent part of the relationship between an employee and a supervisor. The plan's three sections cover what skills the employee needs to develop for the future, what skills the employee needs for the present job, and what job and personal growth skills a person needs to be a multiskilled employee. Because Mazda's training is decentralized, it is difficult to ensure that supervisors and employees develop complete plans, but most supervisors do use them.

Mazda conducted a pilot program for phase one training. This allowed training and development staff to identify logistical problems such as redundant content, incorrect information, or program segments that ran too long or short. In the pilot running, participants saw that the program was flexible, and they gave the program favorable word-of-mouth publicity among their co-workers. The training and development staff found the pilot test so useful that now they will not launch a training program without one.

Step Eight: Evaluate the Program

Mazda is developing a long-term, formal evaluation process to assess the organizational impact of its training programs. The pilot program was followed by evaluations after three and nine months to measure the effect of the training on employees' job performance. Mazda now requires that training presenters give participants reaction sheets to complete after training. In the train-the-trainer courses, prospective instructors are audited through classroom observation by professional trainers and through participant interviews.

As noted earlier, technical training's organizational impact is fairly easy to measure. However, this is not true of the softer skills or cultural growth, and Mazda wants to look at them more closely. Basically, the new evaluation process will monitor a group of new hires six and nine months after their training to determine how they are using new skills and how that benefits the company. Training department staff will also consult each participant's manager or supervisor to track post-training progress.

Development and preparation of phase one training took six months. Phase one implementation, including delivery to more than 3,000 employees, took a year and a half. As of May 1988, phase two training delivery was under way, and Mazda expected to complete this phase in two years (Ken Kumiega, telephone interviews, May 1988).

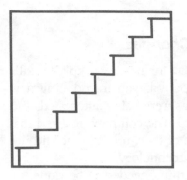

Resource B:
An Established Plant View:
Case Study from Harrison Radiator
(The Applied Approach)

The following case study of the Harrison Radiator Division of General Motors is a scenario for using the applied approach that is probably common to many companies in the United States. The Harrison Radiator facility in Lockport, N.Y., where this program was initiated, has been operating since 1908 and has had an active union presence for a significant part of that period. This contrasts sharply with the Mazda case study, which documents the establishment of a new plant that initially did not have a union presence. Although the two cases deal with organizations at different stages of maturity and with different operating philosophies, both demonstrate successful use of this book's methodology to implement positive and aggressive workplace basics programs.

Harrison Radiator is a $2 billion company that manufactures automobile climate control and engine-cooling components. There are four Harrison Radiator locations in the United States and three abroad. The Lockport facility, which is the site of this training program, houses five plants and an administrative and engineering building and employs 6,800 workers. This facility has been in operation since 1908, and the current buildings were built from 1947 through 1964.

Harrison Radiator's Lockport facility has operated its basic workplace skills program, the Skills Enhancement Lab, since April 1988. The lab offers courses in math (basic and advanced, through trigonometry), reading, writing, English as a Second Language, computer literacy (through Lotus 1-2-3), and communications (five-step problem solving, public speaking, group and personal dynamics, and socio-technical systems). Employees may take courses to work toward a GED or entrance into a college program, or to brush up on skills needed for their jobs. The program is available from 12:30 P.M. to 5:30 P.M. four days a week, Monday through Thursday. These hours overlap both shifts, enabling all workers who want or need attention to participate.

The Skills Enhancement Lab is closely linked to the company's technical training program. Employees who are unable to handle company-specific technical training because of basic workplace skills deficiencies are referred to the lab for "upgrade training."

Over 1,000 employees have participated in the Skills Enhancement Lab programs. Long waiting lists and high demand indicate that the number of participants will steadily increase.

Step One: Identify Job Problems or Changes

Harrison Radiator began to identify the need for basic workplace skills upgrading as early as 1980, when the company began introducing new technology into the workplace. Many positions were being automated, and the assembly line was becoming computerized. The company realized that the changes were causing problems for some of the workers, who did not have the skills needed to deal with the new technology.

There were several indicators that something needed to be done:

- Productivity was low,

- Sales were down,

- Quality was poor, and

- Warranty costs were high.

In sum, Harrison Radiator's competitive position was deteriorating. At one point in the early 1980s, the company laid off 2,300 people, and the future looked bleak, with little hope of improvement. If the company wanted to survive, it realized it would have to change.

One change that Harrison Radiator began to make in the early 1980s was in its institutional culture. The company wanted a more democratic workplace and began to implement a more participative management approach. This change required that employees up and down the line improve their communication skills in addition to more advanced technical skills.

The company believed that training could alleviate most of its problems, make employees more productive, allow them to claim ownership in their jobs, and improve overall quality.

Prior to the present Skills Enhancement Lab, Harrison Radiator had operated a limited GED program for three years, during which only seventy-five employees had taken advantage of the program. The program had difficulty in succeeding for a number of reasons: Advertising for the program was poor, and many employees were not aware that it existed; the instruction was ineffective because it was not geared to the needs of the workplace; and employees felt that, instead of providing support and encouragement, the instructors made them feel inadequate. As a result, employees who were interested in the course frequently showed up for only one class and then dropped out. The quality of work life coordinator, who was responsible for the GED program, requested in the summer of 1987 that the program be suspended so that a needs assessment could be done.

That needs assessment was in the form of a survey of 10 percent of the employee population at Harrison Radiator. It was believed that this random sample represented an accurate cross-section of the groups of employees in the Lockport facility.

From the survey interviews, Harrison Radiator learned some interesting facts. For one thing, its work force was both more educated and older than the national average; it was assumed that this was due in large part to the fact that the company had not hired new employees since 1977 (a ten-year period). The company also learned that although most of its employees had high school diplomas, they had received them so long ago that their skills needed to be refreshed.

Step Two: Build Management and Union Support

Building management support for the basic skills program was not a difficult task at Harrison Radiator. Because the support for organizational change at the company came from the top, there was already strong support for developing a basic skills program. In the auto parts industry, resistance by top management to change has been common, but Harrison Radiator's top management holds the philosophy that it is essential to retrain employees in order to keep pace with technological change and maintain market share.

Although there was no resistance from top management to implementing a basic skills program, line and midlevel managers did display some resistance. Managers were reluctant to release employees from work to attend training programs, fearing productivity in their work areas might suffer. Realizing that support for training cannot be mandated from the top, the company has worked to build lower-level management support through the implementation of a reward system for managers that encourages them to develop their employees. Twenty-five percent of each manager's regular performance appraisal addresses training, development, and productivity of subordinates; managers, therefore, know they are held accountable. As a result, managers have become active in encouraging their workers to participate in training.

Harrison Radiator also courted union support for the basic skills program. This was not difficult to get because the company's relationship with the union has historically been a very cooperative one. Harrison Radiator is served by United Auto Workers (UAW) Local 686, Unit One. The 1973 labor-management agreement between Harrison Radiator and the UAW initiated a discussion on training that opened the door to further discussions in 1980 about implementing a basic skills program.

As Harrison Radiator moved toward implementing the basic skills training program, it encouraged the union to be actively involved. Local 686 tends to be conservative, but it is the perception of management at Harrison Radiator that the company has a better relationship with its union than most other companies. The union and the company have a lot in common, and their differences provide a good system of checks and balances. Harrison Radiator's philosophy is that there are two ways to look at the union—as a hindrance or as a partner. Harrison Radiator has chosen to make the union a partner. Therefore, the union agreed to help with the basic skills program. Currently, the union and the company share equally in all decisions involving training, including developing curriculum and hiring instructors. In fact, the union is moving away from its traditional reactive approach to change and is moving toward a proactive approach.

This partnership between management and the union is clearly evident in the structures in place at Harrison Radiator that promote institutional support for the basic skills program. One structure for building institutional support is the union's Joint Action Committee. This committee is the umbrella group that oversees all aspects of work life at the Lockport facility and is one of the most important committees in place at Harrison Radiator. The group, which meets once a week, is crucial for building training program support as well as overseeing other activities in the plant.

The members of this committee include representatives from both management and labor: three plant managers, three personnel directors, the president of the union local, the chair of the bargaining committee and six committeemen at large, the top person in the engineering department, and an industrial relations representative and one of his or her support staff. The actual membership of the committee fluctuates but is usually around fifteen people. Various subcommittees concentrate on technical training, quality of work life, customer satisfaction, and similar activities.

In addition to this large committee, each plant at Harrison Radiator also has a separate advisory committee that meets every other week to address external issues that affect work in the plant. These groups identify training needs and work to implement training programs. The composition of these committees varies among the plants depending on the location they serve; at one plant the committee is composed of ten hourly and six salaried employees, at another it is two hourly and four salaried employees.

Because technical training activities are closely linked to the basic skills program, the technical training Needs Analysis Task Force is another important committee. Each trade group has its own such task force, and there is a plant-wide committee composed of task force members selected from each trade group to plan the plant-wide technical training programs.

Step Three: Present Strategy and Action Plan

Harrison Radiator used the results of the employee survey to formally inform managers of the educational needs of their work force. The employee survey, together with a plan of action and a budget proposal, was presented to a regular meeting of the Joint Action Committee in January 1988, one year after the group had given the quality of work life coordinator the OK to suspend the ineffective GED program and study the training needs of the Harrison Radiator work force. The coordinator, who had administered the survey, told the committee what additional basic skills training employees at Harrison Radiator needed. The survey was well received, and the climate was right to introduce a basic skills program, so the committee gave the go-ahead to implement the program.

Two in-house employees were selected to staff the program. The quality of work life coordinator was designated co-director of the program, and the chairwoman of the union's Education Committee, who was a production employee at the Lockport plant, was brought off the floor to be the other co-director. She had extensive contacts with the education community, which was useful in developing necessary linkage with those institutions.

Step Four: Perform Task Analyses

Harrison Radiator conducts informal task analyses on a regular basis, usually when new equipment is brought into the plant. However, the first formal and extensive task analysis was done in the summer of 1988 using three outside certified teachers as investigators. The first job family the investigators analyzed was the model-maker group, using a task analysis designed and developed by the Buick-Olds-Cadillac (BOC) Group of

General Motors Corporation. The BOC task analysis was also used to conduct a subsequent task analysis for the inspector-plate-layout group in the fall of 1988. Although the BOC task analyses were successful, Harrison Radiator plans to experiment with the effectiveness of the DACUM task analysis when conducting its third formal task analysis, which will be for the machinists tool-room/boring-mill group.

Before conducting the formal task analyses, Harrison Radiator already had an indication of the jobs and job tasks in which employees were deficient from supervisor reports saying that employees could not handle the new technology being introduced. The training provided by Harrison Radiator is geared toward both job families and job tasks, depending on the needs of the work unit or the individual requesting training.

Step Five: Design the Curriculum

Most of Harrison Radiator's training programs are performance based, including courses on statistical process control and computer literacy. The company emphasizes performance-based instruction so that participants learn functional skills that will directly relate to their job requirements. The company believes that job-related instruction is the most useful and contributes significantly to the overall success of a course; all of their instructors are trained in the functional context methodology.

In order to ensure that all course materials provide a functional context for learning, Harrison Radiator has designed the course textbooks or supplements to textbooks so that they provide the trainees with applications of the skills as they relate specifically to jobs at Harrison Radiator. Instructors visit the work areas to talk with employees and find out what the problems are that necessitate training in order to incorporate real examples into the course curriculum. After a course, the company wants trainees to be able to apply what they have learned in the classroom to the problems they encounter on their jobs.

Criterion-referenced tests are used in almost all of the courses to measure student progress. The one exception is lecture courses, where such tests have not yet been implemented. The criterion-referenced tests were developed both externally and internally. A local college aided Harrison Radiator in developing the criterion-referenced tests for the courses in the basic skills program. The course developers who prepared the program for Harrison Radiator also developed the criterion-referenced tests for the technical training course.

Harrison Radiator received a grant from the state of New York to fund its basic skills program. In 1988, $2 million was available to employers in the state of New York through the Workplace Literacy Special Grants Fund authorized by the New York legislature. Approximately seventeen projects were funded; Harrison Radiator was one of them. The funds came from the state's Education Department and were set aside to enhance the competitive position of companies in New York.

Harrison Radiator received $102,000 from the state for the period from April through August of 1988. The company received the same amount for the period from September 1988 to June 1989, as well as an additional $31,000 left over from the first grant. These funds are supplemented by

$100,000 from the company's budget, which covered costs associated with the initial employee survey, program development, mailings, supplies, and the salary of one of the co-directors of the program. Harrison Radiator was assured of receiving a state grant at least through August 1989. After that, the company planned to continue the program using company funds if necessary, so strong is its commitment to the Skills Enhancement Lab.

Harrison Radiator keeps track of participant progress in the program both on computer and manually. These systems make it possible to determine who was in training, what training they were in, when they participated, what they were doing, and how well they performed. Each participant also keeps a personal folder of his or her own progress.

Step Six: Develop the Curriculum

Some of the curricula used for the basic skills programs were developed by Harrison Radiator, some were developed by the outside teaching staff using Harrison Radiator materials, and some were obtained from other sources such as vendors and consultants and then customized to meet the needs of the company. Material is continually updated and customized for the Skills Enhancement Lab program.

Harrison Radiator uses many teaching methodologies for its classes: hands-on, lecture (although it tries to limit this), stand-up, computer-based, and self-paced. None of the classrooms have desks; instead, they all have tables so people can work together in teams.

Although the technical training program is conducted primarily in-house at an on-site technical training center, the basic skills program is conducted by Harrison Radiator staff at the Niagara County Community College's Industrial Training Complex. The off-site location is necessary due to a lack of space for additional courses at the technical training center. At this time, Harrison Radiator has no plans to build a facility on-site for the basic skills program, in part because employees seem to like the idea that they are taking college preparatory classes at the local community college.

Step Seven: Implement the Program

Participation in Harrison Radiator's basic skills program is voluntary, although employees are frequently encouraged by their managers to attend. Employees are frequently motivated to attend courses because they know that promotions and pay increases can be jeopardized by skill deficiencies. Employees who might choose not to attend could be reassigned or suffer a wage cut (it is unlikely they would be laid off). So far, the program has been very positively received, and most employees are eager to receive the additional training. Employees pay the course fees, but Harrison Radiator pays all other related program costs (books, transportation, and the like).

The basic skills program is targeted to the entire employee population, although most of the participants are hourly workers. About 5 percent are salaried, and most of those participate in the computer courses such as Lotus 1-2-3.

The basic skills program was marketed to employees by sending a letter to their homes inviting them to attend a general information session about the program. Posters were placed on the union and company bulletin boards, announcements were made on an electronic sign in the cafeteria, and advertisements were placed in several employee publications. Once the program began, positive comments from participants became an important and effective advertising tool.

In February and March of 1988, after approval was given by the Joint Action Committee to implement the program, the program coordinators hired four professional, certified teachers and two instructors who had previously taught math courses for the technical training program. The math instructors are skilled trade workers who have been pulled off the line to teach courses to their peers. They teach after hours while continuing their regular duties at the plant.

A counselor was also hired; she has a doctorate in education and counseling. The teachers and the counselor were trained before the program began and continue to receive training as new instructional technology is introduced and new training needs are identified.

Harrison Radiator does not have formal learning contracts, although when employees sign up for the program, they schedule a meeting with the counselor to discuss their deficiencies and the training they will need. The employees may schedule meetings with the counselor as often as they like during the semester; if she doesn't hear from them, she initiates a midsemester meeting. Employees also meet with the counselor at the end of the semester. Employees may also discuss their educational goals with their supervisors.

Harrison Radiator did not run a pilot course for the basic skills program. However, it had looked extensively at what other organizations were doing as well as at its own previous efforts, and it knew what did not work. The company built upon its previous experiences to develop and implement the basic skills program.

Step Eight: Evaluate the Program

Harrison Radiator monitors and evaluates the basic skills program only informally. After each section of a course, participants fill out a ten- to twelve-question survey. The co-directors of the program visit the classrooms regularly, at least once a week, to meet and talk with teachers and administrators.

As part of the state grant used to fund the program, the New York Department of Education wanted to conduct a study of Harrison Radiator to determine the effectiveness of the program. The University of Buffalo was contracted to do the study and received a portion of Harrison Radiator's grant. However, there were some problems with the administration of the study and the results were not available as of this writing.

The Center for Industrial Effectiveness is also working with Harrison Radiator to look at the effectiveness of the entire operation at Harrison Radiator; training programs, including the basic skills program, will be one of the areas under investigation.

The perception both inside and outside the company is that Harrison Radiator's basic skills program is excellent; the company has been contacted by many other employers interested in implementing a similar program.

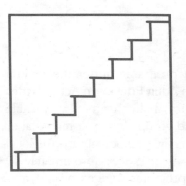

Resource C:
The Providers:
Where to Get Help for
Workplace Basics Training

Research indicates that as a general rule most providers of training services are identified through informal networking among training personnel within specific industries. Employers frequently choose providers based on referrals from peers and information passed on through professional associations or trade shows. Often when the providers are consultants, they have come from the ranks of former employees or individuals whom trainers have come to know over the years. Usually these providers are local.

There are several services available to aid employers in locating training consultants. One such service is TRAINET, available to members of the American Society for Training and Development. This computer data base provides information on many available training services. Two other sources that list training consultants by subject area are the *Consultants and Consulting Organizations Directory* and the *Training and Development Organizations Directory,* both published by Gale Research. Some contacts for other types of providers are listed at the end of each relevant section below.

Training providers, public and private, are constantly marketing their products and services. Employers are bombarded daily with phone calls and mail encouraging them to use a particular service. Employers might follow up immediately on these promotions to find out more about a specific program, but usually a call for service is not initiated until after an internal need has surfaced.

The individual in the employer institution who actually makes contact with a provider varies from company to company. If the training is done by a central training department, the contact person will usually be located in that department. If a functional unit is responsible for the training, the person making the contact will usually be from that unit. Sometimes the training department assists the functional unit in the selection process.

Within the provider groups themselves, it is more difficult to pinpoint who the contact person is since it varies from organization to organization. For adult education offered through the secondary schools, a good initial contact is the local superintendent of schools, who can make an appropriate referral; for community colleges, it is the director of business, industry, and government programs or the director of continuing education; for the military, the commander of the local military installation is a good place to start; for Job Training Partnership Act training, call the Private Industry Council number listed in the local telephone directory and talk with the director.

Local School Districts

Local school districts offer adult education programs under the federal Adult Education Act (Public Law 91-230). The Adult Education Act provides grants to state educational agencies that, in turn, make this money available to local educational institutions, agencies, and groups for adult remedial or basic skills programs. The state maintains oversight responsibility; the local agency develops and operates the programs. As of 1986, approximately 40 percent of those enrolled in adult education programs were employed, and 44 percent were unemployed but looking for work.

Using the guidelines set forth in the Adult Education Act, these programs enable adults to:

- Acquire basic skills necessary to function in society,

- Complete secondary school education if desired, and

- Become more employable, productive, and responsive citizens through training and education.

Adult education programs tend to focus heavily on the traditional skills of reading, writing, and arithmetic, with little or no emphasis on the other basic skills important to employers such as teamwork and problem solving. The three most common programs funded under the Adult Education Act are:

- Adult Basic Education (ABE)—programs to teach basic reading, writing, and arithmetic;

- English as a Second Language (ESL)—programs for immigrants and others for whom English is not the primary spoken or written language; and

- General Equivalency Diploma (GED)—programs to enable individuals to pass tests that measure individual knowledge of information taught in high schools, such as history, English, and mathematics.

There are currently more than 14,000 local ABE programs operating in all fifty states and seven U.S. territories. More than 60 percent of the participants attend classes in adult learning centers and schools, community colleges, vocational schools, churches, libraries, and correctional facilities. Slightly over 30 percent attend sessions in elementary and secondary schools.

About three million people enroll in ABE programs each year. All adults sixteen years of age and older with less than a high school education are eligible to participate in adult education programs. Out-of-school youths aged sixteen to twenty-four account for 40 percent of the program participants. Persons twenty-five to forty-four account for another 40 percent, while ages forty-four and over account for the balance. The overall enrollment is nearly equally divided between men and women.

Historically, business involvement with ABE programs have been limited to employers publicizing opportunities for employees to enroll and allowing participation to be considered a reimbursable expense under a company's tuition assistance program. Until recently, few ABE programs have incorporated job-related materials or vocabulary. One of the few exceptions, and a model for other ABE programs, is the Albertville, Ala., ABE program.

As many as twenty companies per year from the Albertville area work with the Alabama State Department of Education to develop and present basic curriculum material leading to a GED. To the extent possible, job-specific materials are utilized that relate to each of the companies' specific needs. Some of the companies recently involved in this three-year pilot program (which began in 1986) include Kendall Mills, Arrow Shirt Factory, Heil Company, Earthgrain Bakery, two local steel plants, and a hosiery factory. The companies pay for the teachers' salaries, provide the teachers with company-specific materials, and make available on-site training facilities. Employees attend classes for two or three hours once a week between shifts or as a part of a work release arrangement. The companies pay the cost of GED testing and convene a special banquet to recognize those employees who are certified; they also pay bonuses to those who pass. The statistics from a recent class of fifty-five show that thirty-five took GED testing and all passed. Overall, 75 percent of those who take the classes complete the training.

The motivation for involvement of the companies is a need to improve worker retention and morale; to improve the companies' competitive edge in the labor market; to increase employee services; and to improve the quality of training and employee completion rates.

Contacts for adult education programs include the following:

Division of Adult Education
U.S. Department of Education
Reporters Building, Room 522
400 Maryland Avenue SW
Washington, D.C. 20202
(202) 732-2959

Northeast Alabama Adult Education Program
P.O. Box 977
DeKalb Board of Education
Ft. Payne, Ala. 35467
(205) 845-0465

American Association for Adult and Continuing Education
1201 16th Street, Suite 301
Washington, D.C. 20036
(202) 822-7866

Community and Junior Colleges

A growing number of community and junior colleges now offer employer-specific customized training both in traditional institutional settings and at the employers' work sites. However, the majority of training currently being provided by community colleges for businesses is vocationally or technically oriented with only a small (but growing) percentage geared toward basic workplace skills. The potential for community college participation in this type of training is enormous.

There are currently over 1,200 community colleges in the United States and territories, and the majority are located within thirty minutes of most individuals. These colleges maintain close ties with the communities they serve and are considered to be particularly responsive to business, industry, and community needs.

Recently, the American Association of Community and Junior Colleges published a report entitled *Building Communities: A Vision for a New Century* (1988) that is essentially a blueprint for increasing involvement with local businesses. Furthermore, a survey conducted by the association shows that 40 percent of all community colleges already have campus-based business-industry-labor councils and that two-thirds have on-campus business-industry coordinators. The councils coordinate activity between the academic and business sectors in order to facilitate the development of customized training for businesses. The survey estimates that 75 percent of all community colleges provide some customized training for private-sector employers.

Community and junior colleges are also the second-largest providers of ABE programs (after local school districts). According to many educators, basic skill instruction to out-of-school populations should and will shift from school districts to community colleges even though at the present time ABE is considered to be under the purview of secondary rather than post-secondary education. Advocates of the move argue that community colleges can better utilize business-related information in curriculum design—a critical element in the effectiveness of basic skills programs. In five states (Iowa, North Carolina, Oregon, Wisconsin, and Washington), community colleges constitute the major or exclusive system for delivering publicly funded basic skills training to out-of-school adults. Several other states (Alaska, California, Florida, Idaho, Kansas, Nebraska, Nevada, New Mexico, Texas, and Wyoming) give community colleges a significant role in delivering ABE instruction. Community colleges in states not providing adult basic skills training frequently have state laws prohibiting such involvement.

In light of today's educational trends, more community colleges are already focusing on adult educational services in order to stem the tide of declining enrollments. One outstanding example of a community college that has advanced well beyond offering the traditional academic and vocational course load is Dundalk Community College in Maryland.

Dundalk Community College has been at the forefront of employer-oriented training for the last ten years. The school maintains a pool of trainers in addition to existing faculty, and this has allowed local employers to eliminate or cut back on their internal training departments in some instances. Dundalk actively markets training programs and supplies trainers with a steady workload, thus reducing their trainer costs.

Dundalk also supplies technical and organizational development consulting services to businesses within its catchment area. For example, Dundalk worked with General Motors (GM) and the United Auto Workers (UAW) to develop a literacy program that prepared GM employees to enter a retraining program. Due to changing technology and marketing trends, GM and its union determined that the only way to avoid a plant shutdown in the Maryland operation was to retrain workers for newer equipment. GM and the union analyzed worker needs and decided that while many workers had good work habits and met quality standards, their reading skills were insufficient for retraining.

The UAW has a national reputation for quality training for its members. However, in this instance, the level of creativity shown is a tribute to the synergy that can emerge when business, labor, and education unite in a cause. Participants enrolled in a six-week, full-time basic skills training program. They were paid to go to school with union health and welfare funds. Dundalk instructors were paid by GM and the union. In order for the plant to continue operations, shifts were rescheduled and laid-off workers recalled so that the assembly line continued operations. The average student improved his or her reading comprehension by several grade levels, and all the students viewed the program as a positive experience. The program appears to be a winner for everyone involved: The company retained quality workers, the workers gained improved skills, the union provided a positive service, and Dundalk delivered that service to everyone's satisfaction.

Contacts for community college programs include the following:

American Association of Community and Junior Colleges
One Dupont Circle NW
Washington, D.C. 20036
(202) 293-7050

Dundalk Community College
Director of Retraining and Community Development
7200 Sollers Point Road
Baltimore, Md. 21222
(301) 285-2967

Private Industry Councils

The establishment of private industry councils (PICs) is a guiding principle of the federal Job Training Partnership Act (Public Law 97-300), the nation's largest federally funded civilian job-training program, which serves only unemployed individuals who meet specific eligibility requirements. The act requires that PICs be established within each service delivery area and that 51 percent of the membership and the chairman be selected from among private-sector representatives. Over 11,000 business representatives currently serve on the councils nationwide.

The administration of program funds on the local level is through a joint partnership agreement between local elected officials and the PICs. This is a change from prior legislation, by which training was provided under the direction of local elected officials alone. The most recent legislation, passed in 1982 and implemented in 1983, reflects the conviction that local employers are the best judges of what kind of training is needed within a local community. The unemployed populations specifically identified to be served under the act include the disadvantaged (adult and youth, including special summer youth programs); dislocated workers; Native Americans; migrant and seasonal farm workers; Job Corps–eligible youth; veterans; and older workers.

The act assigns to the local PICs specific responsibilities for providing policy guidance and exercising oversight of local job-training activities. The major types of training conducted under the act fall into the following categories:

- Classroom training, which consists of basic education, occupational skills training, or a combination of the two.

- On-the-job training, which involves skill training in a specific occupation in an actual work setting with a commitment beforehand that the employer enjoying the benefits of the act's reimbursement provisions will hire the trainee for full-time employment upon successful completion of training. Employers are reimbursed for one-half of a trainee's wages for a period of up to six months.

- Job search assistance, which helps recipients learn how to locate, apply for, and obtain employment.

- Work experience, which is short-term or part-time subsidized work designed to assist eligible participants in entering or reentering the labor force or enhancing their employability.

All of these types of training can be packaged in many different ways. Frequently the act's funds are used to leverage funds from other federal, state, and private sources for complementary specialized services that make the difference in allowing both employers and trainees to participate in a program.

One of the most effective ways for employers to take advantage of federal job-training funds is through customized training in which PICs consider training program proposals from individual employers or groups of employers who agree to hire a minimum number of unemployed individuals upon successful completion of a designated training program. This process tailors each program to the unique training requirements and employment needs of a particular firm or industry where projected numbers and types of new job openings can be clearly determined and identified. Many of the basic workplace skills are integrated into the vocational training that is provided under this customized training concept. One such customized training program funded by the San Diego, Calif., PIC includes in its training vocationally related reading, writing, and computation skills.

The San Diego area has been a leader in the development of plastics composites and their utilization in both commercial and industry applications. There are over 100 companies in San Diego involved in plastics development, manufacture, and repair, with an overall employment of 2,600 and an annual estimated growth rate of approximately 10 percent. The projection in 1986 was for a manpower requirement two to three times their on-board staffing level. There was also a critical labor shortage of qualified personnel, particularly at the entry level, where no training programs were available. The proposed customized training program was to train and place unemployed participants in permanent, unsubsidized employment as entry level plastics fabricators at an appropriate starting wage with good opportunities for upward mobility.

The program is run by a local third-party private training organization, Comprehensive Training Systems, which has a successful track record in operating this type of training program. The initial start-up of the plastics fabrication training program was accomplished through the establishment of an industry advisory board composed of plastics fabrication employers. The board designed the curriculum, established equipment needs and program standards, and donated materials, supplies, and equipment. It meets on a quarterly basis to ensure program quality and success. Other costs such as recruitment, supportive services, staffing, program management, and related services are paid for through federal funds.

The course is eight weeks long with a total of 280 hours of training. There are two sections: The first covers basic math and job-related basic geometry and precision measuring; the second covers shop training, including safety, blueprint reading and drawing, applications, and quality assurance. Training is industry simulated using General Dynamics attendance policies. (General Dynamics is a major employer of program completers.)

In its first year of operation, the program was funded to place 130 low-income participants in employment at an average wage of $5.60 per hour. Actual placement was 122 at an average wage of $6.17 per hour. In its second year of operation the program placed 113 of 120 participants at an average wage of $6.83 per hour.

Contacts for federally funded job-training programs include:

National Association of Private Industry Councils
201 New York Avenue NW
Washington, D.C. 20005
(202) 289-2950

Comprehensive Training Systems
663 Palomar Street, Suite E
Chula Vista, Calif. 92011
(619) 426-2010

National Job Training Partnership
1620 Eye Street NW
Washington, D.C. 20006
(202) 887-6120

Four-Year Colleges and Universities

Four-year colleges and universities offer customized training to the business community and often become involved in specific projects such as learning laboratories to test adult learning or skills training theories. Further, specific departments or divisions within a school may develop expertise that can be tapped by business. For example, Boston University's Sargeant School of Physical Education has been involved in designing programs to improve the physical stamina and condition of employees in everything from fire departments to the construction industry.

In addition, many schools encourage and actively solicit business input into curriculum design and delivery. Many colleges have established divisions called management development institutes or metropolitan colleges that offer specific seminars and evening courses for students. Management development courses are frequently open to nonsupervisory as well as management and supervisory employees. Bryant College in Rhode Island runs a seminar program that covers a variety of topics including stress management, teamwork, effective oral communication, negotiating, and coping with difficult people. About 50 percent of the attendees are nonsupervisory staff. Bentley College in Massachusetts has also established a reputation as a business-oriented and creative institution. Bentley regularly offers seminars in areas of emerging interest to business including time management, controlling benefit costs, and leadership. The programs are run by the continuing education department and are often taught by leaders in business. The school estimates that 50–60 percent of enrollees are nonsupervisory staff.

Many individual professors at colleges regularly consult with companies on particular training efforts. Often this consulting is sponsored by the college. Increasingly, colleges are offering customized training to particular firms provided the company can guarantee a particular class size. Rutgers University in New Jersey has recently contracted with the Communication Workers of America and Bell Laboratories to provide ESL training and reading improvement for workers. Both the company and the union noticed that entry-level positions were increasingly attracting immigrants who often had a limited ability to understand or speak English. In establishing the program with Rutgers, the union and the employer wanted to improve attention and performance rates for these workers. Rutgers set up a self-paced, individualized reading improvement program available to all employees. The ESL program is open to employees for whom English is not the native language.

Contacts for programs at four-year institutions include:

Director of Office on Educational Credit and Credentials
American Council on Education
One Dupont Circle NW
Washington, D.C. 20036
(202) 833-4770

Program in American Language Studies
Rutgers University
3 Bartlett Street
New Brunswick, N.J. 08903
(201) 932-7422

Volunteer Literacy Organizations

Volunteer literacy organizations have begun to play a major role in upgrading the basic skills of the American work force. These organizations focus on one-on-one tutoring for adults who read and write below the fifth-grade level. Tutors are trained by state or national staff. In addition to one-on-one tutoring, these groups often sponsor library reading fairs and are beginning to offer on- and off-site customized literacy training to local businesses.

Recently, voluntary literacy agencies began working with businesses to reduce the stigma attached to illiteracy by asking employers to publicize and support literacy programs. Employees interested in learning to read are listed with local volunteer literacy affiliates and notified about enrollment without the intervention of a supervisor.

Two of the major national organizations addressing adult literacy in the workplace are the Literacy Volunteers of America (LVA) and Laubach Literacy Action (LLA). Both organizations are, coincidentally, headquartered in Syracuse, N.Y. In both organizations, state-level affiliates organize and oversee local chapter operations, while the local chapters recruit the tutors and deliver services.

LVA operates about 340 tutoring programs in thirty-six states. Its central staff supports the programs with tutor training assistance, management help, and audio-visual materials development. LVA's curricular approach emphasizes the use of materials built around the needs and interests of individual students. LVA uses materials developed by its central staff, by tutors in local LVA programs, and by commercial organizations where appropriate.

LLA, the larger of the two organizations, has forty-five state chapters, 750 local affiliates, and over 68,000 volunteers. Taking a more traditional approach, LLA focuses on developing reading and writing skills through grade-level appropriate materials. In 1987, LLA reached over 100,000 adults. One example of the LLA approach to workplace literacy training is occurring in Hampton, Va.

The city of Hampton, with 1,200 city employees, began using LLA materials and methods to train its work force at the end of 1985 as a result of realizing the need for literacy upgrade training. This realization occurred when the city decided to go to direct deposit of paychecks but found that many employees did not have checking accounts. When they investigated to determine why this was so, they found that many of their employees did not read at a level that enabled them to take advantage of this service. At this point, the city decided to implement a voluntary literacy program.

Hampton used the local literacy council as its primary resource in determining how to establish the program, and the council recommended LLA materials. At the request of the city's human relations department, the literacy council trained city employees to be tutors. City employees are currently being trained using LLA materials supplemented with job-specific resources, such as standard forms and manuals that tutors obtain from trainee supervisors.

Both the trainees and the tutors are given work release time and must receive permission from their supervisors to participate. Very few problems have arisen as a result of this since the program has a good reputation and most supervisors have been very supportive. In the few cases where a problem arose, the program coordinator talked with the supervisor in question and a solution or compromise was worked out.

In 1989 there were eighteen pairs (one trainee, one tutor) participating in the program, and the number has gone as high as twenty-five pairs. Through participation in the literacy upgrade program, many of the trainees have been able to make strides in other related areas. For example, they can now access the adult basic education programs available through the public education system. As a result, approximately twelve people have gone on to complete their GED.

There has not been a formal evaluation of the program, but meetings have been held with supervisors, tutors, and trainees to obtain their reactions. The results show that supervisors believe the efficiency of their work units has increased due to three factors: increased self-esteem and self-confidence among trainees; the fact that they can now give written rather than verbal instructions, which takes less time; and the fact that the tutors feel good because they believe they are doing something worthwhile.

For the first year the program was funded by a grant from the state library system. Since the beginning of the second year the city department of human resources has picked up the tab.

Hampton plans to continue offering the program for as long as it takes employees who need it to reach the level of literacy required by their jobs. The city has also expanded the program to include tutors and trainees from the community at large.

Contacts for volunteer literacy programs include:

Literacy Volunteers of America
404 Oak Street
Syracuse, N.Y. 13203
(315) 474-7039

Laubach Literacy Action
1320 Jamesville Avenue
Syracuse, N.Y. 13210
(315) 422-9121

Department of Human Resources
City of Hampton
22 Lincoln Street
Hampton, Va. 23669
(804) 727-6407

The U.S. Military

The U.S. military is the single biggest deliverer of education and training programs to adults. In fiscal 1985, the five military services spent over $25 million on basic skills training alone (reading, writing, computation). Sixty-two percent of the total is attributable to the army.

Since its inception the military has been training people to perform specific jobs and has developed job-oriented materials for people with varying levels of basic skills. The Department of Defense, as the umbrella agency concerned with military readiness service-wide, has played a seminal role in encouraging the development of functional-context basic literacy and occupational skills training to serve the needs of all service branches. The earliest effort in this direction was entitled Project 100,000, which was established during the Vietnam War to induct substantial numbers of marginally literate men into active-duty military service.

More recently, the Defense Department has formed the Joint Service Manpower Research and Development Program to more rapidly develop specific responses to training needs. One of the more interesting prototype programs is called Computer Handheld Instructional Prototype, or CHIP. The CHIP program has several advantages: It has multi-service applications, it is a low-cost training technology, and it will improve training effectiveness. The benefits of the system are that it makes productive use of downtime, it increases skills retention, it improves unit performance, and it is susceptible to technology transfer.

In addition to the basic and specialized training provided by the military, each service branch has developed cooperative arrangements with civilian schools to enable service personnel to earn high school diplomas or work toward college degrees. Several credit-by-examination and correspondence programs are offered also. The army, navy, and marines have also developed registered apprenticeship programs that enable enrollees to receive credit for their service experience in civilian apprenticeship programs. The military uses distinctive training technologies and methods of delivery. Its principal contribution to the nation's learning enterprise has been and continues to be to develop training practices and technologies and disseminate them to civilian education and training institutions.

The army, for example, maintains a competency-based approach to education through its Job Skill Education Program. This program seeks to ensure functional literacy by applying basic skills in reading, writing, and problem solving to daily job tasks. It is a microcomputer-delivered basic skills program designed to teach military personnel the basic academic skills necessary to perform specific jobs. Developed by Florida State University and Ford Aerospace, it presents job competency measures for ninety-nine different occupational specialties within the army. Because of its applicability to the civilian sector, the U.S. Department of Labor and the U.S. Department of Education jointly awarded a $628,000 grant to Florida State's Center for Educational Technology to test the feasibility of adapting the program for civilian use.

Taking a somewhat different approach, the navy promotes remedial education so that recruits who need it can complete their technical training. For example, the naval air station at Millington, Tenn., developed the short-term, total-immersion Academic Remedial Reading program. All recruits participating in the program read below the sixth-grade level when they entered the seventeen-day program. Upon program completion, recruits increased reading levels by an average of 2.3 grades; two-thirds qualified for enrollment in navy technical schools.

As a result of the program's success with navy recruits, the navy joined in a coalition with Project Literacy–Memphis in an outreach effort to bring the program to the neighboring communities. A navy admiral chaired the coalition. Twenty employees from the Memphis Sanitation and Parks Department were invited to participate; potential participants were expected to read between the third- and fifth-grade levels. Sixteen people applied for a ten-day program; eleven of the sixteen participants were nonreaders. The students were predominately black, middle-aged, and married and had an average of four years of schooling. All participants had an annual income of less than $18,000.

On entering the program all participants expressed confidence in their ability to perform their jobs but not in their ability to learn reading; all had experienced failure in traditional classroom settings.

Participants were paid to attend the ten-day training session at the naval air station. A bus picked up the students at their job site, took them to the air station for training, and then returned them to the workplace at the end of the day. During their time in the program, participants did measurably increase their reading levels. Participants also improved their self-images and their esprit de corps; faster learners tutored slower learners in order to bring about successful results. Fifteen of the sixteen students enrolled in the city ABE program for follow-up classes. The program's success led the Memphis Literacy Coalition to recommend program expansion to the hard-core unemployed, inmates of correctional institutions, high school students, and local businesses.

Employers interested in using the military as an on-the-job training resource should contact the commanders of nearby military installations. For further information, contact the education headquarters of the individual services at the following locations:

U.S. Army
Army Education Center
2461 Eisenhower Avenue
HQDA
Education Division, Room 1434
U.S. TAPA
DAPC-PDE
Alexandria, Va. 22331-0472
(703) 325-9806

U.S. Air Force
Education, Training, and Personnel
HQ USAF-DPPED
Pentagon, Room 4D228
Washington, D.C. 20330-5060
(202) 695-7816

U.S. Navy
Director, Total Force Education and Training
Arlington Annex, Room G831
Columbia Pike and Southgate Road
Arlington, Va. 20370
(703) 694-5216

Community-Based Organizations

Community-based organizations that provide training traditionally represent constituencies underrepresented in the established political system. These organizations are usually formed around a central issue and represent a particular segment of the population. Most community organizations operate on shoestring budgets ranging from $15,000 to $200,000. Community-based training organizations all share several characteristics: They have evolved in response to some social or economic need from within their community; they are independent of affiliation with any other group; they are private and nonprofit in structure; and they are concerned with the community as well as with the individual.

For many such organizations, training or enhancement of skills is seen as a mechanism for attaining individual, organizational, or community objectives. Thus, training and education programming often occurs in conjunction with other activities such as classes for families of alcoholics, battered women, or other constituency groups. Often training focuses on assertiveness training or building self-esteem.

For the most part, these organizations are confined to their own communities, and employers who might be interested in using their services should contact them there. There are, however, several community organizations that have achieved national prominence. Three such organizations, the National Urban League, the Opportunities Industrialization Centers, and SER–Jobs for Progress, are somewhat more accessible than most community-based organizations because they operate local organizations linked through a national network. They all focus primarily on employment and training services. These organizations serve constituencies with poor basic workplace skills who have failed to learn through traditional teaching methods in classroom settings. These organizations see themselves as helping constituents obtain gainful employment by providing job training and job placement.

Headquartered in New York, the National Urban League currently has 112 local offices. The league concentrates on preparing poor people for jobs through remedial education and technical skills training. Opportunities Industrialization Centers, headquartered in Philadelphia, has more than eighty local offices. It operates basic skills and upgrading programs to help constituents obtain and retain jobs in fields such as word processing, health, bookkeeping, computers, and electronics. SER–Jobs for Progress operates basic skills and upgrading programs in eighty-three cities and places special emphasis on addressing the needs of Hispanics in the areas of education, training, employment, business, and economic opportunities.

Most community-based organizations have business representatives on their boards of directors at the national and local levels, and many have reached out to employer organizations to involve them in the design of curricula so they can better meet local business needs. For example, SER–Jobs for Progress, recognizing a need and a potential for interacting with the corporate sector, brought together a small group of major Fortune 500 corporations in 1973 to form a corporate advisory council known as Amigos de SER. This council has become an important partner in the organization's development.

Community organizations are singular resources with a good track record. Employers looking to provide training that will enhance worker self-esteem, increase motivation, teach goal setting, and build employability skills may find them useful for both potential new hires and current employees. The Aetna Institute for Corporate Education in Hartford, Conn., has found local community organizations so helpful that it has developed a two-pronged approach to using them. The institute uses the particular strengths of these organizations both to recruit potential employees from their constituent communities and to train them in preemployment and self-esteem skills.

Contacts for community-based organizations include the following:

Association for Community Based Education
1806 Vernon Street NW
Washington, D.C. 20009
(202) 462-6333

Opportunities Industrialization Centers
100 West Coulter Street
Philadelphia, Pa. 19144
(215) 951-2200

National Urban League
500 East 62nd Street
New York, N.Y. 10021
(212) 310-9000

SER–Jobs for Progress
1355 Riverbend Drive, Suite 240
Dallas, Tex. 75247
(214) 631-3999

Employer-Funded Consortia

An individual employer such as a small business may not have the
resources, the know-how, or the time to put together a program to train
workers. However, there may be several businesses, small or large, in the
same geographic area with related occupational and/or basic workplace
skills training needs. This convergence of interests frequently makes it
desirable to put together a training consortium run by a third-party training
organization and funded wholly through private funds to conduct training
tailored to the needs of the participating employer institutions. One such
consortium of employers that has succeeded in doing this is the Continuing Education Institute in Boston.

The Continuing Education Institute (CEI) is a privately owned, nonprofit educational corporation. Since 1981, nine companies in the Boston
area (Blue Cross/Blue Shield, Bank of Boston, Data General, Digital Electronics, Millipore Corporation, and four area hospitals) have funded and
contracted with the institute to provide a diploma program for their
employees. All courses are conducted on company premises after work
hours. The programs also incorporate nontraditional skills such as critical
and analytical thinking, problem solving, teamwork, and career
development.

Once the companies had committed their resources to this project, a
meeting was set up with company supervisors for general orientation. The
program was advertised within the companies, and interested employees
were encouraged to sign up. An important part of the program is that the
companies give full tuition assistance, which can go as high as $3,000 per
participant for a full two-year enrollment, if that is what the employee
needs and the company wants. The results of the program show up in
improved self-esteem, more promotions, and improved job performance,
as well as in a positive impact on employees' personal lives.

Due to the success of the adult diploma program, the institute now
offers company-specific training, particularly in English as a Second Lan-

guage (ESL). Companies positively impacted by the core program have requested company-specific or, in some cases, department-specific ESL programs. Further, the institute has rewritten some company manuals and communication materials to ensure that the reading level is not too high for the target audience.

For information on employer-funded consortia contact:

Continuing Education Institute
33 Ship Avenue
Medford, Mass. 02155
(617) 396-8817

Union Training

Unions have long been leading activists in upgrading the workplace skills of the nation's workers. Today, unions are meeting their memberships' skills needs through innovative collective bargaining agreements worked out with management. These agreements emphasize education and training programs for both active and dislocated workers. Training programs resulting from these agreements are developed in-house as well as by outside providers.

The training program model worked out between the United Auto Workers (UAW) and Ford, General Motors, and Chrysler is one of the more successful collective bargaining arrangements. The model established a reeducation trust fund that uses employer contributions to support the Employee Development and Training program. This program provides an opportunity for union members of car-manufacturing companies to upgrade basic and technical skills in order to make each company stronger and more competitive. The program was developed in two stages. First, each company contributed 5 cents to an education fund for each hour worked by nonexempt employees (later increased to 10 cents per hour plus 50 cents per hour accrued for overtime in excess of 5 percent straight time). Second, each company established a basic skills enhancement program for employees to continue basic education, brush up on academic skills (such as math and communication), and learn new skills.

Many other collective bargaining agreements also include joint training programs to improve nontraditional basic skills. For example, the American Federation of State, County, and Municipal Employees (AFSCME) District Council 37, New York, operates one of the most innovative and comprehensive membership education programs in the country. The union's commitment to training and education is underscored by the fact that a campus of the College of New Rochelle has been established at union headquarters. As with the car companies, employer contributions are placed in a benefits trust for reeducation. These reeducation funds are applied to:

- Basic skills enhancement,

- College education for union members and their families,

- Job-specific training (office practices, including answering phones, filing, communications and writing, and teamwork), and

• Leadership development (negotiation, parliamentary procedure, and contracts).

In addition, AFSCME District Council 37 fosters career development for its members. It has tailored programs for paraprofessions such as hospital aides and developed a career ladder and job comparability system for analyzing worker skills.

In a third union initiative, District 1199C of the National Union of Hospital and Health Care Employees established the Training and Upgrading Fund—a nonprofit educational trust supported by employer contributions; grants from the U.S. Departments of Education, Labor, and Health and Human Services; state and city adult education programs; and local Job Training Partnership Act funds.

The fund focuses on postsecondary education for fifteen health care occupations and offers literacy training to approximately 200 adults a year. Union members may also enroll and receive funds for health-related training in any college or university. Basic skills programs include reading, writing, math, and computer literacy.

Contacts for union-funded training programs include:

1199C Training and Development Fund
1319 Locust Street
Philadelphia, Pa. 19107
(215) 735-5555

UAW–Ford National Training Center
P.O. Box 6002
Dearborn, Mich. 48121
(313) 337-7464

AFSCME, District 37
140 Park Place
New York, N.Y. 10007
(212) 766-1530

Trade and Professional Associations

Most industries have trade and professional associations that offer courses for line and management personnel, but very few offer courses that address the nonsupervisory worker or workplace basic skills. There are some that do, however, and while industry-specific models vary somewhat, the process and strategy is similar to that offered by the American Institute of Banking (AIB).

The American Bankers Association, parent organization of the AIB, has been active in banker education opportunities through local chapters, study groups, and correspondence courses. While core programs are targeted to certification, remedial and compensatory training is the current focus of educational services. In determining the need for literacy programs, AIB also addressed the need for support services such as testing, tutoring, and counseling.

In designing its program, AIB has taken into consideration that different bank jobs may require different competencies—teller jobs are different from those of operations clerks, and so on. Therefore, AIB developed its instructional materials by using the actual entry-level manuals for each job, which allowed employees to develop their literacy skills to match their job needs.

Although AIB has prepared materials in job-specific remedial education, it has tried to make its members aware that beyond specific basic education competencies, they also need to address the psychological barriers that may interfere with worker performance, such as fragile self-esteem, fear of failure, and fear of change. AIB began offering its basic education courses in the fall of 1988. It has taken particular care in designing these courses to avoid terms that may imply a negative connotation such as remedial, illiterate, and so on.

Contacts for training offered through trade and professional associations include:

American Society of Association Executives
1575 I Street, NW
Washington, D.C. 20005
(202) 626-2723

American Institute of Banking
1120 Connecticut Ave., NW
Washington, D.C. 20036
(202) 663-5430

Consultants and Vendors of Training

One look in the American Society for Training and Development's *Buyer's Guide* provides proof enough that there are hundreds of private for-profit or nonprofit consultants and training organizations that offer both off-the-shelf and customized training programs in every imaginable business-related subject. However, research shows that most of the training in the basic workplace skills discussed in this manual is only now beginning to be offered to employees below the supervisory level. As employers demand more such training for their nonsupervisory employees, the market will move to fill the vacuum, and courses in a variety of basic workplace skills will be developed specifically for the nonsupervisory worker. Some training companies are already providing such services.

Training consultants and vendors exist for the sole purpose of providing training to employers and their work forces. They are probably the most responsive of all training providers in that they will come to the employer's site regardless of where it is, and they are flexible in their scheduling and in the types of programs they will do.

There are many kinds of training organizations offering a broad spectrum of skills training. A few representative examples include Communications Skills, a small communications consulting firm that customizes training workshops in oral, listening, and interpersonal skills for all levels of employees; Applied Behavioral and Cognitive Sciences, which provides job-specific workplace literacy education and training to industry and government; the United States Basic Skills Investment Corporation, which takes a high-tech approach to basic skills mastery and is just beginning to market itself to employers with a computerized management tracking system and an open-entry, open-exit format that is particularly useful for accommodating the needs of adult learners and their employers; and Learning International, one of the largest consulting firms in the world, with clients among the Fortune 500 companies. Learning International offers sales training as well as training in management, supervision, problem solving, decision making, and a variety of other courses to all levels of employees in training modules that last from half a day to three days.

These are only a few of the training organizations that exist in the marketplace. An employer organization that wants a particular type of training and is having difficulty finding it should contact consultants and vendors who offer similar or related workshops and discuss the possibility of having specialized training courses developed to fill the vacuum.

For information on vendors of training programs contact:

American Society for Training and Development
1630 Duke Street
P.O. Box 1443
Alexandria, Va. 22313
(703) 683-8100

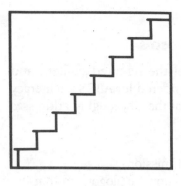

Resource D:
Sample Request for Proposals

Background

Provide potential training providers with approximately one to two pages of information about the basic skills training program your organization plans to operate. Include one paragraph to address each of the following points (sample text for each is given in parentheses):

1. Who is sponsoring the training program and what their goals are.
   (The proposed job literacy program represents the collaborative efforts of ABC Company and the XYZ union to assist workers in increasing their technical skills to improve their job performance.)

2. The time frame of the training program.
   (The job literacy program will be offered to employees year-round, as ninety hour units of instruction, for a duration of nine weeks each.)

3. The anticipated number of employees to participate and the qualifications for entry to the program.
   (The ABC plant in Smithville employs 5,000 workers. It is estimated that the job literacy program will begin with 275 participants and expand to serve up to 750 employees annually. The program will be open to any employee choosing to participate.)

4. Any conditions that may require special consideration.
   (Much of the work at the ABC plant involves tedious, precision-oriented assembly work. Employees perform a variety of mentally tiring, demanding tasks that require prolonged periods of concentration. Participants in the proposed program will be attending the basic skills training classes each day after completing six hours of their normal eight-hour day.)

5. The major requirements and underlying training philosophy of the program.
   (To ensure that all participating employees will be able to transfer reading improvement to their actual on-the-job reading tasks, the basic skills training program will have to be *contextually based, individualized, process-oriented,* and *distinguishable from the traditional school setting.* As currently conceived, the training program would be conducted in a learning lab environment and would be *incorporated into two hours of every work day, Monday through Friday, for a total of nine weeks per instructional unit.* Motivation must be sufficiently compelling to maintain the active involvement of employees in the learning process.)

Note: Adapted from RFP guidelines for solicitation of educational providers developed by Public/Private Ventures, Philadelphia, Pa., 1987.

Required Format for Submitting Proposals

Provide training providers with an outline of the required content and maximum length of their proposals. To be considered for ABC's job literacy program, an applicant must submit a proposal that thoroughly addresses the following issues:

1. Background of the Organization
   a. Describe organization's history and mission.
   b. Describe its experience with populations analogous to that of ABC's Smithville employees.

2. Training Services
   a. Describe proposed instructional approaches and rationale for these approaches.
   b. Describe in detail proposed curriculum materials and reasons for using them.
   c. Describe activities proposed to meet the goals of employees; discuss how these activities will fully engage the participation of employees in the education program.
   d. List other equipment or resources needed to conduct the program.
   e. Describe in detail the initial and ongoing assessment techniques to be used to establish goals and to place individual employees in the curriculum. Discuss how potential assessment results relate to the program activities described above. Please list assessment instruments you propose to use.
   f. Describe the procedures for documenting and measuring employee progress.
   g. Indicate whether the program will include computer-assisted instruction. If yes, then describe how it will address the broad range of educational levels, describe the courseware and software to be used, and give your rationale for these selections.
   h. Describe how you will monitor program performance.

3. Other Activities
   a. Does the organization have the capacity to provide a task analysis before curriculum development is begun? Describe.
   b. Does the organization have the capacity to develop contextually based, functional job literacy curriculum materials? Describe.
   c. What other resources is the organization able to provide to respond to individual employee needs?

4. Staffing and Program Management
   a. Provide the names and experience of the individuals responsible for development and implementation of the job literacy program.
   b. Describe procedures for selecting instructors. What instructor characteristics and experience will be sought for this program?

  c. Describe the role of the instructors in the program you propose.

  d. Provide the names of any other individuals likely to be involved in overall management of the program.

5. Staff Development and Planning
  a. What type of orientation will be given to instructors?
  b. What staff development activities are proposed for instructors?
  c. How will instructor performance be monitored?
  d. When and how will instructors plan day-to-day activities for employees?

6. Location
  a. Where will these training activities take place?

7. Estimated Costs
  a. On the budget forms provided, give a breakdown of proposed costs, including salaries, materials, equipment, and administrative overhead. Costs should not exceed $ _____ for the first year.

8. Supplementary Information
  a. Please limit the proposal to no more than fifteen pages. However, you may include whatever attachments you feel are necessary.

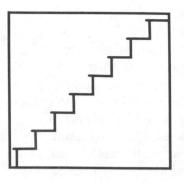

Resource E:
Generic Curriculum Guidelines for Promoting Workplace Basics

Introduction

The curriculum content guides that follow are intended for use by trainers and others who are confronted with the task of establishing training programs in workplace basics and who are generally unfamiliar with the subject matter in each skill area. The guides can be used whether the training is to be developed in-house or through an outside provider. If in-house trainers are used to develop programs, these guides can be a starting point for further research; if an outside provider is to be selected, they can be used to establish a knowledge base against which the subject expertise of a potential provider may be measured.

Although these curriculum guidelines deal with the basic workplace skills as separate and discrete entities, when they are taught in a workplace setting they are almost never taught separately, but rather as groups of related skills that employees need to interact effectively in a work environment. The guides are not all-inclusive, nor do they constitute the only substantive approach to training in each subject area. Final determination of program content and length will be contingent on the requirements of the organization and the needs of the employees.

The ability of individuals to attain job-related competency for most skill areas depends on many variables, such as an employee's prior knowledge in each skill area, the complexity of the skill itself, the required level of skill attainment for a specific job or job family, the design of the curriculum, the commitment of management, and so on. For most of these skills, achieving competency will take anywhere from forty hours to five years. And, in addition, all training should include follow-up and evaluation once the employee is back on the job, as well as refresher courses throughout the work life of the employee.

These guidelines are a starting point for the development of a workplace basics training program.

Approaches to Learning-to-Learn

There are several different approaches to providing workplace training in learning-to-learn skills. They include:

- Training for self-directed learning, which has as its objectives to encourage trainee awareness of self as a learner; to establish that the identification and analysis of learning processes can be interesting and productive; to introduce the learning-style concept and assist participants to gain a perspective on their own learning styles; to prepare participants to carry out and analyze a personal learning project; to provide information useful to participants in conducting their personal learning projects and to meaningfully analyze them; to increase skill in using resource people on a one-to-one basis; to extract transferable strategies from the project each person has conducted; to synthesize what has been learned about self-directed learning; and to encourage post-workshop application of training (Smith, 1982, pp. 145–149).

- Training for collaborative learning, which has as its goals improved membership skills and teamwork development. Training involves helping people to understand the conditions under which adults learn best in face-to-face groups; helping people learn how to learn with and from one another while using other resources as needed; and fostering the development of diagnostic skills and the ability to distinguish content from process (Smith, 1982, p. 152).

- Training through educational institutions, which is geared toward helping participants get the most from programs and resources found outside the employer institution. These courses present and develop for participants an understanding of thinking processes; an understanding and appreciation of nonlinear and intuitive thinking and problem solving; and the ability to assume more authority for their own learning. Experience and research show that six types of training exercises provide excellent training for improving learning-to-learn skills. These are learning, reading, taking notes, writing, taking exams, and self-organization (Smith, 1982, pp. 160–161).

Below is a content guideline for skills that make up the heart of a learning-to-learn curriculum. Subject-specific areas, formal and informal learning strategies, and learning styles are integrated throughout the training process and overtly identified for the training participant where the trainer believes it to be appropriate.

Content Guidelines for Learning-to-Learn Skills Training

(*Source:* Adapted from Smith, 1988, pp. 82–83.)

1. What are the objectives of this training?
   a. To understand the nature of knowledge.
   b. To be able to organize learning activities.
   c. To develop the critical skills of evaluation.
   d. To understand how to apply appropriate thinking (convergent, divergent, critical, and intuitive).
   e. To understand the importance of and be able to do self-assessment and needs assessment.

2. What are cognitive learning-to-learn skills?
   a. Understanding the nature of knowledge.
   b. Organizing learning activities.
   c. Learning critical evaluation skills.
   d. Thinking convergently, divergently, critically, and intuitively.
   e. Relating and recalling information.
   f. Relating and organizing information.
   g. Developing basic skills (reading, writing, computing).
   h. Problem solving.
   i. Understanding the feasibility and usefulness of learning-to-learn or learning process consciousness.
   j. Transferring learning strategies.
   k. Communicating:
      • Active listening.
      • Viewing.
   l. Developing knowledge about resource availability and assessment.
   m. Organizing learning and development activities.
   n. Understanding cognitively the difference between learning and being taught.

3. What are personal understanding learning-to-learn skills?
   a. Understanding self as learner:
      • Preferred styles and adaptations.
      • Personal resources inventory (assessment).
      • Personal awareness and monitoring.
   b. Conducting needs assessment (self-assessment):
      • Sense of direction.
      • Sense of purpose.
      • Life planning.
      • Ability to create resources.
   c. Building confidence, persistence, openness, and flexibility.

4. What are interpersonal learning-to-learn skills?
   a. Accessing and evaluating resources.
   b. Giving and receiving feedback.
      • Seeking information nondefensively.
      • Seeking important feedback.
      • Analyzing feedback.
      • Giving feedback when needed.
   c. Developing strategies for performing contextual analysis.
   d. Developing strategies for using collaborative inquiry.
   e. Understanding how to find and use resources:
      • Expert source.
      • Peer support.
      • Media.

Reading, Writing, and Computation

The achievement of competency in reading, writing, and computation is not usually something that can be accomplished in a one-day or even a one-week workshop. Furthermore, although these guidelines deal with each skill independently of the other, in actuality they are almost never taught separately because each incremental competency achievement by participants in any one skill area contributes to helping achieve competency in the other two. For example, it is impossible to solve mathematical problems without having achieved some skill in reading and writing, while writing clear, competent memos, reports, or bookkeeping summaries requires a certain level of reading. Only at the most rudimentary, nonliterate level are skills likely to be taught completely separately, and then only for a brief period.

The reading, writing, and computation skills that follow have been identified as those most commonly used to perform basic job-related tasks. Research indicates that employers seek out job applicants who have mastered these processes (Pratzner, 1978; Pratzner and Russell, 1984; Smith, 1973; Wiant, 1977). For training to be effective, these skills should be presented in the context of performing simulations of job tasks.

Content Guidelines for Reading Skills Training

(*Source:* Adapted from Philippi, 1988.)

1. What are the objectives of this training?
   a. To improve job-related reading skills as they relate to immediate job requirements.
   b. To improve job performance.
   c. To enhance participants' chances of job stability and upward job mobility through improved reading skills.
   d. To increase company productivity through improving individual reading capabilities.

2. How do you develop skills in literal comprehension?
   a. Identify factual details or specifications within text.
   b. Follow detailed, sequential directions to complete a task.
   c. Determine the essential message of a paragraph or selection.

3. What techniques are used to locate information within a text?
   a. Using table of contents, index, appendix, glossary, systems, or subsystems to locate information.
   b. Locating page, title, paragraph, figure, or chart needed to answer questions to solve problems.
   c. Using skimming or scanning to determine whether text contains relevant information.
   d. Cross-referencing within and across source materials to select information to perform routine tasks.
   e. Using a completed form to locate information needed to complete a task activity.

4. What is involved in learning how to compare and contrast information?
   a. Combining information from multiple sources that contribute to the completion of a task.
   b. Selecting parts of a text or visual materials to complete a task.
   c. Identifying similarities and differences in objects.
   d. Determining presence of a defect or extent of damage.
   e. Matching objects by size, color, or significant markings.
   f. Classifying objects by size, color, or significant markings.
   g. Distinguishing between relevant and irrelevant information in text or visuals.

5. How do you recognize cause and effect and predict outcomes?
   a. Use common knowledge to avoid hazard or injury.
   b. Apply preventive measures prior to task to minimize security or safety problems.
   c. Select appropriate course of action in an emergency.

6. How do you use charts, diagrams, and schematics?
   a. Obtain a factor specification from a two-column chart to find information.
   b. Obtain a factor specification from an intersection of a row and a column on a table or chart. Use a complex table or chart requiring cross-referencing within text material.
   c. Apply information from tables or graphs to locate malfunctions or to select a course of action.
   d. Use a simple linear path of an organizational chart to list events in sequential order.
   e. Use the linear path of a flow chart to provide visual and textual directions for a procedure, to arrive at a decision point, or to provide alternative paths in problem solving.
   f. Isolate each major section presented in a schematic diagram.
   g. Identify the components within each section of a schematic diagram.
   h. Isolate a problem component in a schematic diagram and trace it to the cause of the problem.
   i. Interpret symbols to indicate direction of flow, text points, components, and diagrammatic decision points.
   j. Identify details, labels, numbers, and parts from an illustration or picture.
   k. Identify parts from a key or legend.
   l. Interpret drawing of cross-section for assembly or disassembly.
   m. Follow sequenced illustrations or photographs as a guide.

7. How do you become competent in inferential comprehension?
   a. Determine meaning of figurative, idiomatic, and technical meanings of terms, using context clues or reference sources.
   b. Make an inference from text that does not explicitly provide required information.
   c. Organize information from multiple sources into a sequenced series of events.
   d. Interpret codes and symbols.

8. How do you improve vocabulary?
   a. Recognize common words and meanings.
   b. Recognize task-related words with technical meanings.
   c. Identify word meanings from sentence context.
   d. Recognize meanings of common abbreviations and acronyms.

Content Guidelines for Writing Skills Training

(*Source:* Adapted from task analyses of civilian and military occupations, U.S. Department of the Army, 1988; Mikulecky, 1982; Diehl, 1980.)

1. What are the objectives of this training?
   a. To improve job-related writing skills as they relate to immediate job requirements.
   b. To improve overall job performance.
   c. To enhance participants' chances of job stability and upward job mobility through improved writing skills.
   d. To increase company productivity through improving individual writing capabilities.

2. What are the key production competencies?
   a. Writing key technical words accurately on forms.
   b. Spelling task-related words and abbreviations correctly.

3. What is the process for entering and performing single-step activities?
   a. Enter appropriate information onto a form.
   b. Record essential information in phrases or simple sentence form accurately and precisely.
   c. Record information that involves more than one sentence.

4. What is the process for entering and performing multiple-step activities and sourcing?
   a. Transfer numbers, codes, dates, and figures from equipment or written sources onto appropriate sections of forms.
   b. Write a report including necessary support documentation or classification.

5. How do you learn to translate actions to paper?
   a. Write brief, descriptive accounts of activities or transactions performed.
   b. Outline a situation by identifying key ideas and supporting details.
   c. Summarize essential details for a written communication, using problem-solving or newswriting guidelines (who? what? where? when? how?).
   d. Select relevant details for a written communication.
   e. State general impressions of an event or situation as they relate to specific reporting goals.
   f. Summarize events and precise dialogue in an accurate, complete, and objective manner.

      g. Summarize major points presented in a written
         communication.
      h. Generate a written communication according to a specific
         format (that is, memos, telex, or letter).

6. How do you learn interpretation?
    a. Identify objectives, intent, target audience, and all essential and
       supporting details of a written communication.
    b. Generate a written communication, arranging events
       sequentially.
    c. Write brief justifications for actions taken and provide good
       reasons for rejecting alternative actions.
    d. Appraise a written communication and make adjustments to
       improve clarity.

Content Guidelines for Computation Training

A recent study of over 130 different vocational areas showed high to moderate generalizability (transferability from one occupational area to another) of the mathematics skills that follow.

    Those items with an asterisk (*) indicate skills directly involving the use of problem solving or interpretation.

(*Source:* Adapted from Greenan, 1984.)

1. What are the objectives of this training?
    a. To improve job-related computational skills as they relate to
       immediate job requirements.
    b. To improve overall job performance.
    c. To enhance participants' chances of job stability and upward
       job mobility through improved computation skills.
    d. To increase company productivity through improving
       individual computational capabilities.

2. What procedures do you need to learn to understand how to use whole numbers in the workplace?
    a. Read, write, and count single- and multiple-digit whole
       numbers.
    b. Add and subtract single- and multiple-digit whole numbers.
    c. Multiply and divide single- and multiple-digit whole numbers.
  *d. Use addition, subtraction, multiplication, and division to
       solve problems with single- and multiple-digit whole
       numbers.
  *e. Round off single- and multiple-digit whole numbers.

3. What procedures do you need to learn to understand how to use fractions in the workplace?
    a. Read and write common fractions.
    b. Add and subtract common fractions.
    c. Multiply and divide common fractions.
  *d. Solve problems with common fractions.

4. What procedures do you need to learn to understand how to use decimals in the workplace?
   a. Carry out arithmetic computations involving dollars and cents.
   b. Read and write decimals in one or more places.
   *c. Round off decimals in one or more places.
   d. Multiply and divide decimals in one or more places.
   e. Add and subtract decimals in one or more places.
   *f. Solve problems with decimals in one or more places.

5. What procedures do you need to learn to understand how to use percents in the workplace?
   a. Read and write percents.
   b. Compute percents.

6. What procedures do you need to learn to understand how to use mixed operations in the workplace?
   *a. Convert fractions to decimals, percents to fractions, fractions to percents, percents to decimals, decimals to percents, common fractions or mixed numbers to decimal fractions, and decimal fractions to common fractions or mixed numbers.
   *b. Solve problems by selecting and using correct order of operations.
   c. Perform written calculations quickly.
   d. Compute averages.

7. What procedures do you need to learn to understand how to use measurements and calculations in the workplace?
   *a. Read numbers or symbols from time, weight, distance, and volume measuring scales.
   *b. Use a measuring device to determine an object's weight, distance, or volume in standard (English) units.
   *c. Use a measuring device to determine an object's weight, distance, or volume in metric units.
   *d. Perform basic metric conversions involving weight, distance, and volume.
   *e. Solve problems involving time, weight, distance, and volume.
   *f. Use a calculator to perform basic arithmetic operations to solve problems.

8. What procedures do you need to learn to understand how to use estimation in the workplace?
   *a. Determine if a solution to a mathematical problem is reasonable.

Content Guidelines for Oral Communication Training

(*Source:* Adapted from Elsea, 1988a.)

1. What are the objectives of this training?
   a. To make participants aware of the importance of oral communication in their everyday work life.
   b. To improve participants' oral communication skills as they directly relate to their job.
   c. To teach techniques for ongoing individual self-development of oral communication skills.
   d. To increase participants' value to the organization by helping them to do their job better.

2. How can you *not* communicate: (Know your own style of communication.)
   a. Facts about amount of time spent communicating.
   b. Why it's important to make good first impressions.
   c. Explanation of how first impressions are formed in the first two to four minutes.
   d. What do you look like? (nonverbal communication)
      - Discussion of body language and appearance and the fact that these nonverbals constitute 55 percent of the meaning of the message; note importance of culture, gender, and authority or status.
      - Do practical exercise that highlights importance of nonverbals (for example, have participants check out personal space or whether they like to be touched).
   e. What do you sound like? (vocal communication)
      - Discussion of voice characteristics such as rate, pitch, and loudness; how the voice contributes 38 percent of the meaning in face-to-face interactions and 70–90 percent when one is on the phone.
      - Do practical exercise that demonstrates how rate or loudness can energize or calm people down; if group is small, get brief sample of voices on tape recorder.
   f. What do you say? (verbal communication)
      - While language is worth only 7 percent in first few moments, it will be worth more if receiver gets past nonverbal and vocal communication to choice of words, arrangement of words, and support for ideas.
      - Some word choices are more powerful than others.
      - Importance of consistency between what is said and how it is said; if there is a discrepancy, people believe the how.

3. Are you what you value? (Assess your style of communication.)
   a. Option A: Distribute a self-assessment instrument that measures each participant's style of communication; score it with group, so each participant knows dominant and backup styles.

    b. Option B: Videotape some participants (or all, if small group) in a brief role-playing situation where they respond to a typical job-related situation.

4. What kind of action styles do you use to communicate?
    a. Profiles of four styles of communication:
       • Describe each style briefly or show video (if Option B is used).
       • Have group draw up nonverbal, vocal, and verbal characteristics for each style; this can be done in small groups or large group discussion.
       • Get participants to discuss what physical environment is associated with each style (for example, pictures of family, tidy desk, lots of light).
    b. Brainstorming session: What are the strengths and weaknesses of each style on the job?
    c. Tips on improving body language and/or voice.
    d. Practical exercise using audio or video:
       • Focus on one change participants think should be made in their voice or body language.
       • Give some or all participants one to two minutes before camera or microphone to try out new behaviors.
       • Replay tape and reinforce results; make suggestions for further change. Might have brief critique sheet available for participants to fill out.
    e. Develop activity plan that can improve participants' oral communication skills.

5. How can you *not* communicate? (power of communication)
    a. Facts about interpersonal communication and success in the workplace.
    b. *First* impression, *best* impression: How impressions are formed, and why they are important.
    c. Three key questions effective communicators ask:
       • What do you look like? (nonverbal communication)
       • What do you sound like? (vocal communication)
       • What do you say? (verbal communication)
    d. Trainer gives brief synopsis of each of these three channels of communication, noting importance of culture, gender, power, physical response, and where interactions take place.
    e. Self-assessment instrument.

6. Are you what you value? (Assess your style of communication.)
    a. Scoring the self-assessment instrument.
    b. Profiling four styles of communication—brief overview by trainer of each style.

7. How do you value others? (Understand other styles of communication.)
   a. Problem-solving exercise (individuals meet in small groups according to communication style to draw up a profile of what they look like, sound like, and say, and what their environmental preferences are (for example, messy desks, plants and pictures, chair for guests).
   b. Debriefing (each style reports its profile).
   c. Discussion period (may include contributions and weaknesses of each style in the workplace).

8. What happens when styles collide? (Adjust your style to the styles of others.)
   a. Small group exercise.
      • Each group assigned a style unlike its own.
      • Each group draws up a plan of action to adjust its style to the one assigned; some adjustments might be nonverbal, others vocal, others verbal.
      • Each group also notes what bugs them about the assigned style.
   b. Each group reports its plan, and the participants representing that style react to the adjustments.
   c. Tips on expanding your range of styles and using backup styles.

9. What action styles do you use to communicate?
   a. Case study (assign groups composed of representatives of four styles; give each a brief case study; groups must first discuss solution from point of view of each of the four styles; then group picks best style or combination of styles).
   b. Role playing (using case study as scenario; either in small groups or before entire group) with focus upon making adjustments in one's own style; these can be videotaped.
   c. Discussion (replay video or rework role-playing scenes).

Content Guidelines for Listening Skills Training

(*Source:* Adapted from Elsea, 1988b.)

1. What are the objectives of this training?
   a. To make participants aware of the importance of listening in their everyday work life.
   b. To improve participants' listening skills as they directly relate to their jobs.
   c. To teach techniques for ongoing individual self-development of listening skills.
   d. To increase participants' value to the organization by helping them to do their job better.

2. Was what you heard really what I meant? (facts about listening skills)
   a. Facts about human beings as listeners.
   b. Notes on the listening process: percentage of time spent in listening activities; listening versus hearing; factors that affect listening.
   c. Videotape participants and then replay video and discuss what participants see in themselves as listeners.

3. How do you know which of the four styles of listening is your most dominant? (Profiles in communication: relaxed listening, social listening, active listening, defensive listening)
   a. The continuum of four styles of listening—group problem-solving exercise (trainer divides participants into four groups and assigns one style to each; groups must draw up a profile of assigned style—body language cues, vocal indicators, and typical verbal responses—and be prepared to demonstrate its style).
   b. Debriefing and demonstration of each style and discussion as to when they are appropriate and inappropriate.

4. What are the barriers to effective listening, and how do you remove or reduce them?
   a. Three types of barriers: sender barriers, listener barriers, and environmental barriers.
   b. Group brainstorming session, then problem-solving exercise (trainer divides participants into at least three groups; reviews rules of brainstorming; assigns time frame for each phase; tells group to select one or two key barriers from list and draw up a plan of action for removing or reducing that barrier).

5. What are strategies for better listening?
   a. Four basic strategies for improving listening skills:
      • Learn to empathize and read people.
      • Be flexible in your styles of listening.
      • Pay closer heed to the environment.
      • Get feedback about your listening tendencies from people whose opinion you value.
   b. Practical exercise to increase skills (video, if possible).
   c. Replay video or discuss how to measure improvement.

6. How does listening improve or weaken your health?
   a. Medical findings re listening styles.
   b. Plan action for improving one's individual listening skills and/or those of the team.

Content Guidelines for Problem-Solving Skills Training

1. What are the objectives of this training?
   a. To increase participants' skills in problem solving.
   b. To clarify techniques for individual problem solving.
   c. To introduce new techniques for group problem solving.
   d. To improve on-the-job success and productivity.

2. How do you identify work-related problems?
   a. Define the scope of the problem.
   b. Obtain valid information about the problem in order to identify what it is.

3. What are two alternative approaches to group problem solving?
   a. Fundamental group problem analysis focuses on:
      • Generic group brainstorming to identify the cause of any type of problem.
      • Group input and commitment.
   b. Complex group problem analysis focuses on:
      • Problems that have appeared recently or have always been present with no apparent cause.
      • Group input and commitment.
   c. Both approaches can be used when:
      • The cause of the problem is unknown and needs to be determined.
      • The resources of the group rather than the skills of one individual are needed to address the issues.

4. How do you develop group skills in problem identification, problem solving, and decision making?
   a. Fundamental group problem analysis:
      • Discusses facts surrounding problem.
      • Silently generates causes of problem.
      • Provides round robin recording of causes.
      • Clarifies and discusses causes.
      • Verifies the causes.
      • Carries out corrective action.
      • Reports results of corrective action.
      • If first cause does not check out, moves on to second most probable cause, and so on.
   b. Complex group problem analysis uses videotape to illustrate how to:
      • Set up a deviation statement (see Figure 10).
      • Generate facts.
      • Silently generate causes of problems.
      • Provide round robin recording of causes.
      • Vote to establish probable cause.
      • Compare probable cause to facts.
      • Verify the probable cause.
      • Carry out the corrective action.
      • Report results of corrective action.
      • Move on to second most probable cause if first cause does not check out, and so on.

5. What practices will help you gain proficiency in problem analysis and resolution?
   a. Videotape participants going through each process, and group critique the videotape to emphasize process and conclusions.
   b. Review application of approaches using actual case studies of work situations.
   c. Perform three- and six-month refresher sessions to review process.

Content Guidelines for Creative Thinking Skills Training

(*Source:* Adapted from Rickards and Freedman, 1979, p. 6.)

1. What are the objectives of this training?
   a. To demonstrate to participants why creative thinking is essential for success in the workplace.
   b. To master some techniques of creative thinking that can be used to increase levels of creative response on the job (administer Torrance Test of Creative Thinking at beginning and conclusion of workshop to measure increased performance).
   c. To build skills in applying creative thinking to group and individual problem-solving situations through instruction, practice, and reinforcement exercises.

2. What is involved in problem recognition and definition in creative problem solving?
   a. Trainer and participants examine intuitive problem-stating style.
   b. Participants practice several procedures or parts of procedures for defining problems.

3. What is the process for generating ideas?
   a. Trainer and participants examine idea-generation procedures (unusual uses for mundane items exercise).
      • Select a noun randomly; instruct participants to think of as many uses as possible.
      • Pick a common problem and list as many solutions to the problem as possible.
   b. Participants practice several idea-stimulating procedures or parts of procedures, working individually.

4. What is a basic creative problem-solving procedure?
   a. Trainer facilitates brainstorming-type interactive group session that combines definitional and idea-generating procedures.
   b. Trainer and participants examine methods for evaluating ideas that were generated.
   c. Trainer encourages participants to invent their own problem-solving systems by combining parts of procedures that have been discussed and practiced.
   d. Trainer analyzes elements of day's activity from the participants' point of view as what/why statements.

5. What is the role of interpersonal skills awareness?
   a. Trainer prepares the way for interpersonal aspects of creative problem solving; exercises and discussion topics include Kolb's learning style inventory and active listening.

6. How do you extend and modify basic problem-solving procedures to make them useful in specific situations?
   a. Trainer introduces the concepts of personal accountability for and multidimensionality of ideas, relating these to generalized framework.
   b. Participants prepare and implement personal action plans.
   c. Using a matrix, participants combine material into what/why constructs and apply them to case studies in creative problem solving.

Content Guidelines for Self-Esteem Skills Training

(*Source:* Adapted from McKay and Fanning, 1987.)

1. What are the objectives of this training?
   a. To teach techniques for building self-esteem.
   b. To demonstrate to participants how increased self-esteem will help them improve their work performance.
   c. To perform real-world exercises that will incrementally build self-esteem in participants and help them recognize and avoid self-destructive behavior.

2. How do you determine your self-esteem quotient?
   a. Do a self-concept inventory that describes each participant in the following areas and then put a plus or minus beside each item indicating strengths and weaknesses:
      - Physical appearance.
      - Relating to others.
      - Personality.
      - How others see you.
      - Performance on the job.
      - Performance outside the job.
      - Mental functioning.
      - Sexuality.
   b. Perform an accurate participant self-assessment to include:
      - Acknowledging and remembering strengths.
      - Describing weaknesses accurately, specifically, and nonpejoratively.
   c. Separate out weaknesses and rewrite them using the following guidelines:
      - Use nonpejorative language to describe the self.
      - Use accurate language.
      - Use specific rather than general language.
      - Try to find a corresponding strength.
   d. Acknowledge strengths by recalling the positive things others have said about each participant.

  e. Write a new, realistic description of the self covering all eight areas of the self-concept inventory.
  f. Acknowledge each participant's strengths through:
- Daily affirmation.
- Reminder signs.
- Active integration.

3. How do you combat self-distortion?
  a. Write down self-statements that murder self-esteem.
  b. Examine self-statements for distortions:
- Overgeneralization.
- Global labeling.
- Filtering.
- Polarized thinking.
- Self-blame.
- Personalization.
  c. Write rebuttals about the self using an imaginary support person who can take one of the following positions:
- Be positive.
- Be accepting.
- Be assertive.
- Be rational.
- Be compassionate.

4. How do you avoid the tyranny of the "shoulds"?
  a. Participants compare "shoulds" with their basic value systems.
  b. Determine whether or not "shoulds" are in conflict with values.
  c. If they are in conflict, revise to reflect the reality of needs.

5. How do you handle making mistakes?
  a. Feel good about the self in spite of mistakes.
  b. Perform exercises to raise consciousness about mistakes:
- Realize that everyone makes mistakes.
- Realize that each participant makes mistakes.
- Forgive yourself for making mistakes.
- Visualize mistakes as a natural consequence of living and affirm self-worth.

6. How do you handle criticism?
  a. Discuss how reality influences each participant's view of criticism:
- Innate constitution.
- Physiological state.
- Emotional state.
- Habitual behavior patterns.
- Beliefs.
  b. Discuss the three ineffective response styles to criticism: being aggressive, being passive, or being both.
  c. Discuss the three effective response styles: acknowledgment, clouding (token agreement with a critic), and probing (clarification).

     d. Learn how to effectively counter criticism by removing self-esteem from the picture and comparing the reality of what the critic is saying with what is constructive and what is accurate.

  7. What is your wants inventory?
     a. Develop an inventory of wants to raise your awareness.
     b. Evaluate the inventory and determine those wants and needs where assertiveness and self-esteem seem to desert you, and then negotiate what is important by being clear and assertive.
     c. Each participant should work on three requests they want to make of another workshop participant and then transfer the successful experience to someone in their life who really can fulfill specific wants; practice makes perfect. Some guidelines include:
- Keep requests small.
- Keep requests simple.
- Don't blame or attack.
- Be specific.
- Use high self-esteem body language.
- Mention positive consequences.
- Set a mutually agreeable time for the conversation.

     d. Keep a log documenting details of improvement.

Content Guidelines for Motivation and Goal-Setting Skills Training

The purpose of offering a training program in motivation and goal setting is twofold: to be able to predict and define future employee behavior to meet organizational needs best, and to help individual employees learn techniques for enhancing their goal attainment and needs satisfaction. A model program should include all the skills of self-motivational goal setting while incorporating elements of several of the theories of external motivation.

  1. What are the objectives of this training?
     a. To improve participants' understanding of internal and external motivation as it relates to the work environment.
     b. To help each participant define what works for him or her in motivating for success.
     c. To internalize techniques for goal setting to improve attitude and work performance.
     d. To increase productivity and thereby enhance participant probability for job stability and success.
     e. To improve the bottom line of the organization through enhanced individual motivation.

  2. What are the intangible needs that motivate internal goal setting?
     a. Discuss Maslow's hierarchy of needs:
- Biological needs.
- Security needs.
- Social needs.
- Esteem needs.

- Independence needs.
- Self-realization needs.

b. Discuss how people's behavior on a job is related to their needs:
- Our on-the-job behaviors are the payoffs we want and seek.
- Goal-setting activity is directly proportional to the benefits we think we are likely to receive from the effort expended.

c. Discuss motivator/hygiene theory:
- Job enrichment.
- Opportunities for achievement.
- Recognition.
- Internally satisfying work.

3. How do you set internal work goals?
   a. Setting and achieving goals can give a big boost to self-esteem in the workplace:
   - Develop exercises with simple, short-term goals; for example, getting to work on time.
   - Break the goal down into small steps.
   - Concentrate on observable behavior.
   - Visualize personal struggling.
   - Include positive consequences of accomplishing the goal.
   - Affirmatively spell out the first step.
   - Set a date to implement it.

4. How do you set internal personal goals?
   a. Crystalize your thinking.
   b. Develop a written plan of action with deadlines.
   c. Decide what you really want in life.
   d. Develop self-esteem and learn to behave with self-confidence.
   e. Develop the determination to follow through.

5. How do you keep a log to track the development and success of self-motivation through goal setting?
   a. Select small goals each day.
   b. Write out process for achieving success.
   c. Document actual performance on the road to success.
   d. Document feelings and thoughts as you go along.
   e. Share successes and failures with workshop participants.
   f. Keep trying.

6. What are the tangible job needs that motivate external goal setting?
   a. Tangible needs are the substantive rewards an employee seeks for work:
   - Material payoff (a stock-option plan, a parking space, a new laboratory).
   - Situational payoff (a supervisory position, a lateral move into a new job area).

   b. Discuss the relationship of tangible needs to intangible needs.
   c. Optimally, individual benefits and organizational results should be able to mesh so that both the employer and the employee are rewarded by the work done.

7. How are people extrinsically motivated?
   a. Motivation is about achieving more productive performance, which translates into achieving job goals in the most efficient way.
   b. Using a motivation assessment instrument, ascertain the link between each participant's job goals and her or his needs.
   c. Discuss conditions under which benefits can be realized:
      - Need to motivate for both an intrinsic behavior change and an extrinsic business change; the second won't happen without the first.
      - Provide case studies that illustrate the three E's of work motivation (exchange, equity, and expectancy).

8. What other factors motivate individuals in a work setting?
   a. Discuss external goal setting:
      - Direct attention and action.
      - Mobilize energy and effort.
      - Increase persistence.
      - Develop appropriate task strategies.
   b. Discuss operant learning and conditioning:
      - Demonstrate how behavior elicits consequences.
      - Show how positive feedback leads to desirable work behaviors.
      - Illustrate how stated goals facilitate feedback.
   c. Discuss management styles:
      - Open and respectful.
      - Employee participation.
      - Self-directing.
      - Trustful atmosphere.
   d. Discuss participation:
      - Quality circles.
      - Employee survey feedback.
      - Work teams.
      - Job enrichment.
      - Quality of work life.
      - New design of the workplace.
   e. Discuss expectancy:
      - Rewards expected from action or results.
      - Rewards received from action or results.
      - Change in behaviors because of rewards.
   f. Discuss equity:
      - Fairness perceived in relation to others.
      - Increased work effort because of perceived fairness in relation to others.

9. What are some successful motivation techniques?
   a. Carry out exercises that require a sharp focus on individual skills.
   b. Understand correctly the expected performance.
   c. Develop evaluative criteria and measurements for goal attainment.

d. Measure progress toward goals.
e. Negotiate goals with other participants.
f. Identify resources necessary to reach goals.
g. Constantly revise goals, setting new boundaries.

Content Guidelines for Employability Skills Training

(*Source*: Adapted from National Alliance of Business, 1986, pp. 791–794.)

1. What are the objectives of this training?
   a. To improve participants' lifetime skills for getting and keeping a job.
   b. To teach techniques for daily living that will lead to lessened stress in the workplace.
   c. To help participants understand the benefits and obligations of being employed.
   d. To help participants learn to think ahead about what is required to meet employer rules and standards.

2. When you complete this training, what will you be able to do?
   a. Use multiple sources of job information.
   b. Identify a prospective employer's products and services.
   c. Determine key contacts within a prospective employer's organization.
   d. Identify the free services provided by the state employment agency in helping people find jobs and training.
   e. Determine how private employment agencies operate to help people find jobs for a fee.
   f. Identify the procedures involved in applying directly for jobs at a company personnel office.
   g. Prepare for common types of employment tests.
   h. Identify the purpose of job application forms.
   i. Read and complete those parts of a job application asking for personal facts, job interests and job skills, references, educa-ion, and employment records.
   j. Prepare letters of inquiry or application.
   k. Compile a list of references.
   l. Apply for a social security card, work permit, licenses.
   m. Prepare a resume summarizing experience, education, and job training.
   n. Identify the purpose of job interviews.
   o. Identify the necessary steps in getting ready for a job interview.
   p. Assess prior work experience, career goals, personal character, job references, and personal aptitudes.
   q. Discuss wages and salaries with prospective employers.
   r. Define basic terms about wages and salaries, identify standard paycheck deductions, and do simple computations related to salary.
   s. Identify and describe common company benefits.

t. Identify the purpose of worker's compensation and describe the benefits it provides.

u. Identify the purpose of unemployment insurance and disability insurance and describe the benefits they provide.

3. What work and career planning skills will this training prepare you for?

   a. To correlate the relationship between job and academic skills.

   b. To demonstrate an accurate employment market knowledge of occupational requirements and trends.

   c. To describe what various fields of work are like and what kinds of people are successful in them.

   d. To evaluate the chances of getting a job now and in the future in the fields of work that interest individual participants.

   e. To determine how many and what kind of workers will be needed (now and in the long term) in the local area.

   f. To identify where and how to get specific local labor market information.

   g. To determine the kind of preparation and training needed to get an entry-level job and subsequent promotions.

   h. To identify occupations and professions through appropriate information sources.

   i. To evaluate occupational apprenticeships and other training opportunities.

   j. To evaluate educational opportunities (college, vocational training, home study, and lifelong learning programs).

4. What are the life skills you will be knowledgeable about when you exit this training?

   a. How to use the telephone correctly.

   b. How to tell time.

   c. How to use your local public transportation system.

   d. Appropriate hygiene and dress.

   e. How to use money effectively.

   f. The need for income tax returns and how to compute tax returns.

   g. The major points to consider in renting an apartment.

   h. Banking and financial services available in the community.

   i. How to use sound buying principles for goods and services.

   j. How to define credit and use it judiciously.

   k. What contracts are for and their elements.

   l. Tips for buying and maintaining a car.

   m. How to appraise personal insurance needs.

   n. How to identify and understand appropriate child care services.

5. What does it mean to be reliable at work?

   a. Accrue an acceptable attendance record by being on the job regularly and promptly.

   b. Record timely notice if late or absent.

   c. Complete tasks on time.

> d. Demonstrate responsibility and dependability by carrying out assigned tasks.

6. What kind of attitude and behavior should you display at work?
   a. Arrive at work clean and dressed properly.
   b. Solve personal business problems outside of work.
   c. Arrange for adequate child care.
   d. Demonstrate self-control.
   e. Accept responsibility for your own actions.
   f. Use appropriate language.
   g. Maintain a sense of congeniality.

7. What work habits will serve you best in the workplace?
   a. Prepare and organize job responsibilities.
   b. Arrange materials, tools, and work stations.
   c. Demonstrate consistency in task completion.
   d. Use appropriate job techniques.
   e. Plan time effectively.
   f. Plan reasonable work goals.

8. What will your supervisor expect of you at work?
   a. To be attentive and cooperative.
   b. To request clarification when needed.
   c. To negotiate differences of opinion.
   d. To accept guidance, correction, and constructive criticism.
   e. To recognize and respect another's authority.
   f. To complete instructions and work under supervision.

9. What should you expect of your employer?
   a. To assess employment conditions.
   b. To evaluate work standards and schedules.
   c. To clearly state personnel procedures.
   d. To clearly identify emergency and safety procedures.
   e. To define loyalty.

Content Guidelines for Career Development Skills Training

(*Source:* Adapted from Gutteridge and Otte, 1983, pp. 37–39.)

1. What are the objectives of this training?
   a. To empower participants to take charge of their own careers.
   b. To explore the meaning and practice of career development.
   c. To learn techniques for ongoing evaluation of a career.
   d. To plan for your employment future.

2. How do you do an initial self-assessment?
   a. Who am I? What do I want to do?
      - Self-concept.
      - Clarification of values.
      - Personality characteristics and personal style.
      - Motivational patterns.
      - Occupational interests.
      - Personal preferences.

   b. Where have I been?
       • Personal and educational background.
       • Work experience.
       • Key accomplishments.
       • Peak experiences.
       • Significant life decisions.
       • Satisfying and dissatisfying experiences.
3. What is a future self-assessment?
   a. Where am I now? What can I do?
       • Analysis of current job (behavioral demands; importance of
         various job elements; likes and dislikes).
       • Values, skills, and abilities (professional or technical;
         managerial; personal).
       • Special knowledge or capabilities.
       • Personal qualities.
       • Developmental needs.
       • Sources of satisfaction or dissatisfaction.
   b. Where do I want to be?
       • Occupational daydreams or ideal job description.
       • Desired future accomplishments.
       • Preferred working environment.
       • Ideal lifestyle.
       • Career goals.
       • Personal goals.
4. How do you do an environmental assessment?
   a. What's out there?
       • Organization profile and business outlook.
       • Opportunity structure, job requirements, and selection
         standards.
       • Available career paths.
       • Developmental policies.
       • Other resources and information.
5. How do you develop a goal-directed action plan?
   a. What's the next step?
       • Reconciling self-assessment with environmental assessment.
       • Identifying long-range alternatives.
       • Specifying short-range goals.
       • Setting priorities.
       • Preparing action plan.
       • Developing contingency plan.
6. How do you implement your action plan?
   a. How do I get there?
       • Developing marketing techniques.
       • Establishing career action projects with time frames for
         completion.

Content Guidelines for Interpersonal Skills Training

(*Source*: Adapted from Egan, 1976, pp. 27–33.)

1. What are the objectives of this training?
   a. To improve the skills necessary to interact constructively in a one-on-one and group situation.
   b. To practice these skills until proficiency is achieved.
   c. To help each participant understand his or her strengths and weaknesses in interpersonal skills.
   d. To learn how to continue to grow and master these skills.

2. How do you learn to build relationship skills (trust and risk)?
   a. The individual skill-training phase to establish and develop mutual relationships through the core skills of relationship-building include:
      - Self-preservation.
      - Self-disclosure (an examination of interpersonal style).
      - Concreteness (the more concrete the statements, the more immediate interaction with others becomes).
      - The expression of feeling (discover the place of emotion in interpersonal dialogues).
      - Responding.
      - Accurate empathy (ability to respond actively and with understanding to those who disclose themselves).
      - Respect (examining the quality of respect for others).

3. What are the skills of challenge?
   a. New skills to enhance ability to engage responsibly in the process of feedback and challenge include:
      - Strength identification (recognize the strengths of others and let them know you appreciate them).
      - Advanced accurate empathy (communicate to the other person not only what they say but what they are implying; make the connection between seemingly isolated statements).
      - Confrontation (what a person says versus what is actually done).
      - Immediacy (examine what is happening in the here and now).

4. What are group-specific skills?
   a. Individual skills do not necessarily generalize to group situations, and it is sometimes necessary to learn how to use a variety of skills in a variety of combinations actively in a group:
      - Active response (when contacted by someone in the group, you contribute actively to the dialogue—active listening).
      - Taking the initiative (contacting others actively and not merely waiting to be contacted in order to establish and develop a relationship).
      - Primary-level accurate empathy (spontaneous, accurate, empathic understanding).

- Self-disclosure (revealing the self without actively being requested to do so).
- Owning the interaction of others (acting as a catalyst in the conversation of others in order to help them achieve their goal).
- Using challenge skills (checking to see what is happening in each of the relationships being developed: Where do you and I stand now in our relationship?).
- Calling for feedback (asking others for confrontation or any other interaction necessary to achieve goals).

5. Why do you develop a core contract?
   a. Training structure is reduced to a minimum; pursuit of goals is achieved through an open group experience using newly acquired skills. The core contract is used to provide structure to:
      - Examine each interpersonal style.
      - Observe self-behavior and receive feedback.
      - Acquire or strengthen basic interpersonal skills.
      - Begin to alter interpersonal style to enhance lifestyle.

6. Why do you keep a log?
   a. Enter experiences, behaviors, and feelings that will help improve skills outside of the group experience. Hints for keeping a successful log include:
      - Keep entries concrete.
      - Keep track of what needs to be worked on.
      - Keep a page for each group member.
      - Decide what you want to accomplish in each group meeting.

Content Guidelines for Teamwork Skills Training

1. What are the objectives of this training?
   a. To present participants with an overview of the importance of effective teamwork.
   b. To enhance teamwork in order to resolve specific organizational problems.
   c. To explore the need for improvement in teamwork.
   d. To explore ways in which participants can strengthen their teamwork skills.

2. What is teamwork?
   a. Explain basic teamwork theory.
   b. Consider issues of management style, support, trust, cooperation, and conflict.
   c. Assess individual teamwork styles.
   d. Explore the characteristics of personal effectiveness (intimacy exercise—openness and confrontation).

3. What are the issues around team leadership?
   a. Discuss concepts of participative leadership.
   b. Complete and analyze team leadership style questionnaire.
   c. Discuss the impact of leader's actions on activity of the team.

4. How do you prepare an action plan for teamwork improvement?
   a. Prepare action plans for individual development and group development by splitting participants into small groups.
   b. Present plans to all participants.
   c. Comment on plans and review events.

5. What are the skills particularly relevant to becoming an effective team member?
   a. Communication skills:
      • Oral communication (distribute a self-assessment instrument that measures each member's style of communication).
      • Listening: key ideas.
      • Active listening techniques.
   b. Feedback skills:
      • The concept of feedback.
      • Guidelines for giving feedback.
      • Guidelines for receiving feedback.
   c. Problem-solving skills:
      • Defining the critical issues.
      • Selecting the problem for resolution.
      • Exploring the causes.
      • Analyzing the data.
      • Examining the results.
      • Selecting the solution.
      • Developing an action plan.
   d. Conflict resolution skills:
      • Dealing with feelings.
      • Determining cause of conflict.
      • Choosing strategy to resolve conflict (active listening, assertion, confrontation, creative problem solving).
   e. Team task skills:
      • Setting goals and objectives.
      • Setting standards.
      • Getting and giving information.
      • Processing information.
      • Planning for action.
   f. Team maintenance skills:
      • Keeping communication lines open.
      • Managing conflict.
      • Evaluating team process.
      • Providing for team's physical needs.

Content Guidelines for Negotiation Skills Training

1. What are the objectives of this workshop?
   a. To cover the basics of negotiation.
   b. To better understand how a negotiating session works and what its key elements are.
   c. To help participants understand their own strengths and weaknesses in negotiating.
   d. To help participants strengthen their own negotiating skills.
   e. To explore how a positive negotiating position will sustain a positive collaborative atmosphere after negotiations have concluded.

2. What is conflict?
   a. Two opposed parties actively seeking their own end goals.
   b. Positive and negative uses of conflict in an organization.
   c. Principal causes of conflict.

3. How do you manage conflict?
   a. Identify the problem(s).
   b. Select strategy for resolution (avoidance, delay, confrontation, negotiation, collaboration).

4. When is negotiation appropriate?
   a. When there is leeway to give.
   b. When resources are limited.
   c. When a win-lose stance is undesirable.

5. What are the benefits of effective negotiation?
   a. Improved working relationships.
   b. Enhanced organizational effectiveness.
   c. Enhanced personal effectiveness.
   d. Ability to make better deals.
   e. Techniques for breaking through standoffs and stalemates.

6. How do you prepare for the negotiation process?
   a. Determine the degree of seriousness of the conflict.
   b. Identify organizational and individual self-interest in resolving the conflict.
   c. Establish mutually acceptable negotiating guidelines.
   d. Establish ground rules (time, commitment, mediator, place, food and drink, recording, confidentiality).

7. How do you analyze an opponent?
   a. Determine the BATNA (*best alternative to a negotiated agreement*):
      • Your own and your opponent's mini-max position.
      • What each side is willing and able to walk away with.
   b. Choose an appropriate strategy and tactics and negotiate a win-win resolution based on this information.

8. What are the successful traits of a negotiator?
   a. Evaluate yourself as a negotiator:
      • Planning skills.
      • Ability to think clearly under stress.

- Verbal ability.
- Practical intelligence (street or world wise).
- Personal integrity.
- Knowledge of yourself.
- Ability to perceive and exploit power.

9. What are some effective negotiating approaches for resolving conflict?
   a. Needs theory of negotiation (Nierenberg).
   b. Contract versus contact (Gestalt theory).
   c. Interest versus position (Fisher and Ury).

10. What are some negotiation skills exercises?
    a. One-on-one activity (solo approach); feedback from observer.
    b. Team negotiation:
       - Evaluation and debriefing from each team observer.
       - Learning points.
       - Discussion of elements of activity.

Content Guidelines for Organizational Effectiveness Skills Training

1. What are the objectives of this training?
   a. To increase participants' understanding of explicit and implicit organizational norms, structures, and codes and how they shape the work environment.
   b. To improve participants' skills and abilities to function in these environments in an effective and job-enhancing manner.
   c. To understand how each participant is perceived by others (peers and supervisors) in a way that helps or hinders his or her organizational effectiveness.
   d. To help participants understand how personal and professional values, choices, and behaviors affect their effectiveness in an organization.

2. What are organizational effectiveness skills?
   a. The ability to read and understand organizational cues to better understand the organization's direction and values.
   b. The ability to understand the explicit and implicit structures and codes of an organization to better comprehend its culture and succeed within it.
   c. The ability to understand how compatible or incompatible personal and organizational values and behavior patterns will enable you to succeed in a particular organization; make a decision to leave; or modify your beliefs and style of operating in order to stay and achieve your objectives.
   d. The skill to develop an action plan that identifies how available organizational mechanisms can be used to help increase organizational effectiveness.

3. What will a self-assessment process contribute to improving my organizational effectiveness skills?
   a. It provides a knowledge of work-related skills and abilities such as vocational and occupational skills and personal and professional values, relationships, and interests.
   b. It helps in understanding what one does best and enjoys doing, as well as in making a determination of how marketable these preferences are in today's organizations.
   c. It helps to uncover each participant's personal vision of the ideal work environment by answering the following questions:
      • What am I doing in my ideal job environment?
      • Where am I doing this?
      • What skills do I bring to the job?
      • What results can I achieve?
   d. It answers the questions, How prepared am I to meet the challenge of achieving my vision? and What do I need to learn and know to achieve my vision in this organizational structure?
   e. It uncovers resources, training and/or educational needs, and the ways you and/or the organization can best help you fulfill the vision.

4. How will improving my understanding of how I can grow professionally affect my organizational effectiveness skills?
   a. It helps to match opportunities with career interests.
   b. It develops skills to uncover and create new job opportunities within and outside an organization.
   c. It changes attitudes toward wanting more responsibility— from a feeling of powerlessness to a desire to assume control.
   d. It broadens focus and perspectives on what's important in terms of career and personal life.
   e. It explores how normative behavior standards differ from organization to organization and how behavior affects the ability to do a job successfully.

5. What will this knowledge enable you to do?
   a. Understand your own value.
   b. Enhance your determination (volition) to conduct self-management activities.
   c. Develop options to enhance your versatility.
   d. Make your personal and professional worth more visible to others.
   e. Develop the ability to visualize desirable job and career outcomes.

Content Guidelines for Leadership Skills Training

The following guidelines present one perspective on leadership training. If an organization chooses to implement a leadership seminar in-house or purchase the training from an outside provider, the course may, and probably will, differ from this. The degree of difference will depend on the theoretical approach espoused by the provider or selected by the organization, as well as on the specific training techniques used.

1. What are the objectives of this training?
    a. To learn from the general literature of leadership theory.
    b. To develop a list of generally acceptable characteristics of what makes a good leader.
    c. To develop a consensus on the qualities necessary to succeed in a shared leadership environment.
    d. To explore each participant's leadership strengths and weaknesses.
    e. To strengthen weaknesses and expand strengths in shared leadership skills.
    f. To better understand the dynamics of shared leadership through the vehicle of mini-exercises.

2. What does the new organization look like?
    a. It is organizationally more compact.
    b. It consists of matrix management, cross-functional project teams, horizontal responsibility.
    c. To be competitive it must provide more services or better goods at less cost.
    d. It employs new approaches to motivation.
    e. It pushes leadership functions down through the organization to the point of production or point of sale.

3. What do we know about leadership?
    a. Theories of leadership (functional, visionary, behavioral, and others).
    b. The definition of leadership.
    c. Shared versus appointive leadership.
    d. Manager versus leader.

4. What makes a person successful at shared leadership and team empowerment? (Kouzes and Posner, 1987, p. 14; Hastings, Bixby, and Chaudhry-Lawton, 1986, pp. 92–94)
    a. Challenge the process (search for opportunities; experiment and take risks).
    b. Inspire a shared vision by making it public (envision the future; enlist others to work toward a shared vision).
    c. Empower others to act (foster collaboration; strengthen others to act independently).
    d. Model the way (set the example; plan small wins).
    e. Encourage the heart (recognize individual contribution; celebrate accomplishment).
    f. Help yourself to perform (encourage frank feedback; develop a support network).
    g. Pass the baton (encourage others to take over; don't fear to say you don't know).

5. How do you build a shared leadership style?
    a. Develop an inventory of personal leadership skills:
        • Diagnostic (problem solver, critical and creative thinker).

- Perceptual (communicates well, verbally and through listening).
- Behavioral (teamwork, negotiation, interpersonal, delegation, motivation, coaching, counseling).

b. Develop leadership skills through:
- Case studies.
- Experiential learning.
- Workshop simulations.

References and Suggested Readings

Diehl, W. A., and Mikulecky, L. J. "The Nature of Being at Work." *Journal of Reading,* 1980, *24* (3), 221–227.

Egan, G. *Interpersonal Living.* Monterey, Calif.: Brooks/Cole, 1976.

Elsea, J. G. "Oral Communication Skills for the American Worker." Unpublished paper developed for the American Society for Training and Development, 1988a.

Elsea, J. G. "Listening Skills for the American Worker." Unpublished paper developed for the American Society for Training and Development, 1988b.

Greenan, J. P. *The Development of Strategies and Procedures for Assessing the Generalizable Skills of Students in Secondary Vocational Programs: Generalizable Mathematics Skills.* Springfield: Illinois State Board of Education, Department of Adult, Vocational, and Technical Education, 1984. (ED 248 323)

Gutteridge, T. G., and Otte, F. L. *Organizational Career Development: State of the Practice.* Alexandria, Va.: American Society for Training and Development, 1983.

Hastings, C., Bixby, P., and Chaudhry-Lawton, R. *The Superteam Solution.* Hampshire, England: Gower Press, 1986.

Kouzes, J. M., and Posner, B. Z. *The Leadership Challenge: How to Get Extraordinary Things Done in Organizations.* San Francisco: Jossey-Bass, 1987.

McKay, M., and Fanning, P. *Self-Esteem.* New York: St. Martin's Press, 1987.

Mikulecky, L. J. "Functional Writing in the Workplace." In L. Gentry (ed.), *Research and Instruction in Practical Writing.* Los Alamitos, Calif.: South West Regional Laboratories, 1982.

National Alliance of Business. *A Systems Approach to Youth Employment Competencies.* Washington, D.C.: National Alliance of Business, 1986.

Philippi, J. W. "Matching Literacy to Job Training: Some Applications from Military Programs." *Journal of Reading,* 1988, *31* (7), 658–666.

Pratzner, F. C. *Occupational Adaptability and Transferable Skills.* Project final report, Information Series, no. 129. Columbus: National Center for Research in Vocational Education, Ohio State University, 1978. (ED 186 717)

Pratzner, F. C., and Russell, J. F. *The Changing Workplace: Implications of Quality of Work Life Developments for Vocational Education.* Research and Development Series, no. 249. Washington, D.C.: Office of Vocational and Adult Education, 1984. (ED 240 283)

Rickards, T., and Freedman, B. "A Reappraisal of Creativity Techniques in Industrial Training." *Journal of European Industrial Training,* 1979, *3* (1), 3–8.

Smith, A. D. *Generic Skills for Occupational Training.* Prince Albert, Saskatchewan, Canada: Training Research and Development Station, 1973. (ED 083 385)

Smith, R. M. *Learning How to Learn: Applied Theory for Adults.* Chicago: Follet, 1982.

Smith, R. M. *Theory Building for Learning How to Learn.* Chicago: Educational Studies Press, 1988.

U.S. Department of the Army. *Prerequisite Competencies in Job Skills Education Program.* Washington, D.C.: U.S. Department of the Army, 1988.

Wiant, A. A. *Transferable Skills: The Employers' Viewpoint.* Columbus: National Center for Research in Vocational Education, Ohio State University, 1977. (ED 174 809)

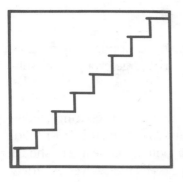

Glossary

Analysis of existing documents: The analysis of existing documents involves a critical review and evaluation of materials, documents, manuals, and work instructions for how work is to be performed in order to determine competencies needed for the job.

Behavior modeling: Behavior modeling is a process in which learners work through a step-by-step model for handling a given interactive situation, followed by a demonstration of the steps, usually on video.

Case study: A case study is a description of a work situation in writing, on audio-tape, or on videotape that the trainees study and discuss under the guidance of the instructor. A case study usually has no right or wrong answers but rather a number of different solutions, each with particular advantages and disadvantages.

Closed questionnaires: Closed questionnaires are surveys composed primarily of questions for which a limited set of responses is provided.

Competencies: Competencies are the knowledge, skills, abilities, and attitude standards required for success in a particular job.

Computer-based training: During computer-based training the learner interacts with a computer program that presents subject matter, allows for practice exercises, gives feedback, analyzes performance, and provides special assistance as needed.

Course outline: A course outline is a description of the structure and sequence of the instructional program.

Criterion-referenced tests: Criterion-referenced tests are evaluation instruments designed to measure the exact objective and the specific behavior required to accomplish a particular task.

DACUM: DACUM (*developing a curriculum*) is an approach to occupational analysis that specifies in detail the tasks that successful workers must perform in their occupations.

Functional context learning: Functional context learning is an approach to training in which subjects are taught contextually (in ways that reflect their actual use on the job). It is designed to produce the quickest, most effective results in the area of improved employee performance.

Group discussion: A group discussion is a planned opportunity for participants to freely exchange ideas or opinions in a large group or in subgroups.

Guided learning center: A guided learning center is a learning facility designed to provide instruction that is individualized and self-paced. Instructors and/or aides are used at particular points, but learners should be able to progress through the educational process by themselves. A variety of instructional materials are used such as print, audio-visual aids, and computer.

Individual exercise: Individual exercise allows learners to independently apply the lesson objectives to their own situation to test their understanding.

Interactive television classroom: An interactive television classroom is a learning environment that involves the use of broadcast video to deliver instruction to the learner, allowing contact between instructors and learners who are geographically dispersed.

Interactive videodisc: Interactive videodisc is an instructional method that uses a video delivery system designed to respond to choices made by the individual user.

Investigator: The investigator is an individual who explores the nature and scope of all reported basic skills problems in order to determine an appropriate response.

Job analysis: A job analysis is a process designed to determine whether a basic workplace skills problem exists that warrants a special training effort for a substantial number of employees.

Job description: A job description is a tool for describing general information about what a person does on a job and the conditions under which she or he works. It is composed of a number of duty statements, that is, statements that describe a worker's major job duties and responsibilities.

Learning contract: The learning contract is a mutually agreed-upon written contract between the program operator (the employer) and the learner (the employee) specifying the learning goals and outcomes expected by both parties.

Lesson: A lesson is a cohesive unit of instruction with a specific learning objective: the acquisition by the learner of defined knowledge or skills.

Lesson objective: The lesson objective is what the trainee will know and be able to do at the end of a particular lesson.

Lesson plan: The lesson plan is an instructor's tool that defines the learning objective, describes the activities (learning experiences) and instructional materials, and provides an evaluation of the degree to which the objective was achieved by the trainee.

Multimedia classroom: The multimedia classroom is a learning environment in which learners have opportunities to use a variety of learning media such as films, tapes (audio or video), slides, print, and radio.

Needs analysis: Needs analysis is a systematic process for determining and ordering goals, measuring needs, and deciding on priorities for action.

Observation method: The observation method is an information-gathering technique that involves a trained person observing workers on the job in order to determine the competencies needed.

Open-ended questionnaires: Open-ended questionnaires are questionnaires composed primarily of questions that cannot be answered by a simple yes or no but must be answered with a personalized narrative.

Performance-based training: Performance-based training is a systematic format of instruction in which skills or competencies to be learned are clearly defined for the trainee and are designed to reflect the skills required to achieve and/or retain employment. In addition, the skill mastery requirements for each task are stated prior to the beginning of instruction.

Performance objective: A performance objective is a description of the performance the learner is expected to exhibit before being considered competent.

Presentations and lectures: Presentations and lectures are structured one-way communications from the instructor to the learners.

Program monitoring: Program monitoring is an ongoing process that channels information back to program operators on how effectively the instructional process is operating. Where program efficiency and effectiveness are determined to be less than optimal, changes can be made to improve performance.

Role playing: Role playing is an exercise in which learners simulate a real or hypothetical interactive situation. A discussion and analysis follow to determine what happened and why. Role playing can be used to analyze the learners' customary ways of dealing with the situation but more often is used to allow the learners to apply newly learned procedures or skills.

Self-study: Self-study involves the learner's use of a package of printed material that includes readings, exercises, and tests for self-evaluation.

Simulation: A simulation is an exercise that represents a real job situation and allows the learners to practice skills or application of knowledge within a limited time frame and in a risk-free environment (the classroom).

Task analysis: Task analysis is the process of breaking down a task into smaller units and then sequencing these units in an order of priority based on their importance in performing the job.

Task detailing: A task detailing is a systematic breakdown of each task to determine the skills, sequencing, knowledge, and attitude an individual needs to perform a single task successfully.

Task force exercise: A task force exercise is a method of training in which a group of three to eight trainees work together on a problem and present their solution to the class.

Task inventory: A task inventory is an instrument used to verify the tasks of a job.

Task listings: Task listings are statements describing the work activities of employees in specific jobs or occupational areas.

Traditional classroom: The traditional classroom is an instructional situation in which the learners are seated individually behind desks or tables facing the front of the room, where the instructor operates behind a desk or lectern with a blackboard, overhead projector, flip chart, and other audio-visual aids.

Validation: Validation is the process that confirms that the information gathered in the task analysis process is consistent with the circumstances of actual job performance.

Written exercises: Written exercises are activities that involve giving learners written materials to which they respond in writing.

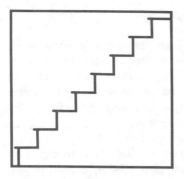

Index